Dr. Spencer-Hwang's commitment to share wisdom gathered from Resiliency Capital members is the start of a revolution in holistic parenting. Filled with practical methods to help us begin creating a wellness mindset at home, *Raising Resilient Kids* reminds us that as caretakers and guides for our children, we're entrusted with a miraculous opportunity—the chance to lead by example and show our kids how to live each day with genuine appreciation for this adventure called life. You will learn how to help your children see that caring for body, mind, spirit, and soul one choice at a time can lead to a lifetime of good, especially when it comes to triumphing through adversity.

> **JUNI FELIX**, member of the Behavior Design Teaching Team created by Dr. BJ Fogg; founder and director of Stanford University's Behavior Design Lab; author of *You Are Worth the Work: Moving Forward from Trauma to Faith*

Even the premise of this book—capturing the wisdom of the ages from centenarians to guide today's young parents—is intriguing. Rhonda Spencer-Hwang has distilled an amazing array of advice from those over 100 years of age into a useful set of principles for raising resilient children. With practical references to scientific literature and an engaging writing style, she carries the reader through her own life experiences while sharing simple guidelines for healthy living. Parents of all ages will enjoy and benefit from the wisdom in these pages.

> **RICHARD H. HART, MD, DrPH**, president, Loma Linda University Health

As a family physician, I see patients ranging in age from newborn to elderly, or "from the cradle to the grave," which gives me the privilege of seeing people as they age. I have often asked my older patients who are doing remarkably well what their secrets are. This book, which is filled with wisdom from centenarians, is written in a very down-to-earth way with funny anecdotes, which makes it easy to read. Its advice will help you raise your children so they can bounce back from the challenges they will face in a less-than-perfect, ever-changing world.

The book is well-researched and breaks the findings down into sensible and thorough solutions to help your children build successful and meaningful lives. I highly recommend it as an entertaining and effective tool to help you raise confident, optimistic children.

JANINE HWANG, MD

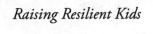

Raising Resilient Kids

DR. RHONDA SPENCER-HWANG, DrPH, MPH

RAISING

RESILIENT

KIDS

8 PRINCIPLES FOR BRINGING UP

HEALTHY, HAPPY, SUCCESSFUL CHILDREN WHO CAN

OVERCOME OBSTACLES & THRIVE DESPITE ADVERSITY

TYNDALE
MOMENTUM®

The Tyndale nonfiction imprint

Visit Tyndale online at tyndale.com.

Visit Tyndale Momentum online at tyndalemomentum.com.

TYNDALE, Tyndale's quill logo, *Tyndale Momentum*, and the Tyndale Momentum logo are registered trademarks of Tyndale House Ministries. Tyndale Momentum is the nonfiction imprint of Tyndale House Publishers, Carol Stream, Illinois.

For information about special discounts for bulk purchases, please contact Tyndale House Publishers at csresponse@tyndale.com, or call 1-855-277-9400.

Library of Congress Cataloging-in-Publication Data
A catalog record for this book is available from the Library of Congress.

ISBN 978-1-4964-4508-7

Printed in the United States of America

27 26 25 24 23 22 21
7   6   5   4   3   2   1

*This book is dedicated to my husband, Joe,
and our children, Jayden, Joelle, and Julia.*

CONTENTS

A NOTE BEFORE YOU BEGIN

RAISING RESILIENT KIDS INTRODUCES YOU to eight healthy habits that centenarians (people one hundred years or older) have practiced since childhood and that may improve your family's overall health and resilience as well. Before making major changes to health practices such as diet and exercise, however, be sure to consult with your physician.

FOREWORD

WHEN THE CORONAVIRUS CRISIS of 2020 forced the world to stop and retreat indoors, parents and experts alike began to worry about how living through a pandemic would impact our children's development.

COVID-19 created an adverse childhood experience (ACE) for nearly every child on earth. What would this mean long-term for a global generation of children?

Research on ACEs is of growing importance as we learn more about their potential lifelong effects on health. Equally important, if not more so, is knowing what protective actions can counter the impact of early life adversity and build resiliency. Fortunately, not long before the pandemic struck, Dr. Spencer-Hwang completed her study of the childhood habits of another generation that had grown up during perilous times—the centenarians who were born around the year the previous global pandemic struck and whose youth was shaped by the Great Depression and Second World War.

In this innovative approach to capturing and distilling the salient life experiences of a vibrant and active community of centenarians, Dr. Spencer-Hwang lays out a blueprint of eight strategies to create a hub of resilience in your own home. The lessons she has gleaned from her interviews are consistent with habits known to mitigate the effects of ACEs and improve overall physical and mental health. As a busy mom herself, she offers practical suggestions on how your family can begin incorporating all of these principles in your daily life. Although technology has altered our lifestyles since the childhoods of these treasured sages, these concepts are timeless and adaptable—and possibly never more important to us than now.

As you reflect on how the cascading impacts from unavoidable life circumstances such as the COVID-19 pandemic may be influencing your children, family, and other loved ones, be encouraged by the compelling and inspiring vignettes shared in this work. Be empowered to have faith, set goals, and take action, knowing that these adversities do not preclude living long, healthy lives; rather, this stretching and molding we are all enduring—and how we choose to intentionally respond to our challenges—may strengthen and equip us to stay the course and enjoy many more decades of a joyful, blessed, and healthy life.

Celeste Philip, MD, MPH
Deputy Director for Non-Infectious Diseases
Centers for Disease Control and Prevention

The views expressed herein are those of the author and do not necessarily reflect official positions of the Centers for Disease Control and Prevention.

INTRODUCTION

ON A MILD CALIFORNIA WINTER'S DAY a few years ago, I sat on the patio watching my youngest child, one-year-old Julia, babbling away in the sandbox. Her brother and sister were already at school, and I had no classes to teach that day. I didn't have to rush off to a meeting, answer an email, give a health presentation, drive car pool, or settle sibling disputes. I relished this unhurried moment of calm.

Yet I felt uneasy. I knew something was not right and I was headed for trouble. I was teaching public health at a university but privately devouring and feeding my kids junk food. I was teaching the importance of physical exercise and movement but spent most of my time sitting at my desk working while my kids sat in front of the TV. I was dedicated to my church, but my family and I were missing more services than we attended. I had lost my direction—and worse, I was setting up my kids to follow the same rocky path.

Watching Julia dig her way to China with her plastic shovel, I thought about how far our family had drifted from a healthy lifestyle. Like so many other parents, I was overwhelmed by the endless bombardment of daily challenges, accompanied by heaping doses of exhausting stress. As a working wife and mother in a two-career household, dealing with the hectic scheduling demands and conflicts of three children, I found myself making one subconscious decision after another.

Fast food just this once. I'm too tired to cook.
A marathon of TV for the kids just today. It's sure to settle them down.
Skipping church just this week. We've got so much to do.

Such days had turned into months and months into years, until these continual "exceptions" to the rule had *become* the rule—and soon characterized our daily lives. Making matters worse, my husband and I were paying for those unsettling selections not only with our own personal health, but with our kids' health as well.

As a public-health professor, I knew what our choices meant. Many of the consequences that accompany such split-second decisions are readily apparent—like a burgeoning waistline. Others remain hidden—potentially wreaking havoc inside the body—becoming evident only later in life. I understood these facts well, and I worried for my kids. Life hadn't always been this way, and somehow, I knew I needed to find my way back. Yet I lacked direction and felt paralyzed to make a change.

Ironically, I live and work in Loma Linda, California, a community known worldwide for the health, extraordinary resilience, and longevity of its citizens. Often referred to as a longevity hot spot, Loma Linda is one of only five regions in the world—and the only one in North America—with clusters of centenarians, men and women who have reached a vibrant one hundred years of age.[1]

As a working mom, I wanted to do much better at promoting the health and well-being of my own kids. As a professor in the School of Public Health at Loma Linda University, I began to think critically about how to promote health and resilience among all children. After all, many studies have shown that our habits and experiences in childhood lay the foundation for our health as adults. What childhood practices had protected the centenarians in our community from the stresses of hardship and encouraged their accomplishments? I suspected that these senior citizens had much to teach today's parents about how to raise healthy kids, so I embarked on a study that centered on interviews with as many of the centenarians in my community as I could find.[2] My quest? To learn how their childhoods had set them up for resilience and success throughout their lifetimes.

WHAT THIS BOOK CAN DO FOR YOU

Through my research, I discovered eight resiliency principles common to all the centenarians I interviewed. Each is important for immediate and long-term health and resilience, not just for adults, but especially for children. Resilience—the body's ability to maintain itself both mentally and physically, either preventing disease, illness, or pathological changes in the first place, or bouncing back when illness or disease strikes—is a key factor in our families' wellness and wholeness. When supported by a positive mindset, resilience (physical, emotional, mental, and spiritual) enables people to reach their potential, whether in academics, extracurricular activities, or careers. It also promotes health within the entire body.

> *When you learn, teach. When you get, give.*
>
> MAYA ANGELOU

The resiliency principles help boost the immune system and protect us from everyday stressors, and they provide some degree of protection from ever-present environmental stressors like air pollution and viral outbreaks like COVID-19. I had no idea what was coming in early 2020, but I know that by putting the centenarians' wisdom into practice, my family and I were better prepared when that pandemic overtook the United States.

By adopting the eight resiliency principles, you and your family will experience immediate and long-term health benefits. Too often we parents practice à la carte health. We pick and choose the health habits we'll try to adopt—whether because we like them best, they conveniently fit into our schedules, or they support the idea of who we feel our family should be (hello, lacto-ovo, Friday-only pescatarian vegetarians). But choosing just a couple of habits will get you only so far. We need to practice whole health.

Because I know from personal experience how hard it can be to begin and remain committed to lifestyle changes, I provide a number of tools to help you along the way. I've included a survey in the back so you can take stock of the areas where you are strongest and where you could benefit most from improvement. You'll find several other tools there to help you evaluate your progress along the way, as well as healthy recipes developed by a dietitian and executive chef.

Chapters 1 and 2 give you an inside peek at how a conflict within the Loma Linda community ultimately helped lead me to compromise my family's health—and how I took back control. Chapters 3 through 9 will walk you through one new principle each week. The final chapter will give you the tools to help you and your family keep up your new healthy habits. In these chapters, you'll discover what I learned from the centenarians and how you can begin to apply those lessons in your own family. I encourage you to use a notebook or journal to record your responses to the questions and prompts in each chapter, which will help you track your progress along the way.

Though you can practice one new principle each week, don't worry about covering them all in eight weeks if that's not feasible. Also, if you are pressed for time, look for the "In a Pinch, It's a Cinch" section in each chapter, where I provide you with strategies for kick-starting that specific resiliency principle.

As you complete the program, you and your family are likely to see improvement in three areas of your life: resilience, happiness, and performance (from academics to athletics and beyond), with the added bonus of immune systems that are better prepared for the next epidemic looming on the horizon. Through my university-affiliated health education programs and guest presentations on this topic, I have helped thousands of parents, childcare providers, and school educators put these powerful principles into action. Now it's your turn. This has been a life-changing journey for me, and it can be life-changing for you as well.

PART 1

GET READY...GET SET

WHY RESILIENCE? WHY NOW?

CHAPTER 1

A MOM IN HIDING

*What you do makes a difference, and you have to decide
what kind of difference you want to make.*

JANE GOODALL

IN 2011, A FIGHT BROKE OUT in the Loma Linda community. Just a few years after we'd been honored and lauded for being named the only Blue Zone in North America, a major fast-food chain approached our city council, seeking to open a location in town. Big Macs and McNuggets in the land of longevity? Though we did have one other fast-food establishment, it didn't begin to approach the cheeseburger juggernaut that was the Golden Arches, and at least that other restaurant made sure to highlight a vegetarian option. For some in my community, the Golden Arches were the greasy epitome of fast food in America—just empty, salty calories with no redeeming qualities.

My colleagues at the university, many of them close friends, urged me to join them at the city council meeting. "Make sure you mark your calendar!" I was told. "We need as many people there as possible to stop this monstrosity from rolling into our city." Even little children were quoted in the local newspaper as saying things like "Our Blue Zone is going to die!"

Me? I sat quietly on the sidelines. After all, who could stop this corporation? Wasn't fast food—particularly *this* fast food—woven into the fabric of America? Its presence in our community was unavoidable; indeed, it was inevitable. Sure enough, despite the protests, it wasn't long before those ubiquitous Golden Arches were displayed prominently on the busiest street in Loma Linda.

For me, a noncombatant in the burger war, the chain's arrival was no big deal. What's another fast-food joint? So shortly after their grand opening, I decided to take my kids for a visit—I was probably one of their first twenty customers.

"Do you guys want an ice cream cone?" I asked my two older kids—both under ten at the time. I told myself that a simple soft-serve ice cream cone wasn't a burger. I remained a semi-practicing vegetarian, right? Very rarely had my kids been exposed to fast food, so I thought of our visit as a harmless taste of American culture.

"Yeahhhh!" they said immediately and in unison, as if they'd waited for this moment their entire lives.

Even with my "no big deal, let's have an ice cream cone" attitude, that first time in the drive-through was a real nail-biter. I kept looking over my shoulder and out the side window like a guilt-ridden criminal. What would my colleagues think if they saw me—a health professor, a researcher, and a dedicated mom—feeding my children fast food?

At the speaker window, I quickly and quietly announced, "Three cones, please."

"Can you please restate your order?" came the staticky voice through the speaker.

"Three cones to go!" I snapped.

"Hold on." After pressing what seemed like dozens of keys, the cashier gave me the total, and I pulled my minivan to the first window to pay and receive our guilty pleasures.

As I drove up, I dug through the little tray in the console to count out the exact amount; I didn't want to wait a minute longer for the cashier to make change. Every minute I sat there was a minute closer to getting caught. I placed the money in the hand of the cashier, a teenage girl with glasses. And then I waited.

And waited. And waited. *What are they doing, churning the ice cream?*

Uneasy, I peered into the rearview mirror at the cars behind me in line.

"I'm so sorry it's taking me so long. I'm still learning the system," the girl said, adjusting her glasses as if that might somehow help her master the process. The stress radiating off me didn't help her concentration—she managed to fumble even more with the cash register.

Finally she handed me a receipt and asked me to drive to the next window, where the three vanilla cones were quickly produced. As the food attendant handed me the cones, she smiled and urged me to "have a wonderful day."

Wonderful? Hardly. My first fast-food purchase on the road to ruin.

Never again, I declared to myself. My kids hadn't been the ones who'd asked me to stop; this sacrilege was all my idea.

Before long, however, my children were routinely begging me to go for shakes, french fries, or hamburgers. Though I resisted their pleas for several weeks, one afternoon while we were driving, the kids spied the Golden Arches.

Maybe just this one time for a treat, I thought. *What's the harm?*

Obliging them, but still feeling guilt ridden should any of my colleagues catch me in the act, I searched my car for a disguise. This was no ice cream outing, I realized. This was Operation Eat and Retreat. I dug out sunglasses and, believe it or not, a wig—part of a costume from my work helping kids learn healthy habits. Crumbs from my children's back seat snacks clung to the top of the wig. No problem. I picked off most of the debris and donned my costume. Once past the drive-through and without being noticed—I hoped—I removed my wig and glasses and turned onto the main drag.

And so it began: a hidden habit our family secretly enjoyed—and felt we couldn't quit. The more I got away with it, the easier it became to get dinner on the table by passing by the take-out window. As my kids became involved in more after-school activities, I typically felt rushed and at a loss for dinner. If I lacked any set plans, my kids recommended picking up nuggets or a burger. Too often, I obliged.

Then one evening when I was beating myself up for my fast-food sins, my husband chimed in with his two cents: "Don't worry about it; we don't go that often." And so I didn't worry and carried on with our family's secret habit.

Our "not that often" became more often than I would care to admit. What had started as a rare treat had turned into a weekly treat and eventually a twice-a-week treat. As the days got busier, I gradually let go of other practices that defined my community's lifestyle—hikes, leisurely vegetarian meals, weekly Sabbath services. Once I resigned myself to accepting my fate as a harried mom, along came the baggage of guilt and regret.

ON THE MAP

When I first moved to Loma Linda for college, the community's health-oriented way of life was brand new to me. Having grown up in the Pacific Northwest with its lush cover of fir, cedar, and pine trees, I hated the sight of palm trees, which seemed more like movie props than actual trees. I swore to myself that, after earning my degree, I'd return to life in the verdant, aromatic forests of Oregon. But then I met Joseph, aka Broken Leg Joe—a nickname he picked up after breaking his leg in a mountain-biking accident. Joe was a Chinese American with a great athletic build who grew up in Loma Linda and loved the outdoors. We met at the sprawling university gym, where I was enrolled in graduate school in the School of Public Health at Loma Linda University. Before long, Joe was dragging me off for one outdoor adventure after another. Once we fell in love and got married, leaving Loma Linda was the last thing on my mind, and I gladly accepted a faculty position after I'd graduated.

By our fifth anniversary, we had two children, Jayden and Joelle, and the pace of our lives switched into a whole other gear—like going from a brisk walk to a sprint. We had less and less leisurely time to spend in each other's company. The comforting hours spent cooking a meal together or playing a game became distant memories. Suddenly there was no time for baking homemade bread, plucking oranges from trees, kicking back with family, or enjoying simple meals together. Like many other parents today, we ran ourselves ragged just trying to keep up. By the time our surprise baby, Julia, arrived, we were so busy speeding through our days that we were unable to see how chaotic and pressured our lives had become.

Something was happening in my own quiet community as my life sped up. In 2005, Dan Buettner had thrust Loma Linda under the bright lights and onto center stage. This journalist, who had salt-and-pepper hair, a blindingly white smile, and a fondness for black hiking boots, had strategically traipsed the globe along with an investigative team on assignment for *National Geographic*. They were on a quest to discover the longevity hot spots around the world—and they found five of them. Buettner called these hot spots "Blue Zones." In these exceptional communities, people lived extraordinarily long and healthy lifespans.

My quiet community of Loma Linda had been identified as one of the longevity hot spots. The others include the Mediterranean island of Sardinia, the city of Nicoya in Costa Rica, and the islands of Okinawa in the Sea of Japan and Icaria in the Aegean Sea.

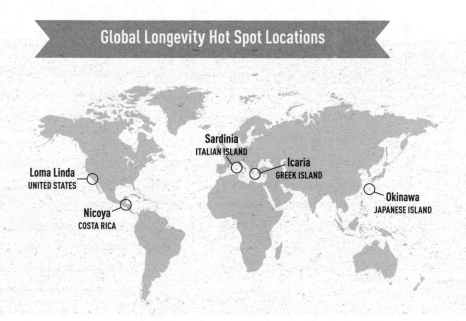

Global Longevity Hot Spot Locations

So how did Loma Linda get on the map? When I arrived here, most of my friends back home had never heard of the town or would have had difficulty finding it in an atlas. Even Siri (had she/it existed then) might have had trouble directing someone here. There were no professional sports teams, no national monuments. At the turn of the twentieth century, however, the Seventh-day Adventists (SDA), a Protestant denomination known for celebrating the Sabbath on Saturday rather than Sunday, bought a failed resort in the town and turned it into a sanatorium, nursing school, and medical school. Before long, Loma Linda became home to a large group of SDA practitioners and health professionals known for their healthy lifestyles.

Seventh-day Adventists tend to consume a plant-based diet, one rich in nuts and beans; refrain from smoking, taking drugs, or drinking alcohol; and on average are more physically active than the general population. Their tradition of health is so well established that many SDAs train to become doctors, nurses, dentists, physical therapists, and other health-related specialists. Over 1,400,000 Adventists live in the United States, with the largest group living in Loma Linda.

The Adventist Health Study, launched in 1974 and funded by the National Institutes of Health, is one of the largest ongoing lifestyle studies in the world.[1] Through this investigation, researchers at Loma Linda University discovered that our community's healthy habits were linked to a longer life. And we're not talking about a few months, a year, or even two; my community members typically live up to ten years longer than the rest of the United States population.

When the curiously high number of centenarians in our community hit the national news, reporters sought out my expertise in public health to help explain the lifestyle that had made our city internationally famous overnight. The unique diets and lifestyles of our elderly residents have been examined by several highly regarded scientific studies and investigative reports, but media coverage of the Blue Zones put our city on the map. My phone rang as TV news reporters and journalists—including CNN's Dr. Sanjay Gupta, ABC's Diane Sawyer, and Oprah's pal Dr. Oz—interviewed our residents and discussed our community on nationally televised shows. A video crew came from Finland to shoot footage of our little town, while a Belgian crew contacted me about taking part in a documentary. Researchers from countries across the globe emailed and called me, wanting to set up meetings, compare notes, and answer questions. Visitors stopped by my office regularly, and complete strangers requested guided tours of the town.

A FAMILY ON THE RUN

Ironically, even as I explained our town's healthy habits, my norm became stress, sadness, and a pounding headache, driven in part by my food choices, but stoked also by many other aspects of our family's frenzied lifestyle. Hardest hit was Julia—my bonus baby—forced to keep up with our family's hectic and demanding schedules. I couldn't help but notice her growing temper tantrums and increasingly whiny tone. Rather than making time for the open-ended sandbox sessions and endless afternoons spent looking for bugs in the backyard that her siblings had enjoyed, I dragged Julia along to their sports practices, piano recitals, and a million other activities.

Our daily lives can become disconnected from the hopes and dreams we hold for our family.

KIM JOHN PAYNE

To keep Julia occupied and happy, I had not one but two electronic devices, each in a colorful case, as if she needed any further enticement. I even bought a larger purse—like a Mary Poppins carpetbag that produced endless surprises—to conceal all the electronics and my hoard of sugary and salty snack foods, which were more hidden habits. If I needed some time to catch up on work, I didn't think twice about giving all three children computer time or letting them watch television for a few hours. When they were Julia's age, I never allowed my older two children to use, much less have, iPads and smartphones. Now, before the age of two, my youngest was an expert on my iPad and iPhone and worked the TV remote control like a professional couch potato.

To make matters worse, my husband was diagnosed with high blood pressure and high cholesterol. His pill containers became a routine fixture in our pantry, stored above the Oreos. Every time I opened the pantry and saw those bottles, I felt a knot in the pit of my stomach. While heart conditions did run in his family, I knew our "convenient" lifestyle wasn't helping the matter.

And he wasn't the only one with elevated cholesterol. My yearly screening required by insurance revealed that while my weight was fine, my cholesterol was well above the acceptable range. I was scared and stunned. My husband and I were highly active—we rode mountain bikes at least three times a week and walked together daily. We ate almost no red meat. How could our cholesterol be so high?

The news got worse. In addition to addressing our soaring parental cholesterol levels, our pediatrician recommended that our son focus on his physical fitness to address his rising weight. Me, my husband, and my child—what was next? I worried that all my children could be experiencing hidden health problems. Here I was, a public health professor—someone who wrote grants and developed health programs for parents and their children. I felt the anxiety churning within me, spinning like a merry-go-round. I had to do something. And I knew one thing from my work in public health—I wasn't alone, either in my unhealthy habits or my unease over how my parenting was affecting my family's well-being.

This concern is warranted: About thirty-two million kids in the United States have at least one chronic health condition (such as asthma or obesity).[2] In fact, a leading journal on health policy declared that the prevalence of chronic conditions in children has reached epidemic levels.[3] Not only that, but the American Psychological Association reported that stress among families has been rising dramatically, particularly as a result of the COVID-19 pandemic.[4]

Each chronic condition, such as diabetes, asthma, obesity, depression, and anxiety, is marked by a state of increased chronic inflammation in the body, which can be measured by elevated inflammatory markers in the blood or tissue. In addition to chronic health conditions, continual stress and environmental contaminants (like air pollution) are linked with increased levels of inflammatory markers. Alarmingly, scientific studies show that harmful physiological changes from ongoing stress can begin in childhood.[5] These markers signal that the immune system is being taxed, which sets children up for a range of poor outcomes, and not just in their physical health. Scientists think inflammation may potentially affect mental health by driving the development of depression.[6] The negative effect of chronic inflammation doesn't stop there; one study of children ages seven to thirteen found that a number of elevated inflammatory markers are linked with significantly lower academic performance.[7]

Most moms and dads sense that something has gone wrong. A national survey of parents found that 90 percent of mothers and 85 percent of fathers worry and feel judged about what others think of their parenting practices, and 69 percent say if they knew more positive parenting strategies, they would use them.[8] A second survey of teens found that 75 percent

Do You Relate?

Which of the following experiences and feelings do you identify with?

- ☐ Hectic family schedules
- ☐ Frequent on-the-go dining
- ☐ Hidden habits
- ☐ Worries about what others think of your family's lifestyle choices
- ☐ Concerns about your child's health and/or their success in life
- ☐ Routine feelings of exhaustion and being overwhelmed
- ☐ A chronic illness experienced by you or a family member
- ☐ Extreme concern for family and your ability to thrive when faced with an epidemic or other disaster
- ☐ Concerns about what the future holds for you and your family

of kids would like their parents to live healthier too.[9] Yet all too often, we fail to do what is necessary to make that happen. I know; I was one of those parents.

MAKING THE CHANGE

With all this interest in my community, I felt forced—okay, maybe not forced, but some days it sure felt that way—to live a double life. Here I was a member of the only longevity hot spot in the United States and a university professor who was teaching others how to live healthier lives. Yet I kept the truth of how my own family lived stuffed in a closet, along with the Pringles, Cap'n Crunch, and Oreos. As life turned upside down, I grew more aware of my own struggles and growing unease.

As uncomfortable and guilt ridden as all the media attention made me feel, I might not have noticed my family's gradual descent into the unhealthy modern lifestyle if it hadn't been for my town's sudden celebrity, which made me a little more aware of my surroundings and prodded me to change my habits. And baby Julia, just by digging her way to China in our sandbox, had shown me that what a young child needs is not another Big Mac, iPad, or TV show, but a life lived in the style of those who'd made our community a longevity hot spot. She and my other children deserved not just a centenarian's many years; they deserved the good health that made those years so rich and wondrous.

Sitting there on my patio watching little Julia play, I realized that I felt exhausted from all the hiding and the baggage that came with it. I knew I could do better—I *wanted* better for myself and for others!

As I quietly prayed for change, an answer slowly began to form in my mind. It was time to come out of hiding. I couldn't keep worrying what people would think of me if they knew the truth about the lifestyle I'd created for my family. It was time to put to work my years of training in public health. I felt a spark ignite inside me, and the flame kept growing.

I strapped Julia into her stroller and began meandering through my quiet neighborhood. It wasn't long before I spied a couple of seniors I knew—two women who were best friends, both in their nineties and one

Picture It

Imagine the benefits of the Resiliency Program for you and your family:

- family schedules that don't leave you stressed and tired;
- improved relationships with family and friends;
- increased happiness and harmony in the home;
- enhanced academic performances;
- a boost in health and resilience;
- being better prepared for disastrous events and epidemics;
- the potential for vibrant longevity; and
- many more amazing benefits of the resilient centenarian lifestyle!

of them nearing one hundred. They were out and about for a stroll, gabbing away, delighting in the early morning sunshine. I maneuvered into the empty street, giving the two complete access to the sidewalk. Nearing them, I smiled and waved. The older of the two, Berra, a warm Filipino grandmother, paused for a moment to peer down at little Julia.

Looking back up at me, Berra asked, "Where's your father? We haven't seen him walk in a while. He's getting lazy."

I laughed at their comments about my own dad. In his seventies, he was a mere youngster in their minds. "I'll encourage him to get out and send him your way!" I said.

We chatted briefly and as I left, it occurred to me that those women were just two of the many seniors I saw strolling the sidewalks in the calm, tree-lined neighborhoods, or walking on the trails amidst the natural, wild beauty of the nearby hills, or heading for an outdoor swim at the local gym. In their nineties and hundreds, they remained vibrantly energetic and engaging—always with a warm smile and a wave, especially for baby Julia.

I wondered, *What if there was a way to increase resilience and health in our children by following the wisdom of our community's centenarians?*

Scientific studies show that harmful biological changes begin to take place in childhood and that the experiences of a child can lay the foundation for health, resilience, and lifespan in adulthood. What habits had my elderly neighbors developed as children that prevented the buildup of inflammation and stress? What childhood practices protected them from the detrimental effects of hardships and encouraged success?

Researchers from prominent universities and institutions across the nation—like Harvard, Kaiser Permanente, and the Centers for Disease Control (CDC)—are learning more about how early childhood experiences influence the development of diseases at all ages and determine how long we'll live. There's a growing consensus that health as an adult is strongly linked to one's childhood, yet we have barely scratched the surface of understanding how our early experiences create the foundation for a resilient life.

As a scholar, I decided to do what I do best. When I got home that afternoon—and on the many days and evenings after—I dived into my research. Given the important role that childhood plays in creating a foundation for resilience and even longevity, I expected to find countless studies looking into the childhood experiences of centenarians. They have, after all, survived for a whole century; how many people can say that? But even with the help of my university library, the many databases available to faculty, and the all-powerful Google search engine, I came up with only a handful of research studies. Even the longevity hot spot researchers focused on the centenarians' health habits as adults rather than on their childhood experiences, and not one study focused on a whole group of centenarians like those living in my famous community. Opportunity knocked—and soon so did I, on many of the centenarians' front doors. Little did I realize that I was about to embark on a journey in which I'd experience a complete paradigm shift—one that would change my family's life for the better.

If you, too, are tired of living life on a merry-go-round and want a better way for your family, take this journey with me as I introduce you to the resiliency principles I uncovered from my interviews with the centenarians. In the chapters that follow, I will tell you more about the discoveries

I made, the lessons I learned, and the eight-week crash course my family began when I decided to apply those lessons to our own lives. Best of all, I will unpack the remarkable change we've enjoyed in our health, happiness, resilience (especially our ability to thrive in the face of an epidemic), and so much more.

HOMEWORK TIME

1. Remembering back before you had a family, how did you imagine your future family life? How did you picture your home with children? How did you imagine yourself as a parent? And how does your current experience match—and/or differ from—what you dreamed it would be?

2. What do you think are your family's pressure points or times when your family members are most likely to experience intense feelings of stress or chaos? What do you do in response to those demands? Does it alleviate the stress or add to it?

3. Write down three ideas for what you think would make your family life better. For each idea, write down one small step you could take toward that goal.

CHAPTER 2

A RESILIENCY CAPITAL: UNCOVERING THEIR SECRETS

A vision is not just a picture of what could be;
it is an appeal to our better selves, a call to become something more.

ROSABETH MOSS KANTER

WITH JULIA SITUATED ON ONE HIP and my overly stocked diaper bag slung over my opposite shoulder, I walked between two giant gumdrop evergreen trees on my way to the front of a white house. Accompanied by Joe and his mom, I was en route to interview a special centenarian about her childhood—my husband's great-aunt, Mulan Tsai.

Finding very limited research on the childhood experiences of centenarians, I had decided it was time to meet some of my celebrated community centenarians to see what advice they could provide young parents today. Loma Linda offered me a robust group of centenarians I could turn to for help, including my husband's great-aunt. At 100, Auntie Mulan was free of any chronic diseases, lived independently, and still drove her car.

As we reached the front door, I fumbled with the strap of my diaper bag, attempting to make it more comfortable. Inside I had stashed a tape recorder and an odd assortment of pens and paper along with diapers, wet wipes, Cheerios, a change of baby clothes, and one brightly colored giraffe.

I had everything I thought I'd need to survive this adventure—and maybe even a week or two in the woods.

Auntie Mulan's house was an inviting single story with large jade plants and colorful potted orchids lining the entry. We rang the bell, listening to the delicate chimes inside as we waited. Soon Auntie Mulan and her son, James, opened the door and with engaging grins simultaneously said, "Hello!"

"Come in, come in," James quickly added. "It's too hot out there."

As we stepped inside, James guided us to the first room on our left, the formal living room.

"Let's sit in here. There's lots of space for us all," James said.

Sun shone through the windows, and the room was simply decorated with beautiful Asian furnishings. I noticed how neat and tidy everything was. And it was quiet, with no loud television blaring. That was quite different from my own hectic home, with toys strewn all about and a dog and three kids running around, filling the house with constant chatter.

I gently placed Julia on the floor, and she quickly made herself at home. Spying a white, fluffy lambskin rug, she crawled over and began rolling around on it. She ended up on her back with her chubby legs in the air, grabbing at her toes and thoroughly enjoying herself. Watching her, everyone laughed loudly. I chuckled a little, too, relieved that no one was upset. Then I began to realize that Julia just might steal the show. I rather liked the thought—no eyes staring intently, waiting for me to say something intelligent.

With all the excitement and attention on her baby gymnastics, Julia quickly tired out and crawled over to my legs. I picked her up and rocked her in my lap, where she went right to sleep.

My nerves calmed, I began asking questions. I considered this my trial run. My fellow researchers and I planned to replicate this interview with many more centenarians. My goal was simple—to find out about the positive and negative aspects of their childhood experiences. Mostly, I was intent on interviewing them about the healthy habits (like a more vegetable-based diet) they had developed back then, but I thought I should ask a question about hardships on the off chance any of them had experienced an adverse childhood experience (ACE) or two.[1]

Sitting next to Auntie Mulan, I asked her, "Could you describe what life was like for you as a child?" Joe gave me an encouraging nod.

"Sure," she replied. "I wasn't born here in the US but in southern China. Things were simpler back then because we didn't have much. We were very, very poor. We ate whatever we had on hand. Once in a while we'd have fish. I sewed and tended to the other children to help my mom."

I asked, "Auntie Mulan, were there any especially hard times that you remember as a child?"

Auntie Mulan's voice grew softer. "Yes, it was hard when my father passed away. I was only seven years old when it happened. A year or two later my mom remarried, but things weren't so great with my stepdad. He wasn't very nice. Plus, we still didn't have much money. Then by the age of eleven, I was sent away to a boarding school. To help pay the cost of going to school there, I worked in the laundry room. It was really tough."

We continued talking throughout the afternoon as Auntie Mulan relayed a story of extreme adversity, accompanied by joyful recollections of working hard and aspiring to a better life. Through those tough early years, she never wavered in her optimism that, for all the hardships, she was on a path toward something greater. There were moments of pain in her voice and eyes, but never a moment of self-pity or anger. I marveled at how strong she must have been to overcome such tremendous adversities and to exude such calm and clarity.

Her bright demeanor and positive spirit sustained her even into adulthood. Eventually, Auntie Mulan and her husband relocated to the United States to be closer to their grown children and expanding family.

By the time I wrapped up our interview, I knew I'd leave Auntie Mulan's house much more serene than I'd been when we arrived. In telling me her story, she had taught me something I wanted to apply to my own life: She had led a life of indescribable hardship and pain, but she hadn't let those adversities destroy her. Instead, she let them build her character and resiliency, which had helped her cope with the other, more common hardships that life delivers. I realized that her positive attitude had lifted me out of my own self-concern and anxiety.

Talking with Auntie Mulan also gave me the confidence I needed to go forth and meet with more—many more—centenarians. To better understand the perspectives and experiences of the centenarians and other seniors living in the Loma Linda region, I wanted to develop a team to carefully collect and analyze data extrapolated from one-on-one interviews and focus groups with this target group. As an epidemiologist, I knew I needed many interviews if I was going to discover any rules or patterns that might explain their resiliency.

When I shared my plan in a meeting at the university, however, I was met with heavy skepticism. One of my colleagues, an epidemiologist himself, challenged the idea.

"I doubt you'll be able to make any kind of difference," he said. "Besides, you're only collecting stories."

I understood his perspective well. Epidemiologists like to count and measure things. We like to find clear, identifiable patterns and associations that explain health and disease in objective, unambiguous ways. Stories just don't do that. But I sensed that it would be the stories, more than the numbers, that would help us understand how these men and women had lived so long—and with such clarity of mind and joy of spirit. Their stories wouldn't muddy the waters, I reasoned; they would draw us closer to those health habits that would encourage healing and promote resiliency.

Needing to garner support for my research and without a dime in my pocket, I put word out that I was looking for volunteers to assist me in my quest. It wasn't long before an assorted group of graduate students and public health research professionals responded.

I developed a semi-structured interview guide, which now included open-ended questions designed to measure economic hardship, family dysfunction, and community violence.[2] After interviewing Auntie Mulan, I thought I might need to ask more questions related to ACEs.[3] Those were supplemented with questions on resiliency factors (RFs), such as diet, rest, time outdoors, and healthy psychosocial relationships. Each of these helps people adapt well in the face of adversity, stress, or trauma. I received ideas on additional questions from my newly formed research team, including some from moms like, Did the centenarians eat sugar? Chicken? How about breastfeeding? How much sleep did they get?

Next, my team had to identify our centenarians. Since there was no directory or database list, we had to do some detective work. Fortunately, I'd learned to locate people from my previous employer, the county health department. Back then, the people I was tracking were spreading infectious diseases, which took me all over the place from hilltop mansions to prisons in the valley—an experience that had served me well.

We used our collective resources to locate centenarians living in the Loma Linda area, connecting with churches, senior living centers, and a local senior community center, as well as friends and family members. Searching high and low, far and wide, we soon found them (and would continue to find them many years later). From a housewife to a surgeon, from a medical social worker to a farmer, with each centenarian interviewed, we were more intrigued by what we learned.

IT'S A HARD-KNOCK LIFE

After months of traipsing all over the place meeting with centenarians, we finally completed the interviews. We then adhered to specific research methods for studying these interviews—recording and transcribing each, word for word, and then analyzing the transcriptions. It was tedious but necessary work. We allowed the interviews to guide us as we looked for consistencies and patterns. For months, my team and I pored over the interview field notes and transcripts. Thousands of parents with kids still at home participated in additional informal interviews to shed light on the stress in households today, as well as dealing with chronic conditions such as asthma. (Some of these parents' stories are included in this book as well, though I've used pseudonyms to protect their privacy.) We also interviewed pediatricians, some of whom were overwhelmed by the need to treat chronic conditions like obesity, diabetes, and depression in their young patients. Finally, the results were in.

It was clear that the centenarians' early-twentieth-century lives were far different from the cluttered consumer- and technology-driven, sedentary, and isolated childhoods that today's children typically experience. Through their hundred-year-old eyes, I'd caught a glimpse of a much more quiet and connected time. They had been raised in slower-paced, do-it-yourself (DIY) communities—with an emphasis on community. Families didn't go it alone—they depended on one another. They also relied on much simpler forms of technology to communicate and get things done.

While today's technologies are supposed to make life easier, they tend to lead to increasingly hectic lives, demanding even more of our professional and personal time. When we connect with friends only through texts or Facebook while on the run or multitasking, we are often oblivious to the people around us. Meanwhile, children spend most of their time indoors, glued to computers or watching TV, rather than playing outside in nature or with their friends.

In contrast, most of the centenarians had been raised in farming families who maintained an active outdoor lifestyle immersed in physical activity from dawn to dusk. The centenarians had baked bread, cared for younger siblings, and helped their families garden and raise livestock. Their diets were simple; they consumed what they grew themselves—mostly vegetables. Due to their farming way of life, their sleeping habits were highly structured, with routine bed and waking times. Perhaps most importantly, they spent time with family and friends, helping one another from an early age. Often these relationships provided emotional support and understanding, especially in times of great adversity. During their childhood, all the centenarians we talked with had been connected to faith-based activities and communities, either through family practices at home or through regular attendance at church or temple and involvement in church-related activities. Lastly, no matter their circumstances, the centenarians had positive mindsets as children. They believed that their actions would result in positive outcomes.

What surprised me, however, was not the many health-related practices they spoke of, but something else. Frequently, just like Auntie Mulan, the centenarians talked about the tremendous adversity they endured in their childhoods as if it was a simple challenge that they went through and overcame. These hardships included deaths in their immediate family and parents who had divorced or who were addicted, mentally ill, abusive, or neglectful. Many of the centenarians had endured economic hardships early in life and often went without much food. While much is made of contemporary violence, the centenarians didn't necessarily live lives of peaceful innocence. Some were witness to unspeakable, constant community violence and brutality during their childhoods. Though they'd lived through these adverse experiences almost a century earlier, many such situations are quite prevalent in households and communities today.

The centenarian hardship responses came not from any specific questions I asked, however. I learned of these stories when I got out of my epidemiological mindset and just asked them to share about their childhoods. I never imagined they'd recall so many traumatic events in such detail. In my naiveté, I'd reckoned that to live to one hundred without any chronic conditions, they must have had an easy start in life. Now I realized how wrong I'd been. Not only did they face psychologically related stressors, they endured harmful environmental conditions to boot—like routinely breathing polluted air before the Clean Air Act was ratified or working long and grueling hours in dangerous conditions before labor laws protected adult and child workers. The centenarians have lived through countless disease outbreaks, with many experiencing at least four pandemics themselves, including the 1918 Spanish flu. They also survived the Great Depression, which flung many families into economic uncertainty and took away their livelihoods.

Everyone has a story that will break your heart. And, if you are really paying attention, most people have a story that will bring you to your knees.

BRENÉ BROWN

What I had stumbled upon was not merely a longevity hot spot or a fountain of youth, but something much greater. This was a *Resiliency Capital*—a region or community in which members show biological signs of having overcome tremendous hardships, chronic psychological stress, harmful environmental conditions, viruses, and even the daily struggles of living. They had been able to bounce back from all these childhood hardships to a state of wholeness with healthy bodies, minds, and spirits, and to live extraordinarily long and fulfilling lives.

Stress plays a significant and important role in our lives. Stress can be helpful when we use it as a motivating force for positive change. However, too much of the wrong type of stress can have a detrimental impact. A landmark study by the physician Dr. Vincent Felitti and CDC epidemiologist Dr. Robert Anda demonstrated that significant chronic adverse childhood experiences (ACEs) have been linked to childhood health conditions and chronic health conditions in adulthood, ultimately shortening people's lifespans.[4] ACEs aren't the only factors that cause stress; it results from anything that negatively and chronically affects whole health (like air pollution, poverty, epidemics, and daily life struggles). The centenarians had a plethora of ACEs and other stressors, and yet they'd overcome whatever life threw their way. Clearly, their resiliency started in childhood. Their lives were not only healthy and extraordinarily long, but they were also filled with adventure and a sense of purpose; in some cases, their positive impact had stretched across the globe.

I had to smile when I thought about how my colleague had questioned the value of collecting mere "stories." These stories were instrumental in rediscovering a path—one that had been forged long ago, but forgotten. A path that provides hope and a better way for overcoming what we face today. Through the shared stories of their childhood experiences, I'd gained tremendous insight into the centenarians' resiliency. What I'd found was not something we likely would have discovered through written surveys; instead, the discoveries came as we spent time with them and heard their life stories.

Despite a multitude of technological advancements, life isn't less stressful today. The centenarians—and their childhood experiences—unlock secrets to positively influencing the resiliency, happiness, and success of families and even society as a whole.

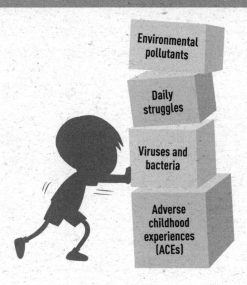

The Childhood Practices of Centenarians Protect against the Stressors of Daily Life

Environmental pollutants

Daily struggles

Viruses and bacteria

Adverse childhood experiences (ACEs)

THE EIGHT RESILIENCY PRINCIPLES

As parents and caregivers, we want the best for our children and families. We want them to experience happiness and joy, as well as academic and extracurricular success. We long for them to find their purpose and be the healthiest they can be. However, we often fail to realize just how interconnected these categories are. Researchers have found associations—for both adults and children—between heightened chronic stress and health problems, decreased happiness, and lowered performance in every area, from academics to athletics to the workplace. Failing to see the connection between these measures of well-being, we try to address each one separately, but in the end, we create more stress for ourselves and slip further away from our goals. We need a new perspective and approach for a comprehensive problem—and my conversations with the centenarians convinced me that the *Resiliency Capital* is our blueprint.

By analyzing the data and stories the centenarians shared with me, I identified eight specific principles each had lived by and which had been planted like seeds early in life.[5] The eight principles are further defined by four major cornerstones—encouraging us to be **Active, Balanced, Connected,** and **Determined.** As a parent, I understand how stretched our minds are by trying to remember appointments, run errands, plan mealtimes, help with homework, and everything in between. That is why I came up with those four cornerstones—basically they're the ABCs for grown-ups. Because the centenarians' lifestyles reflected these values, they likely experienced immediate stress relief and the ability to overcome significant challenges from childhood on. They also increased the likelihood that they would live healthier, more vibrant lives, filled with increased happiness and a greater sense of purpose, and reach successes they would never have imagined possible.

Each of the eight resiliency principles works independently as well as collaboratively to dampen stress and inflammation, promoting health for the mind, body, and spirit. By practicing many of these resiliency principles daily, the centenarians were helping their bodies recover from

Eight Resiliency Principles and Their Cornerstones Are:

- Active Movement
- Nature Engagement

Active

- Simple Foods
- Resting Reset

Balanced

- Nurturing Relationships
- Faith Foundation

Connected

- Positive Mindset
- Helping Hands

Determined

The Positive Ripple Effect of Reducing Chronic Stress

Goes beyond Increasing Resilience

| Decrease Impact of Chronic Stress | = | Increase Resilience | + | Increase Happiness | + | Increase Positive Performance |

all the stresses they faced and maintain balance—a state of what I call *wholestasis* (from the terms *homeostasis* and *wholeness*), in which the body, mind, and spirit are daily made healthy and whole. Furthermore, scientific studies provide evidence that the resiliency principles act synergistically, meaning that when practiced in tandem, the positive protective effects on the body are magnified. By helping your children put all of these principles into practice, you will not only help them immediately increase their resilience, happiness, and performance, but you will also be setting them up for greater health and success later in life.

Of course, no one wants their children to experience extreme hardship, but sometimes in our efforts to protect our kids, we raise them in a bubble of comfort, inadvertently planting seeds of dependency and anxiety rather than seeds of resiliency. As I reflected on my own parenting practices, I realized I was raising my children indoors, insulating them from life's adversities, and feeding them food that practically wasn't even food. I didn't want to continue along that path. So the first thing I did to prepare my family for this journey was to write down all the ways I was shielding them from self-reliance and discomfort. For example, what chores did they do? How often did they do them? Were they taking initiative? What toys did I buy? What toys did they play with? How was I teaching them to handle conflict? Did I swoop in to settle a fight or let them settle it themselves? Was I inadvertently taking any shortcuts in my attempts to help them get ahead?

When I looked at my list, I saw that I wasn't preparing my children for real life—I was preparing them for TV life! Their life of ease didn't feel so easy to me because I took care of everything, which meant that when Mom was gone or busy, things got out of hand. How would my kids handle real-world stress if they never learned to handle small-world stress? And yet the truth was, I settled the conflicts or did the chores myself because I was so tired that it was usually just easier to do them than to leave it up to my kids. It saved me time.

Furthermore, our lifestyle wasn't doing any favors for our immune systems, which are even more important to help us thrive in today's stressful world and prepare us for future epidemics. Chronic stressors (like ACEs and air pollution exposures) have been found to promote systemic inflammation and disrupt the immune system—potentially making a person more susceptible to infectious diseases—a concerning fact, given the recent worldwide virus outbreaks (like SARS, H1N1, and COVID-19).[6] A study by Johns Hopkins University found that children exposed to frequent household stress were at greater risk for illness, especially fever-related ones.[7] As we like to say in epidemiology, given global travel, the next infectious outbreak is just a plane flight away. For that reason, it is more critical than ever that we be better prepared and become as resilient as possible. The centenarians' resiliency principles have been found in independent scientific studies to boost the immune system, enhancing one's ability to fight off infectious diseases. That's especially important when there isn't a vaccine.

After considering how my parenting was affecting my kids' self-reliance, I thought about the difference in families' priorities today as compared to a century ago. To get a sense of what drove my family, I tracked how we actually spent our time for a few weeks. As we began practicing the resiliency principles, I noticed that we were investing more time and wasting less. The change in our lives was remarkable. Before I knew it, we were living a twenty-first-century centenarian lifestyle—and you can too, by introducing your family to the Resiliency Capital principles.

PLANT YOUR OWN SEEDS

Are you ready to increase your family's resilience? Do you want to reduce stress and increase happiness? Would you like to be better prepared for future epidemics by boosting your immune system? Do you have adversities of your own that you worry about?

You have now learned that the centenarians endured many challenges and adverse childhood experiences (ACEs), which science tells us probably should have shortened their lives but did not. You have also been introduced to the resiliency principles they began practicing as children, which potentially protected them from the worst effects of their hardships, poor environmental conditions, and risk of developing disease or infections. While practicing these principles won't guarantee perfect health for your family, it will increase your odds of achieving resiliency and, as a bonus, put your kids on the path to overall improved mental, physical, and spiritual health. In the next chapter, you can begin drawing on the collective wisdom of the centenarians we interviewed to learn how to put the first of these powerful principles into practice with your own family.

The ease in practicing all eight of the resiliency principles (and the benefit from their synergistic protective power) comes from experiencing them in an overlapping manner.

To begin this journey, start by taking a quick survey (see appendix A) to help identify which of the eight principles are already strengths for you and your family and which need some improvement. Every family is different, so the survey will help you better understand your family's needs and know which principles might be the most challenging.

There is one last but very important thing to consider as you begin this program. Take the time you need to go through this process wholly invested.

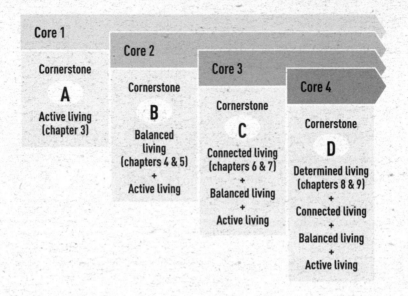

Resiliency Principles: Each Week Builds on the Previous One

Core 1

Cornerstone

A

Active living
(chapter 3)

Core 2

Cornerstone

B

Balanced
living
(chapters 4 & 5)
+
Active living

Core 3

Cornerstone

C

Connected living
(chapters 6 & 7)
+
Balanced living
+
Active living

Core 4

Cornerstone

D

Determined living
(chapters 8 & 9)
+
Connected living
+
Balanced living
+
Active living

Don't make major life decisions. Work to reduce extraneous shopping habits. Simplify your life where possible. Don't take on extra duties or positions at work. The whole point is to gain clarity and resilience, so avoid distractions and extra stress. If your boss asks you to take on extra responsibilities, say no for now. This journey is too important, and you and your family deserve your attention.

Get ready—you are about to launch your eight-week Resiliency Program. In those eight weeks, you'll not only be able to gradually begin practicing each of the resiliency principles; you will have the time you need to develop new habits and be well on your way to sustaining them. With a "learn it," "live it," and "evaluate it" approach, each week will introduce you to a new resiliency principle, guide you as you incorporate it into your family's life, and then provide you with an opportunity to evaluate your experience. Starting with a double dose the first week, you will begin with not one but two resiliency principles to kick things into gear. After that, you'll build on what you've done the previous week to establish lasting change. During the eighth week, you'll evaluate your family's progress and learn tips for staying connected to your purpose and building your family's legacy.

Build up your weaknesses until they become your strong points.

KNUTE ROCKNE

Even though I call it a program, these eight resiliency principles are so much more—by adopting them, you will discover a whole new way of life. Going through this journey can be life altering— I know, because this experience turned my family's life around, got us off the couch and outdoors, enabled us to give up eating artificial food in favor of real food, and helped us come together as a family and community, both socially and spiritually.

Now it's your turn!

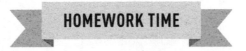

HOMEWORK TIME

Before moving on to chapter 3, set up your family for success by preparing for the adventure ahead. Grab a notebook and pen to answer the following questions and begin tracking your family's resiliency journey.

1. **Spend one week tracking your family's health and relationship habits.** This will enable you to evaluate how things are *currently done* in your household. Ask the hard questions:

   • Where and how does your family spend time?

   • Do you spend that time together or separately? Indoors or outdoors?

   • What do you typically eat? When and where do you eat it?

   • How do you encourage one another and/or others in your community?

   • How do your family members experience sleep? Do they have any particular habits regarding sleep?

   • In general, how does your family feel about these experiences?

At the end of that week, review what you've written. Don't judge yourself for your shortcomings. Simply acknowledge them. Reflect on how you are spending your time. Each day is like a metaphorical time closet. You only have so much space for things. When new things go in, old things have to come out or you'll risk becoming like my real-life closet—crammed so full of stuff the hinges are literally falling off. Throughout the program, you can refer back to your journal log to help identify areas and opportunities for change.

2. **Write down your personal statement as you prepare to begin the program.** Write just two or three sentences, perhaps using these questions as prompts: What are your goals? What is driving you? Are you looking for better health for your family? More joy in your lives? More time spent together with family and friends? A stronger immune system to withstand future outbreaks of disease? This statement is your "why."

Post your statement where you can view it each day. Better yet, create a vision board and post your "why" in the center. To create your vision board, gather pictures and quotes that inspire you to work toward your goals. Glue them on a poster board or pin them up on a corkboard. You can find great-looking framed boards at craft stores. Display in a place you will see daily. Connect often with your reason and motivation for wanting to launch this program.

Now compare your "why" statement with the household practices you wrote about in your journal log. Are the experiences and practices you wrote about supportive of your "why" statement? If the answer is no, whether to a few practices or to the majority, just make a mental note for now and know that these will become opportune areas for change. Your journal log and staying connected to your "why" will become powerful tools to help guide you throughout the eight-week program.

PART 2

GO!

LIVING THE RESILIENCY PROGRAM

WEEK 1:
DIGGING GOATS AND GARDENS

In every walk with Nature, one receives far more than he seeks.

JOHN MUIR

AN EXPLOSION SHATTERED THE SILENCE, followed by a scream.

Some sort of incomprehensible babble in a language not quite human made my toddler daughter chuckle. It was the language of Sims—simulated humans—from a popular computer game of simulated people living simulated lives. My kids loved it.

"I said," I repeated, hands on my hips, "let's get going!"

I cleared my throat, ready to raise my voice, when my older daughter shot back a half-hearted response. "I'm not going, and no one else wants to go either!" Joelle said, not bothering to look up as she slumped in a chair and twirled her hair on her index finger. Jayden reclined on the couch with his oversize "man feet" up on an armrest while Julia was sprawled out on the floor with clumps of peanut butter stuck to her chubby fingers. My three kids were "playing together," which is to say, they inhabited the same room, each mesmerized by the virtual worlds on their own electronic devices. This was not how I imagined our vacation in Portland, particularly on a pleasant sunny day like this one.

I was the mom, and that meant time for fun. As I defined it.

"Come on. You'll like it, I promise," I pleaded. Seeing no movement, I changed tactics. "I've been planning this for weeks, so let's get going."

I stood firm. "I'm not asking," I calmly told them. "I'm telling you. Now get up."

Slowly, their bodies began to show signs of life. I began hunting for hats and shoes to a soundtrack of groans and complaints. "You always make us do crazy things," Jayden declared. "You don't even care about what we want."

I ignored the comment and figured that, once we got going, happiness would follow. Since embarking on my research and applying the lessons I was learning within my own family, I felt as if I were always nudging my kids out of their comfort zone and into new ways of living. They had resisted at first, as they did now, but I was learning that the more I dismissed their resistance, the more readily they accepted that the electronics were to be turned off and we were going outside.

The moment we stepped out the door, the aroma of gardenias and freshly cut grass enveloped us. I inhaled their perfume as if I could capture it forever. After a morning spent in frosty air-conditioning, the sun warmed my face and arms. By the time we reached the family van, I knew this mission was a go. We were on our way—me, the kids, my husband, and even my dad.

The van hummed along, frequently slowing for all the pedestrians, bicyclists, and red lights we encountered. The fast-food signs we passed were like the ringing bell for Pavlov's dogs, making my kids salivate just thinking of the MSG-laden cheeseburgers and chocolate milkshakes they imagined waiting for them.

"Can we stop at a drive-through? I'm hungry," Joelle whined.

"What? We just had lunch!" I said. Not only that, but fast food was no longer an option. Along with being determined to get my kids outside more, I had established another rule—we were eating real food.

Five minutes later, I pulled up in front of my sister's house and parked beneath the shade of a large green oak tree.

"Let's go," I said as I grabbed my purse and flung open the van doors. We marched up the concrete steps and received a warm welcome from my niece, eight-year-old Jenevieve.

My sister's backyard was a rather eclectic adventure, with all kinds of oddities from an outdoor piano and manhole sewer covers that doubled as stepping-stones, to a gang of little kittens and a couple of the neighbor's chickens darting around through the weeds.

We'd been there only a moment when we spied the pygmy goats walking up the path. Jumping, jerking, and walking with a spirited energy, they bounded into my sister's backyard from the path beyond. They possessed more energy than all our group put together. At first glance they looked like dogs, but their awkward mannerisms indicated otherwise. The closer they got, the stronger their smell—that funny farm, animal hair, and hay aroma.

My sister had "rented" the two young pygmy goats, one jet-black and the other a creamy tan and white. With any luck, they'd mow her lawn. But there was no time for that now. The kids had discovered the kids. Joelle patted the head of the black goat, feeling its little horn nubs and scratching behind its soft ears. The pygmies' bellies, like giant balloons, made them look like cartoon characters, their comical round weight supported by skinny legs and little black hooves. The girls handed out a few apples, quickly devoured with much slobbery goat saliva as my sister tethered the two animals together with a single retractable dog leash. What else do you use to take goats for a neighborhood walk? She gave Joelle the opportunity to hold the leash, an offer immediately accepted. Little Julia climbed into the orange stroller, clapping her hands, and we were off.

We meandered down the tree-lined streets, heading for Reed College, which is surrounded by a beautiful forest. Once we were on the campus, more and more students took notice of our clan. "Do you guys know that's a goat?" one student asked, as if we might be oblivious to its species. Several students came close, eager to pet and talk to the animals. Even members of the animal kingdom appeared taken aback by the sight of our four-legged pack. A yellow Labrador retriever passed us, slowing to stare and sniff the air, pondering the goats' presence. Persuaded they were no threat, or a threat best unchallenged, the Lab hurried off.

As we headed to the park surrounding the college, a group of female students ran out of their dorm, holding their phones aloft like mirrors to their faces to video record us, no doubt hoping to create a viral YouTube video.

We wandered through the shady trees trimming the ponds scattered across the campus, the electronic sounds of computer games a distant memory. Our mood lifted, we followed the trails and hurried to keep up with the goats, now off their leash. Joelle ran to the front of our pack. After receiving an unexpected goat nudge to her rear end, Joelle tripped over a root and fell smack-dab into a stinging nettle plant. *Ouch!* Without a cry or word of complaint, she got right back up. After dusting herself off and picking some prickles off her hand, she began walking the goats again.

We continued on, soon nearing a large field where we took in a quick picnic and ate apples we picked right off the tree. I now understand the bewildering fancy of goat yoga—just add goats to any activity, and it becomes epic.

That day, one that had begun with moans and groans, ended with a lingering joy that lasted as I tucked my children into bed that night. I felt somehow closer to my centenarian friends—out in nature, spending time with farm animals, connecting with family, and eating apples straight from the tree. I knew it was time to take the wisdom that these elders had gained through a century of living and plant some seeds of my own. I was determined to make these outings a habit, not a rarity.

WEEK 1: ACTIVE KIDS AND FAMILY

Are you ready to draw on the wisdom of these ancient elders, the centenarians, and raise your children and your family to be as unstoppable and strong as those who live in the brilliance of the Resiliency Capital? If so, then let's begin, right here, right now. With or without the goats!

In the previous chapter, you learned about the hardships and adverse childhood experiences the centenarians endured—difficulties and adversities so great that science tells us these traumas probably should have shortened their lives. You also learned about the resiliency principles they practiced, which potentially protected them from whatever life threw their way. While these resiliency principles won't guarantee perfect health, making them part of your daily life will increase your family's odds of achieving resilient health, happiness, success, and longevity. In this chapter, you will learn how to begin putting these powerful ideas into practice and how to make them a natural and effortless part of your daily lives.

The first week is represented by the cornerstone letter *A*—*A* for *Active* in nature. This represents the first and second resiliency principles—active movement and nature engagement. Tied closely together, these two principles focus on a physically active lifestyle immersed in natural outdoor environments. The centenarians' childhoods centered on being physically active in the great outdoors. Over 90 percent of the centenarians interviewed described spending several hours a day in outdoor physical activity.

These first two principles form a foundational childhood habit. In his *New York Times* bestselling book, *The Power of Habit*, author Charles Duhigg coined the term *keystone habit*, which he defined as those routine practices with the power to positively influence other habits and activities.[1] For the centenarians, outdoor activity in childhood and across their lifespans was linked to all the other resiliency principles practiced—which is why it is a keystone habit and presented in the first week of this program. Now let's think about how you and your family can center your own life around the keystone habit of the centenarians: getting outdoors and becoming active in nature.

PRINCIPLES #1 AND #2—ACTIVE MOVEMENT AND NATURE ENGAGEMENT

Nearly every centenarian I spoke with painted a detailed picture of their early engagement with nature. Most of them spent their childhoods outdoors—living on farms or in farm-like settings in rural environments. Life on the farm meant a physically active lifestyle from sunup to sundown—preparing soil, planting seeds, maintaining plants, and caring for livestock. Their active lifestyles helped both girls and boys develop strong bones and muscles, avoid depression, and increase their energy levels, confidence, and life skills.

"I loved to work on the farm," said Lidia Reichel, a 100-year-old Resiliency Capital member, "[whether digging] in the soil or getting the cows and milking them. We used to do everything around the house. It's not like these days—you go to the supermarket and buy food. . . . As soon as we learned how to walk and talk, we had to work. My mom would dig into the soil and plant, and I'd help her."

For Lidia, memories of working alongside her mother, plunging her hands into rich soil or milking the cows, brought back feelings of love and joy, not drudgery.

While you don't have to buy a farm or force your kids to plant fields and harvest crops, if you want your family to have increased resilience and better health, take a lesson from the centenarians and get moving.

When it comes to being active in nature, one Loma Linda centenarian stands out from the rest. By the time she died in 1997 at 101, Hulda Hoehn Crooks was world-renowned for scaling some of the highest mountains in the world—something she regularly accomplished well into her nineties! Hulda holds the record as the oldest woman to climb Mt. Whitney, which at over 14,000 feet is the highest mountain peak in the continental United States. What's remarkable about Hulda's story, however, isn't her childhood. In Hulda's case, the lesson she has to teach us is something we parents need to hear. That's because Hulda first climbed Mt. Whitney at the age of sixty-five—and scaled it another twenty-two times—making her final climb at the age of ninety-two. Just the year before, at ninety-one, she climbed Mt. Fuji, the highest peak in Japan. Hulda became known as "Grandma Whitney," and in 1991 Congress named a peak in the Mt. Whitney area after her.[2]

Hulda's story is inspiring to all adults who think that they're too old to be active. But her story is also an important reminder of how early childhood can build the foundation for an active life. Her remarkable strength and fortitude can be traced to a childhood spent outdoors, where she worked and played hard. Born to a family of eighteen children in

Saskatchewan, Canada, Hulda grew up on a farm, living in a simple log-and-sod house on the banks of the Whitesand River in the Canadian Northwest Territories.

When asked about her early childhood, she described herself as "strong as a young colt" and active, qualities that still characterized her life at eighty, which she described in her memoir, *Conquering Life's Mountains*: "Early to bed and early to rise. Out jogging about 5:30 a.m. Jog a mile and walk it back briskly. . . . Do some upper trunk exercises, work in the yard, and walk to the market and work."[3]

Clearly Hulda Crooks—with her early childhood rooted in the outdoors—was a champion of the two keystone principles, active movement and nature engagement. What began as a childhood expectation to help out on her family's farm planted in Hulda a love for being active, for reaching her goals, and for taking pride in her strength and resilience. Whether or not you scale mountains into your nineties, by cultivating an active outdoor lifestyle in your family, you can scale heights you never thought possible.

In contrast to Hulda and many other centenarians, our generation has been slowing down, and the generations that follow us may never know the health that comes from moving outdoors. This downward trend is concerning, given the important health benefits of spending time in nature. Instead of being active outdoors, we join gyms, take classes, and even invest in technology that tells us when to stand up and walk! Of course, any form of active movement is good for us—I'm not suggesting you throw out your Fitbit and kettlebell or cancel your gym membership—in fact, I'd encourage you to get a Fitbit, kettlebell, and gym membership. But our movement *indoors* is not nearly as health-enriching as activity *outdoors*. Rather than making physical movement a natural part of our daily lives, these physical fitness routines make moving our bodies yet another thing we have to do. No wonder it's so hard for many people to stay fit.

But if you make active movement a daily routine that begins early in your children's lives, you'll find—and they'll find—that staying fit is something that just happens. Combining active movement with nature engagement makes the whole thing pretty effortless. More important when it comes to our children, encouraging outdoor activity will have lasting health and spiritual benefits as they learn to move their bodies and explore the natural wonders of our world so that as they grow, they will continue to move and engage in the world outside.

Alarmingly, however, over the past thirty years, children's physical activity has significantly declined, and not just in the United States. A recent study conducted by the World Health Organization (WHO) found that the majority of adolescents around the world (a whopping 81 percent) are not sufficiently physically active, putting their health and future at risk.[4] You might be curious to know, just how do US children stack up against kids from other nations? Well, a research group from Canada has the answer. They conducted a review of published journal articles using 177 studies from 50 different countries. They compared the 20 meter (66 feet) shuttle run times of children between the ages of nine and seventeen.[5] They lined up their results and created a theoretical foot race of kids around the globe. The outcome was not great for Americans—no gold, silver, or even bronze medals here. The US children finished almost dead last. Out of 50 countries, we placed ahead of only three others: Latvia, Peru, and Mexico. Time to get moving! Children who are aerobically fit— like those who perform well in the shuttle run—tend to be healthier in general and better able to reach their potential.

In the US, children once were not only physically active outside of school, but they had more time for gym and recess during the day, which helped them release energy so they could sit still and focus during class. Today, however, we force children to sit in classrooms all day long with little exercise, if any at all. Researchers have discovered that while physical activity in schools has diminished, in part because of a growing emphasis on student performance and academic testing, decreased physical activity is actually related to *decreased* academic performance.[6] Even so, physical education is rapidly disappearing from schools across the US, the UK, Australia, and Canada. What's at stake? Our children are at risk of losing their physical literacy—their motivation, confidence, knowledge, and ability to move for physical activities.[7] Gone are the days of sweating it out in gym class, struggling to climb the rope dangling from the ceiling while classmates cheer (or egg) you on. Even recess has been sharply curtailed in many schools, leaving young children with little or no outlet for their energy.[8] The result? They wiggle and squirm and won't sit still—they aren't paying attention to their teachers because their bodies want to move!

Sadly, a childhood spent outdoors and physically active is fast becoming a relic of the past. A survey by the National Trust Foundation found that children today spend half the time their parents did playing outdoors. According to the Child Mind Institute, children spend on average just four to seven minutes a day in unstructured play outside![9] More alarming, they spend an average of seven hours per day sitting and staring at electronic screens, moving nothing but the distal digits of their fingers. Author Richard Louv coined the term *nature deficit disorder* to describe this phenomenon, which sets our children up for possible health problems.[10] Fortunately, your children don't have to suffer from this disorder— once they start getting outside and moving more, you will discover that the increased activity in nature positively influences their academics, health, and resilience.

If we want our kids and ourselves to get healthier, smarter, more resilient, and better prepared for life's challenges, we have to embrace these first two principles. I knew it and adapted our everyday practices, and once my family made the needed changes, our bodies and our spirits thanked us. Remember when I told you that one of my kids was told he needed more physical fitness? Getting him off the computer and out the door was all he needed—that's because our bodies naturally want to move.

Encourage your kids, your partner, and your own sedentary self to get up from the computer, get out of the car, and get moving—before the cobwebs form. Walk away from the TV and engage in a wide variety of physical activity and cardioactivities to help build strong bones and muscles. Parental involvement in kids' physical activity makes a big difference. The more you care and the more you encourage your children to become physically active and get outdoors, the more likely these will become lifelong habits.

You'll likely find that once your kids go outside, they quickly discover that it's not punishment at all but an imaginative adventure. One centenarian, Dr. Robert Bolton (a 105-year-old Resiliency Capital member), recalled his love of building and flying kites with special messages attached. His dad helped him and his brothers build the kites from old fence posts, binder twine, and pieces of soft cloth. "We loved to fly kites," he told me. "One of our favorite things was to put a sheet of paper on the string and then the wind would blow it slowly upwards until it reached the kite." They were so excited to see the paper with their secret message soaring high up in the air.

During the centenarians' childhoods, the outdoors held a world of possibilities—rocks became children filling a classroom just waiting for their teacher to arrive, corncobs and their husks became dolls with beautiful flowing dresses, water spigots enabled a fleet of firemen to fight a blazing inferno, and barnyards became vast territories surrounding immense fortified castles. A world of imagination awaited them whenever they ventured outdoors.

So as you nudge your kids out the door, be prepared for protests, but also be prepared to change your life for the better once you put the keystone principles into practice.

Ready, set, go!

The first step to developing daily habits of kinetic activity is to become aware of your body—particularly when it's not engaged in movement. Notice how much time you and your children spend sitting—whether sitting at the table, at your desks, in the car, or in front of the television. Also note how much time you spend indoors. Get a stopwatch (most smartphones have them), and spend your waking hours one day timing yourself whenever you're in a sitting position or lying down—whether working on your laptop, driving in the car, sitting in class, or lying on the couch watching television. Then count the hours of your waking day and calculate what percentage of those hours you spent in a sedentary position. Repeat this process for your kids.

Pretty scary, isn't it? Unless you have a job that keeps you on your feet and moving, chances are, you spend 75 to 90 percent of your waking hours in a sedentary position—and then go to bed for another six to eight hours of sedentary rest. That level of nonmovement is, frankly, unsustainable. It sets you and your family up for a range of health problems, including obesity, diabetes, depression, early-onset arthritis, heart disease, muscle aches and pains, and chronic fatigue.

Don't despair. Instead, take some advice from King Julien in the movie *Madagascar* as he gyrates his arms, legs, and torso while singing at the top of his lungs, "You've got to move it, move it!" *So move it!* Get your family up and going today!

THREE FUNDAMENTALS FOR APPLYING THE ACTIVE MOVEMENT AND NATURE ENGAGEMENT PRINCIPLES

1. Develop Your Outdoor Purpose	2. Use Your Feet for Travel	3. Simplify Your Requirements for Getting Outdoors
Develop a purpose that encourages your family to get outdoors every single day and connects you with the natural elements.	Increase the use of your family's feet to travel about.	Reduce your dependence on materialistic items for getting your family active and outdoors.

Modern Times Call for Modern Methods

Studying the lifestyles of centenarians presents an irony. The very fact that they are centenarians means that they experienced childhood nearly a century ago! Think how our world has changed in the last hundred years. For the centenarians, even going to the bathroom as children meant donning coats (if it was winter) and heading outdoors to use the family's outhouse.

Today most people no longer live on farms, many have small or no yards at all, both parents may work full-time jobs, and children receive much more demanding homework and have longer school days than the centenarians ever did. Add to that the many structured activities for kids, from organized sports to extracurriculars, and the challenge grows greater. Most children work indoors from sunup to sundown, with little time or opportunity to get outdoors. We lack the freedom the centenarians once had to roam the countryside without parental supervision, knowing they'd more than likely come home safe and sound for supper. So getting your children out the door—spending time together outside when you have work to do yourself—might seem a higher mountain to climb than any Hulda ever summited.

Here's the good news: Just because the world has changed does not mean you can't engage with nature. Just commit to getting outdoors and being active, and you'll find strategies to make it happen. In this next section, I take you through a few of the centenarians' guidelines to living a life interacting with nature and show you how to adapt these traditional ideas to modern times.

To get started, do as the centenarians did: Keep it simple. You don't need to do everything I've suggested, and you definitely don't need to try each idea immediately. In fact, you *shouldn't* tackle them at all once—if you make too many changes right from the start, you'll be more likely to give up, rather than making permanent changes. Instead, take incremental steps. With time, you'll find that by beginning with just a few small adjustments to your daily life, you can achieve profound lifestyle changes.

A few years back, I met Camille, a physician working her way through medical residency. When she heard about my research, she realized she needed to find ways to get her daughter playing outdoors. She wanted her family—which included her husband and three-year-old daughter—to embrace the centenarians' keystone habit. However, both Camille and her husband worked long hours. Their engagement with nature was literally through a bedtime story about forest animals.

The first thing I had Camille do was look at her schedule and identify days and times when she, her husband, or both could take their daughter outdoors, even if just for fifteen minutes. I asked her if she could tie that experience in nature to something her family needed, like recovering and reconnecting at the end of a busy day. She identified two evenings during the week when she and her daughter could spend thirty minutes together in their backyard. She marked those times on her calendar, and those dates became "nonnegotiable" appointments. Eventually her husband joined them, and today they head outside with their daughter four days a week—either in their backyard or with a brisk walk to a nearby playground. They never fully grasped how important it was to have this keystone habit in place until the COVID-19 pandemic hit. This nightly ritual helped Camille and her husband decompress at the end of long shifts at the hospital.

Now let's take a closer look at the three essentials for applying the practices of the resilient centenarians with your own family:

1. Develop your outdoor purpose

The centenarians spent active time outdoors each day, but they didn't need to be encouraged; it was their way of life. Evelyn Reickman (100-year-old Resiliency Capital member) remembers going outdoors each day to take care of her family's cattle on their hundred acres. "There was no fencing on the farm, so it was a big job," she recalls. Salma Mohr (101-year-old Resiliency Capital member) would walk barefoot into town every morning before breakfast to fetch milk in a coffee can for her family—ten children in all. Without her efforts, there would have been no milk for the day. Beyond outdoor work, they found trees to climb, ponds to fish, and woods to explore.

Instead of thinking only of exercise you can do indoors, start thinking of things you need or want to do that require physical activity outdoors. This can provide the immediate purpose for getting outside each day. Start with fifteen minutes a day. Walk around the block to mail that letter. If you do have a yard, go outside and clean it up, plant something, weed something, do something! If all you and your kids have is a balcony, rotate time out there with them. One child could repot plants with you, another might deadhead the flowers, and yet another could do homework outdoors.

Try getting a dog, caring for a farm animal, or planting a garden. Gardening, for instance, provides an immediate purpose for getting outdoors each day. Consider planting a garden with a theme—an herb garden, an aromatic garden, a garden of flowers that bloom only at night. Try making a fairy garden by building miniature houses from twigs, bits of bark, pine cones, leaves, and whatever else you can find. If you don't have a yard, try a container garden set on a patio, inquire about local community gardens, or see if you can start one at your kids' school.

If you have the space, consider caring for livestock or outdoor pets such as chickens or rabbits. Even if you live in the city, having your own vegetable garden or some simple livestock—like chickens—will put your family on the path toward becoming more self-sustaining, which can be especially important during troubling times (like economic depressions or global virus outbreaks). You can check your local city laws to see what types of animals are allowed and how many.

Will your kids squawk at first about going outside? Will they try it once and think they've made sufficient sacrifice? Probably. Don't let their resistance defeat you. Be firm about your commitment to getting outdoors. The younger your children, the easier it will be to acclimate them to playing outside. Older children, such as my nine-year-old daughter, may resist more. Most need encouragement. Make it clear that staying indoors is not an option. Take away electronics if you have to.

Once you do get outside, don't rush. During their early childhoods, the centenarians escaped the frenetic or competitive sports–like pace of modern life. The meditative quality of their peaceful outdoor time lowered their blood pressure, calmed their nerves, and helped them relax. June Ohashi—a ninety-nine-year-old Resiliency Capital member—recalled the tremendous challenge she faced as a teenager because of her Japanese heritage. World War II had broken out, and the sentiment toward Japanese living in America was not good. June had to decide whether to remain where she was living and attending school or return home. She remembers heading outdoors to a serene nature area and walking all around to help gain clarity on the decision she had to make. During the recent COVID-19 pandemic, spending time outdoors and away from people worked wonders in reducing household tension.

No matter where you live, there's a door to the outdoors. Open it. You never know what you might find. Some kids have even found a purpose for getting active in nature that's tied with a positive social benefit. When he was eight, Caleb Smith began training endangered and rescued rabbits to become therapy animals. By age fifteen, Caleb owned and operated a private twenty-two-acre sanctuary called Peacebunny Island.[11] A smart nine-year-old boy named Robbie Bond, a Hawaiian native, grew up in Oahu and always had a passion for being physically active outdoors. When he heard that the White House was reviewing national monuments and parks, intending to downsize or eliminate twenty-seven of them, Robbie convinced his family to visit as many of these monuments as possible over a six-month period. He not only got himself and his family moving, Robbie started a national movement when he became founder of Kids Speak for Parks, the nonprofit he launched in July 2017.[12]

2. Use your feet for travel

How many times have you found yourself getting in the car to drive less than a mile to visit someone or pick up something at the store that you could easily have carried back home? With car accidents most likely to happen within five miles of your home, you quite literally risk your life to drive less than a mile! Instead of turning the key in the ignition, consider simply putting one foot in front of the other—there's a reason we were created to be bipedal. Our feet get us places.

Centenarian Evelyn Reickman (100-year-old Resiliency Capital member) didn't make a fuss about walking places as a child. Her longest journey each week was a whopping six-mile walk with her family to church and another six miles home. Without ready access to cars, getting around to nearby neighbors, schools, places of worship, and most other activities meant walking many miles—often for two to three hours a day. While walking that much today may seem unrealistic, perhaps you can promote living more like the centenarians by walking your children to school or enjoying a walking adventure to the store or library. If you can sit for an hour, you can walk for an hour. Sitting for an hour will drain you of your energy, while walking for an hour will increase it. Try it for a week and see how much better you feel!

Try not to let the rain or snow deter you. Encourage your children to get outdoors in different types of weather—with appropriate clothing. If they balk—and they will—acknowledge the unpleasant conditions but tell them you're going out anyway. Make the weather challenge a part of your adventure. If it's hot, be sure you've got plenty of water and sunscreen. Then splash in a pool or get out the garden hose. Feel the rain falling on your face and watch the puddles bounce. Of course, don't go out if there's any thunder or lightning—lightning is nothing to play with. But a cloudy day, a nip in the air, a bit of water or snow falling from the sky can turn an ordinary day into an extraordinary one.

Need some additional inspiration? Consider Dr. Ellsworth Wareham, a 101-year-old Resiliency Capital member. The climate in Alberta, Canada, where young Ellsworth grew up, could range from bitter cold with temperatures dropping to 22 degrees and heavy snowfall in the winter to highs in the 90s in the summer and everything in between. Even on the coldest days, Ellsworth would get up each morning around 4 a.m. to fetch the cows and milk them by hand before eating breakfast and heading off to school. In fact, most of the centenarians stayed outdoors throughout the day and in every season, experiencing all kinds of weather. Many indigenous people and peasant farmers continue to live this way in other parts of the world—entire families living in mud homes no bigger than most of our bedrooms. It takes nothing short of a cyclone to keep them indoors. Houses are for eating and sleeping in much of the world; the outdoors is for living. So don't let weather keep you locked up indoors.

3. Simplify your requirements for getting outdoors

The centenarians lived a simpler lifestyle than most of us today. With limited financial income, they connected with the outdoors organically. Strenuous work and limited financial means meant taking a hands-on, do-it-yourself approach to getting things done. In addition to making his own kites as a child, Robert Bolton (105-year-old Resiliency Capital member) helped his father make sleds to enjoy the snow.

Like the centenarians, wear clothing that encourages you and your children to be active outdoors. In warm weather, ditch the heels, sandals, or flip-flops and opt for sturdy tennis shoes. If girls prefer dresses, be sure they wear shorts or leggings underneath so they can climb and run. The same goes for you—get out of your suit, replace your heels with walking shoes, and dress for recreation.

Most of the centenarians grew up extremely poor, so they made do with what they had on hand. Rather than shop at Eddie Bauer before an outing, they simply hiked—knowing the terrain and not putting themselves into risky situations, of course. They didn't buy tents that cost a week's wages; they camped under the stars or made shelters of their own. They often used what they had around them and stayed close to their homes.

Have you ever thought about untapped opportunities that might be available in your own community? Sometimes we have resources that we aren't aware of. Many local communities offer outdoor adventures in zoos, public gardens, forest preserves, and even museums. You might call ahead of time to ask if they have any hidden attractions, tours, or just plain advice to help make your trip even more fun. By seeking insider tips prior to a museum visit in San Francisco, my family and I ended up taking a semi-private and memorable outdoor tour of a flower field surrounding a whale bone graveyard.

The centenarians didn't routinely take vacations, but if they are a treasured part of your family's life, consider heading to local or distant campgrounds and spend time in the "wild." The simpler the camping experience, the better. You don't need a fancy recreational vehicle or elaborate camping gear. A modest tent and simple camp stove will help you temporarily leave modern times behind while you enjoy nature.

Another option: Visit a national park. Make your plans well in advance and reserve a camping space online. Read books on outdoor survival skills that teach you how to live with nature while in it—not how to replicate indoor living or "glamping." Learn to make and cook simple meals over an open fire, to fish, and perhaps even to forage for edible foods (though be cautious). Pack food in tight containers so you don't attract animals, and don't leave your toothbrush out overnight—a lesson I learned when a raccoon used mine as his personal body comb and paw cleaner!

If you live in a cold climate, winter may seem a challenging time to get outdoors, but take advantage of sunny, warmer winter days to enjoy places and activities that are rare (or nonexistent) in warmer climates: ice-skating rinks, sledding hills, and ice-carving festivals. Snow brings out the kid in all of us, so join in with your kids as they build snowmen or snow forts. The Scandinavians even have a saying: "There's no such thing as bad weather, only bad clothing!"

Whatever you choose to do to make outdoor living a part of your natural life, start small. Don't try to conquer Mother Nature your first week stepping out. Try varied activities to discover what works best for you and your family, and where you find your greatest joy. When mishaps occur—and they will—address them and carry on. Don't let skinned knees, bee stings, or mosquitoes keep you from living your life. You belong in nature as much as any other creature.

Be prepared for protests, but also be prepared to change your life for the better once you put the keystone principles into practice. Ready? Here are a few ways to practice active movement and nature engagement in your daily life.

IN A PINCH, IT'S A CINCH: ACTIVE MOVEMENT AND NATURE ENGAGEMENT TIPS

- Park your car on the distant edge of parking lots during the day (avoid doing so at night if it might be dangerous) so you can walk a bit farther. This tip comes from martial arts master Bruce Lee, who never parked near his destination. Sometimes my kids and I use the parking lot voyage to pretend, as we make our way to the store, that we are jungle animals. We've even had teenagers join us!

- Get a jump rope, Hula-Hoop, and resistance stretch bands, and engage your family in competitions on the lawn. Who can jump rope the longest or has the funniest style on the Hula-Hoop? You'll have fun and get in shape. I can almost assure you of laughter and family bonding.

- Get a Fitbit (available for both kids and adults) that will let you know when you need to move. Before I adopted the lifestyle of the centenarians, I was so unfit that after I ordered my own Fitbit online, the bank called to see if my card had been stolen! I took that call to mean it was time for me and my family to get moving.

- Got an old-fashioned Polaroid camera? Or even just a phone with a camera? Older kids may like the idea of capturing wildlife through their lens. Not only can they learn to capture great photos simply by being quiet, still, and observant when they are out in nature, many contests, some with prize money, are open to amateurs, from the National Wildlife Federation to the Nature Conservancy.

- Are your kids learning how to spell? If so, try making the learning process active. Stand on one side of the room and tell the kids it's a pretend lake or field of lava with pillows that have become rocks to aid in crossing. Jump to the pillows for every word correctly spelled. Better yet, do this activity outdoors!

- Need help enticing older kids outside? For teenagers, most everything is better with friends. Encourage them to invite their friends over to play basketball, ride bikes, or go for a local hike. Consider putting up a basketball hoop in the back or front yard (where it is safe from traffic) and watch the magic unfold as neighborhood kids—and your own—are drawn to it.

- If you have a dog—or a pygmy goat—head outdoors with the kids and take them all for a brisk walk. If your kids are old enough, encourage them to hold the leash. And if you don't have a dog, consider getting one—it will keep everyone active and entertained.

- Planning a playdate or visit with a neighborhood friend? Don't drive—walk to your destination. Once you arrive, spend time outdoors, playing kickball in the grass or making mud pies in the dirt.

- Put on upbeat music and dance with your children every day. Dancing during household chores (indoors and outdoors) makes the duty much more fun. King Julien's lyrics can motivate you while you clean up. Simply replace the lyrics "Move it, move it" with "Wash it, wash it," or "Dust it, dust it," depending on your chore. Try singing with different accents. The lyrics work perfectly for housekeeping and yard work!

- Head to a nearby park and fly a kite, bat a balloon around, enjoy the playground, go for a short hike, or sled down a hill (with or without snow). Invite your friends. Have an adventure!

- Drive to another neighborhood for a walk. Pretend to be scientists studying a new ecosystem or anthropologists observing an exotic culture.

- Encourage your kids to build an outdoor fort. Supply old blankets, PVC piping, or anything else you have on hand, and let them get creative. Even better, have them use natural materials, such as tree branches and logs.

- Plan a farm staycation with your family. Search for locations online and take part in working on a farm. Many places allow younger children to get involved. It's funny how doing chores at someone else's house is considered a vacation, but it works to get everyone moving.

Week 1: Active Kids and Family

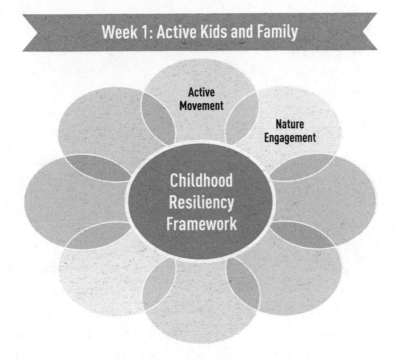

First Resiliency Principle—**Active Movement** (physically active and moving)
Second Resiliency Principle—**Nature Engagement** (spending time in nature)

Want to learn from the centenarians so your family can enjoy improved resilience and whole health? Then get up, get going, and be physically active outdoors at regular intervals throughout the day.

GET YOUR FAMILY'S TRIPLE BOOST

Science tells us that the active outdoor lifestyle that centenarians have led offers many health benefits that extend life and contribute to overall happiness. Putting the active movement and nature engagement principles into practice can help you and your family kick into high gear by:

Promoting happiness: Time outdoors is linked to boosting one's mood and increasing personal happiness.[13] Additionally, being outside enhances children's tendencies to be more self-reliant and to use cooperative tactics in problem-solving. If I ever need to referee my own children when they're arguing indoors, I routinely send them outside and the disagreement quickly resolves. When we get out and connect with nature and friends or family, our own feelings of sadness and isolation decrease.

Increasing resilience: Time in nature promotes heath and healing for the body, mind, and soul.[14] Exposure to the outdoors—especially early in life—helps the immune system develop optimally, though scientists don't fully understand why that is. Studies show that children exposed to farm animals and nature within the first year of life are less likely to develop asthma and other allergies.[15] It not only improves health during childhood, it also sets the stage for health as an adult. A number of studies—and any parent's experience—show that time spent outdoors leads to more physical activity than time spent indoors, which is a major factor in maintaining a healthy weight and preventing obesity.[16] Outdoor play is linked to better sleep.[17] If you take your pets with you outdoors, you also improve their health and longevity. (But you may not want to take your cats along on any walks. They're likely to head for the nearest escape route, leaving you in the dust!) Children exposed to nature early and often are more likely to care—and to promote health—for our planet. If you spend time outdoors with your kids, you'll benefit from a wonderful hidden benefit: a reduction in your own stress and anxiety, which will help you stay healthier longer.

Enhancing performance: Children gain immediate benefits from practicing the active movement and nature engagement principles. Time spent outdoors has been linked to increasing achievement on academic activities, including classwork, homework, and tests. If that sounds counterintuitive, try taking a short break outdoors the next time you are struggling with a work problem. Time spent actively in nature also boosts creativity and imagination.[18] A number of studies have found that children exhibit signs of enhanced resourcefulness and innovation when tackling challenges while playing in natural outdoor settings or experiencing an outdoor classroom.[19] Many highly talented and famous professionals—like photographer Ansel Adams, Amazon founder Jeff Bezos, and writer Annie Dillard—credit time in nature during childhood for their success.

CONQUERING RESISTANCE

As you work on becoming more active and engaging nature, your family may experience a few challenges. Keep the following ideas in mind for overcoming resistance as you begin practicing these first two principles.

Boredom is okay. Life outdoors is not always an adventure. While establishing an agenda will help you stick to it, don't worry about planning every detail for your kids. It's okay if they get bored outside. Boredom lets their minds relax and leads to creativity. When children whine, "I'm bored," tell them that's fine. You might even suggest they count the life-forms they can find; look for things of a specific color, texture, or shape; or just identify the sounds they hear.

Resist the urge to compete. Don't try to keep up with everyone else. Being active outdoors in nature should cost little to no money at all. You'll find the best items for digging and sorting lying around the house: pots and pans, muffin tins, or spoons. Use your imagination—and encourage your kids to use theirs.

Rethink how your kids are spending their time. If their schedules are filled with activities—school, classes, sports, extracurriculars, and chores—consider making changes to allow time for unstructured outdoor play. For example, if your child participates in two indoor after-school activities, consider dropping

Time spent outdoors in nature is linked to physical, mental, and emotional health benefits for both children and adults and may be even more important during times of great adversity.

one. Or find everyday activities your family can enjoy outdoors—even eating outside at mealtime.

Finally, whatever you do outside, expect to get your hands dirty. Ditch the hand sanitizers—just wash with soap and water. We're made to get dirty; enjoy it!

OVERLAP OF THE PRINCIPLES

As you begin learning about new principles over these eight weeks, look for opportunities to use them in tandem. I like to say that "the ease is in the overlap" because the principles will become even more powerful when combined. The centenarians incorporated many of these practices at the same time. Just as you developed a keystone habit by combining active movement with engaging with nature this week, as you overlap them with other principles moving forward, life will actually get easier and the likelihood of success will increase.

HOMEWORK TIME

Now that you've learned about the first week of the program and all its health benefits, put the centenarians' wisdom into practice with your own family. As you encourage your family to live more like the centenarians while implementing the first two principles—active movement and nature engagement—take these three simple steps to get started:

1. **Tie a green string or ribbon around your wrist.** This simple token symbolizes your commitment to live a more nature-engaged life with your family. While it might seem like a silly step, research shows that a small symbolic commitment can lead to a cognitive shift that helps you follow through on your goals.
2. **Establish goals for active movement and nature engagement.** Look at your calendar, and identify days and times you can get outdoors together. Review the journaling you did previously to help identify opportunities for unstructured play outside. Use the ideas listed un-

der "New Base Goal" below or adapt them, but whatever you set out to do, make it achievable. Be specific with the days, time of day, and amount of time to be spent outdoors. Start with small changes and grow from there.

NEW BASE GOAL

Below is a list of sample goals to help you on your way to practicing this first week's principles. As you learn about additional principles in upcoming chapters, you can begin formulating goals that support more than one of these practices, which will increase the likelihood that you accomplish more principles on any given day. For instance, as you model physical activity by being in nature with your kids, you also will be nurturing your relationship with them, the resiliency principle we'll cover in week 4.

- **Active movement and nature engagement principles:** My family and I will get outdoors each day for a thirty-minute walk, ideally at the start of the day.

  Overlapping principles include nature engagement, active movement, and nurturing relationships.

- **Optional new goal 1:** My family and I will park in the parking spot farthest from the entrance of grocery stores and other businesses we frequent during the day.

- **Optional new goal 2:** My family and I will use a pedometer or Fitbit and increase the number of steps we take in a day by 10 percent.

Identify a small reward for reaching the goal. You might decide to bake homemade muffins together, make s'mores over an open fire outside, or plan an outdoor picnic. Find a reward everyone will enjoy. Lay out the plan, mark it on the calendar, and stick to it! Remember, you are making an appointment for yourself and your kids. It's at least as crucial to your health as an appointment with the doctor. Make the appointment—and show up!

3. **Implement and track your success.** Carry out your plans and chart your progress. Each night, just a few minutes before bedtime, record how easy or difficult it was to stick with the plan and whether you followed it closely or deviated from it—and if the latter, in what way. Were you and your family able to get outdoors? Were you able to achieve the daily goal you set for yourself? At the end of the week, review what you achieved throughout the previous seven days. Use the Weekly Evaluation guide (appendix B) to help you track your progress.

Making a point to get outdoors regularly has not only helped everyone in my own family become healthier and happier, it has promoted resilience. Joe and I look forward to evening family walks. We feel less stressed, and those pesky health numbers—like blood pressure and cholesterol—are improving. As we get outside more, we feel better able to cope with daily stress. And best of all, electronic devices no longer rule our home. Try it yourself and see how much more energy, laughter, and enjoyment the experience brings you and your family.

Feel free to revisit—and at any time repeat—this first week. In this personal journey toward living more like the centenarians, every family has different needs. The course of action for your family will likely vary from other families' paths.

Setbacks will undoubtedly occur—for instance, if you or a family member gets the seasonal flu, going outside will have to wait. Don't worry. Jump back into your plans when you or your kids feel better. Just be sure to get back on track as soon as possible, and I guarantee, you'll be glad you did. It takes only twenty-one days to establish a regular habit—get outside those first twenty-one days and you won't think twice about it come day twenty-two!

——— Great Job! ———

Congratulations on completing the first week of the eight-week program! You've taken the first step toward a transformative life by committing to getting yourself and your family out the door and active.

As you go through each week, remember the value in a simple and slow approach to life. Remember that you can repeat week 1 before moving to week 2. Reward yourself and your family when you meet your goal. When you're ready for week 2, you'll learn the third resiliency principle practiced by the centenarians.

For now, just step outside and look up at the sky. It's infinite and it's yours. Enjoy it!

CHAPTER 4

WEEK 2:
CREATING BALANCED KIDS

Balance is not something you find, it's something you create.

JANA KINGSFORD

GLANCING AT MY WATCH, I checked the time: 3:05 p.m. Oh man, I needed to pick up the pace! The faculty meeting had run long once again. After quickly gathering my laptop and lesson plans, I shut my office door and planned my exit. Luckily the hallway was deserted. I took off in a half sprint toward my car. Now I needed to hurry to make it through the pickup line at Joelle's elementary school and then head home to relieve the babysitter. It was going to be tight, especially with bumper-to-bumper traffic and all the other crazy tiger moms who were running late too.

My rushing wouldn't stop there. Once the babysitter left, I would take my two girls to drop off Joelle at her piano lesson. Then I'd quickly head back to the school to pick up Jayden from basketball practice. Once I'd brought Joelle home from her lesson, I'd figure out dinner plans—no easy feat, since my family's dietary habits range from strict vegetarian to complete carnivore. I knew that if I hadn't made any plans for dinner by the time we were all home, I would end up rummaging through my three-inch pile of take-out menus. I needed to feed my ravenous brood before restless appetites turned everyone into grouches.

Eventually, Joe would arrive home, but then he would head to his home office so he could meet pressing work deadlines. Following dinner, Joe would drive Jayden to baseball pitching lessons while I would wash the dishes and help Joelle with her homework—which would take at least an hour. After that, I had my own papers to grade and classes to prepare for.

Your own schedule is likely to be just as hectic as mine, even if you're a stay-at-home parent. For all the modern technologies that are supposed to save us time—from washing machines and dishwashers to cars and computers—life has only gotten busier. We buy more clothes and dishes, so we wash them more. We have cars that allow us to go more places. Computers have managed to ease our tasks while increasing our workloads. And now that women are no longer expected to stay home to care for the family, many work outside the home—but still take on the "double duty" chores of cooking, cleaning, and childcare.

Life has changed drastically since the centenarians were young. Back then, women typically stayed home, and communities were closer than most are today. Everyone knew each other, and the adults watched out for one another's kids. Neighbors often baked breads and pies together, and Sunday dinners were social events. Evelyn Reickman (100-year-old Resiliency Capital member) remembers her family making meals together. "My two older sisters, Mainy and Vila, were the ones cooking, and they would make tomato soups and cook fried potatoes and all kinds of things. I would help with whatever they needed. We all just pitched in."

Another centenarian, Belen Lopez (101-year-old Resiliency Capital member) was the oldest of nine children and born near the town of Veracruz, Mexico. "We'd wake up every day at four in the morning to help my mother crush maize to make tortillas by hand. The tortillas were for us to eat, but we'd also sell them to the nearby farmworkers to help us get by. Without electricity or running water, we had many chores to get done . . . everyone helped."

Centenarian Amy Sherrard (101-year-old Resiliency Capital member) grew up in Burma (now known as Myanmar) as the child of mission-aries. One of her favorite items to make and eat was Indian flatbread. "I always made chapati. I especially loved to tear apart that bread and have it with my breakfast. Not only for breakfast, but any meal. We'd also eat lots of chapati with rice and vegetables." The Indian bread was served at every meal, broken and eaten together by the family (which included her beloved nanny). Ultimately it became a fond food memory for Amy.

We may not be able to return to the communal cooking of the cen-tenarians' past, but we can adopt a few of their practices, such as cook-ing with whole grains and fresh vegetables; minimizing meat, sugar, and processed foods; and eating together every (or nearly every) night. These practices will lead not only to healthier bodies, but also to healthier spirits so that we're better able to weather any storm that comes our way.

Are you ready to discover the healing power of foods and family meal-times? Would you like some tips on how to eat delicious, healthy foods that fit within your budget and time limitations? Do you want to promote resilience and enhance balance in your own family? Are you ready to draw on the wisdom of these ancient elders, the centenarians, and raise your children and your family to be as strong and unstoppable as those who live in the Resiliency Capital? If so, let's get going.

WEEK 2: BALANCED KIDS AND FAMILY

In the previous chapter you learned about the first two resiliency principles—active movement and nature engagement. Now it's time to introduce the third principle: simple foods. The second and third weeks of the Resiliency Program are focused on the letter *B*—for balanced kids and family. The third principle focuses on strengthening the body through nutrition, which unfortunately is becoming harder to do.

PRINCIPLE #3—SIMPLE FOODS

The simple foods principle means just that—simplifying what we eat and how we prepare it. The centenarians' families didn't have the luxury of extra cash, so they cooked and ate the basic foods available, which they prepared at home. The way we feed our families is in sharp contrast to how our grandparents and great-grandparents did it. You may wonder how and why our society has moved so far away from their lifestyle and traditions, which had been followed for hundreds of years.

Our cultural practices have changed in large part because of the increasing role of science, technology, and industry in influencing what we eat. In the 1950s when the government began noticing a shift in the types of diseases Americans were facing—fewer infectious illnesses and more chronic diseases—they responded to these new health threats by increasing research and eventually developing dietary guidelines. Much of this research, however, was funded by the meat and dairy industries, which encouraged diets heavy in animal protein, fat, and lactose. One such guideline came in 1992 when the USDA created the Food Guide Pyramid, intended to assist millions of Americans in their food selection. Dairy even had its own section, making it one of the essential food groups.

When I spotted the Food Guide Pyramid in my child's homework one day, I chuckled and asked myself, *How can dairy be an essential food group when my own kids get diarrhea if they eat just a small amount?* In fact, large sectors of the population lack the lactase enzyme needed for our bodies to process lactose—a sugar found in milk that breaks down into two simple sugars, glucose and galactose, and gives it a sweet taste. Our bodies were created to thrive on mother's milk for the first couple of years—in that way, our species has survived even when there has been little food for infants. However, some individuals may be genetically predisposed to reduce or stop production of the enzyme that processes lactose, an event that typically occurs between the ages of two and five and is known as primary lactose intolerance.[1] As babies, they can consume dairy, but as they grow, dairy becomes harder and harder for them to digest.

The National Institute of Diabetes and Digestive and Kidney Diseases estimates that up to 68 percent of the world's population cannot properly digest dairy products.[2] Even in the United States, the prevalence of lactose intolerance is high, with up to 90 percent of Asians, 75 percent of African Americans, and 13 percent of Caucasians unable to fully digest dairy.[3]

But the industry's influence, combined with American diets based on the foods and animal products we excel at producing, has helped shape the US guidelines, leading us to believe our bodies need dairy products every day when, at best, they are delicious and efficient sources of protein, but not necessarily good for everyone.

Industry leaders are also upping their game by launching campaigns and food products to show how supportive they are of these government guidelines and your health. This dance between government and industry is playing out right before our eyes in the supermarket. Often food packaging includes claims of how the product fights disease—just pick up a box of cereal and read the front.

With all the guidelines and marketing, picking the best food choices is no longer easy. Furthermore, the simpler the product, the more underrated it seems to become—from apples to string beans to water (though not technically a food item). Without flashy labels and health claims attached to them, these natural products are perceived by many people to have less value.

The grocery stores aren't the only ones encouraging us to purchase and eat more. We are bombarded with advertisements and enticements to eat huge portions (Americans eat far bigger portions than most other nations). Sugar, salt, and trans fats are added to most prepared drinks. High-fructose corn syrup is inexpensive but calorie dense. It is found in fruit juices, ketchup, salad dressings, breads, yogurt, canned fruit, and many processed foods. As an epidemiologist, I am concerned about the rise of sugar intake, which is up 20 percent in children and 30 percent in adults over the past thirty years.[4] This rising sugar trend is not just a problem for the US, but for other countries as well (including Germany, the Netherlands, and Ireland) with sugar intake rates well above that recommended by the WHO.[5] Alarmingly, these trends coincide with skyrocketing levels of obesity, diabetes, and other chronic diseases worldwide. If this trend continues unchecked, what will the future health and resilience of our children be?[6] This is particularly concerning because of the potential for future global pandemics, which generally are most dangerous for those with chronic conditions. Now more than ever, as we face this most recent pandemic and prepare for future ones, we need to develop food habits that enhance our body's ability to fight off infection or speed recovery time.

In his bestselling books on modern nutrition, UC Berkeley professor Michael Pollan encourages us to stop consuming "pretend food"—food that is ultraprocessed and created by industry for consumption. The *real* food, such as fruits and vegetables, is often located on the outskirts of the supermarket and doesn't bear any flashy labels.

Pollan says—and I wholeheartedly agree—that we need to take back control and reduce our dependence on processed food. He suggests following the wisdom of our elders when considering our food consumption: Ask yourself, *Is this an item my grandparent would recognize, let alone recommend eating?*

THREE FUNDAMENTALS FOR APPLYING THE SIMPLE FOODS PRINCIPLE

1. Keep It Simple	2. No Food on the Fly	3. Choose Water
Select foods that are in their most natural state and prepare them in a simplified manner.	Prepare and eat meals at home, in a relaxed state, and ideally with family and friends.	Water is the drink of choice morning, noon, and night.

Modern Times Call for Modern Methods

Let's take a closer look at what the Resiliency Capital centenarians have to say about diet and their recommendations for parents today. We'll also explore the essentials for applying the three practices of the Resiliency Capital centenarians with your family.

1. Keep it simple

When it comes to meal planning, cooking, and even dining, the rule of thumb is to keep it simple. As children, the centenarians ate simple meals primarily made up of vegetables and beans, prepared at home. Meals were high in fiber, largely because of the plentiful seasonal vegetables that were raised in family gardens or grown locally. Meat was a luxury item, so they ate little of it. Often the only choice at breakfast was oatmeal, since it was relatively inexpensive. Very little food was processed or prepared by an outside company.

When asked what she ate as a child, centenarian Lidia Reichel (100-year-old Resiliency Capital member) said, "We cooked soup with little meat, and with a lot of vegetables—potatoes, cabbage, corn, and squash, you know—and that was the meal for lunch. And the evening was the leftovers unless we worked hard; something simple . . . maybe fruit, and we baked our own bread."

When we talked with the centenarians about diet, we learned that fiber reigned supreme. One of fiber's major benefits is that it feeds the good bacteria and decreases the bad bacteria in our gut. The gut microbiome, all the thousands of bacteria in our gut, is important to the proper functioning of our body, as well as our overall physical and mental health. Gut bacteria are linked directly to the immune system and can influence a whole number of organs in the body, including the brain. Every time we eat something, we are promoting either the good bacteria or the bad.

These bacteria can be altered within twenty-four hours of a diet change. Within seven days, we can completely transform our gut bacteria biome from one that reflects the modern Western world to one similar to what our ancestors had.

The main way to do that is by eating a wide variety of fruits and vegetables. By eating a range of plant-based foods we provide healthy bacteria the fuel they need to flourish. It's best to eat something from each of the different groups of fruits (from bright red strawberries to dark green avocados), vegetables (from leafy green vegetables to bright purple turnips), legumes, and nuts. Limit meat or use it sparingly to add a little flavor. Incorporate healthier options, like fish, which is high in omega-3 fatty acids and excellent for brain development. To increase vegetable intake, try offering at least two options at dinner or consider making vegetables the main dish rather than a side.

Eating produce that is closest to its natural state is best. Each level of processing—from picking the plants, to transporting them, to transforming them into food products, to packaging and storing them—impacts the nutrients they contain. Keep in mind that foods transported long distances are likely not as nutritious as foods grown and consumed locally because fruits and vegetables begin to lose their nutrient content after harvesting. To eat foods grown as close to your home as possible, purchase them from local farmers markets or grow your own fruits, vegetables, and herbs.

So how else can you keep it simple? I suggest three steps below:

Recognize your current practices. Everyone should begin to "keep it simple" by noting their own eating preferences and practices, even vegetarians who think they're eating well. After all, someone could consume loads of sugary items, cheese pizza, and soda and still technically be considered a vegetarian, though not a healthy one. When Dr. Preet K. Dhillon, senior research scientist at the Public Health Foundation of India, spoke at the Seventh International Congress on Vegetarian Nutrition at Loma Linda University, she explained that research studies of the population in India showed that vegetarians consumed more sugar than nonvegetarians.[7] This phenomenon may occur not just in India, but in other countries too.

So whatever your current diet, take time to review what you recorded about your family's diet during a typical week in the journal you kept at the start of this program. This exercise will give you an idea of your habits and opportunities for change. Another great way to get a bird's-eye view of your dietary practices—and even how they compare to those of the centenarians—is to conduct the kitchen pantry audit, outlined in the sidebar on pages 75–76.

As you consider what foods to keep in your house, think like the centenarians: Their food choices not only promote health and resilience, they also prepare them to endure harsh times like pandemics or economic depressions.

So stock your pantry accordingly. Remember if it's not healthy for the kids, it's not good for you either. Don't store junk food—like soda, chips, and candy—in the pantry because your family will find and consume it.

Kitchen Pantry Audit

Fill in the chart below with the items you have in your refrigerator and pantry and on your countertop. In red ink, add foods you plan to shop for and add to your repertoire. If you are running short of time, you can perform this "pantry test" mentally, without writing everything down.

Fats/oils	Meat/poultry/fish/ eggs	Nuts/beans/seeds
e.g., olive oil	e.g., chicken	e.g., walnuts
Fruits/vegetables	**Grains/high-fiber cereal**	**Milk/yogurt/cheese**
e.g., apples	e.g., whole wheat bread	e.g., sour cream
Snacks	**Drinks**	**Other**
e.g., chips	e.g., soda	e.g., egg noodles

Now evaluate. At least 75 percent of your inventory should be in these three categories:

- nuts/beans/seeds

- whole grains/high-fiber cereal

- fruits/vegetables

How well did you score on your test?

The categories with the fewest items should be drinks and snacks. Be careful of the "other" category, which may tend to include lots of processed, ready-to-go food items (like ramen noodles, boxed pasta-based meals, canned soups, etc.). Those items are quick and convenient but are not great for your body. Work on reducing the "other" processed items from your pantry. If you do make processed items for your kids, offer them fruits and vegetables first to help fill their growling stomachs.

My daughter Joelle taught me not to keep junk food on hand when she was only four. She was so stealthy that she could have starred on the hit TV show *I (Almost) Got Away With It*, featuring criminals who nearly avoided capture. Early one morning, I wandered into the kitchen to put a dirty plate in the sink. Spying the pantry door ajar, I tried to shut it—but it wouldn't budge. I kept pushing and pushing, but the door stood firm. "What in the world?" I asked.

Looking inside, I spied the top of my daughter's head. She was holding my one-pound Trader Joe's candy bar and quickly shoving pieces into her mouth—as if it were going to be the last bar of chocolate she'd ever get!

But what if your pantry sweep leaves you with few of the convenience foods you often rely on to get dinner on the table at a reasonable time? Do you feel as if you don't have the knowledge or the skills to pull off edible meals for your family? Don't worry—even if you are convinced that the only thing you know how to make is toast, you can make delicious meals yourself with little effort. Or perhaps you do feel highly confident in the kitchen and cook dinner every night. No matter which end of the food spectrum you fall on—from complete beginner to total expert—there is likely room for improvement (whether in making healthier meals, adding more variety, spending less time preparing meals, or teaching other family members cooking skills).

The simpler your meals, the better because preparing dinner shouldn't be a significantly stressful ordeal. In fact, having experience in preparing meals may help you make it through tough times. Anita Johnson-Mackey (105-year-old Resiliency Capital member) recalled routinely helping her mother in the kitchen alongside her sisters. Though not vegetarians, they ate a lot of salads, greens, and rice and beans. They ate together every night. When she was only ten, however, Anita lost her mom, who passed away during childbirth. "It was fortunate for me that I had already been trained and was able to help take care of things around the house," Anita recalled. "I was prepared." Are you and your family prepared as well?

Recognize your feelings. The next step toward a simplified eating pattern is an important and often-overlooked step—to recognize your feelings about this subject. If any of your feelings are negative, recognize them for what they are—just a barrier to be overcome.

This may include adjusting your feelings about food preparation. With so many TV cooking shows, it's easy to feel inadequate in the kitchen. After taking a few bites during dinner, my daughter Joelle will sometimes look straight at me and tell me, "You're chopped" if she doesn't think dinner tastes good. Ouch! Talk about deflating my self-confidence!

On the other hand, if you are an expert cook, you might find your kids demanding you serve them a masterpiece every night. If that's the case, reflect on how much time you spend in the kitchen, whether cooking is becoming less joyful and more stressful, and whether or not you demand perfection of yourself. A friend of mine is a single mom who spent so much time trying to make a perfect three- or four-course meal for her daughter every night that eventually nothing she served was good enough—she'd taught her daughter to be as demanding of culinary perfection as she was! Finally, she realized that she no longer loved cooking dinner, and when that happened, she stopped worrying whether it was perfect. She told her daughter that she could eat what she'd prepared or not, but that was what she was serving. Now both mother and daughter are enjoying cooking again, no longer demanding that every nightly meal top the last one.

The goal isn't to become a master chef, or if you are one, to demonstrate all your skills nightly. The goal is to not give up, but to keep pressing forward—making meals that promote wholeness while supporting others along the way.

I am by no means a master chef, but I gained confidence by using "make it yourself" meals delivered to our home from meal preparation services like Blue Apron and HelloFresh. I choose vegetarian or fish dishes. The produce is typically fresh, and I usually add more vegetables to make the dish go further. The instructions with pictures are easy to follow. Using the "make it yourself" meals is a great way to empower yourself and gain culinary skills. Because of the skills I've gained, I now feel different about cooking, even venturing out to create meals all on my own.

Another great way to learn how to prepare quick and easy meals is by watching cooking demonstrations on YouTube. Do some searching, and soon you'll find videos by instructors you like who are cooking foods you like in a style that is accessible to you. One chef I follow is Jamie Oliver, who has a cooking show and cookbook on preparing healthy meals with five ingredients or less. See what meals you can prepare with just a few ingredients. The more you experiment, the more creative you'll become.

A busy pediatrician and friend of mine recommended a great source for vegetarian or vegan recipes—the blog and cookbook *Smitten Kitchen* by Deb Perelman. There are a number of other healthy food blogs out there, and with a bit of googling, you're sure to find some that are a good fit for you. With easy-to-follow directions and excellent photos, it's hard to go wrong with these dishes. Appendix D of this book also contains easy-to-use recipes.

Another important feeling to acknowledge and overcome is that you don't have enough time and are already stressed enough as it is. No matter how skilled you are in cooking, you might find yourself dreading the work if you are pressed for time. Keep your meals simple and consider rotating regular meals a couple of nights a week. I make a pot of beans on Sunday and then use them in meals like burritos throughout the start of the week when things are most hectic. I also make extra and freeze portions of dinners for later. I've frozen veggie enchiladas, lentil soup, and even spinach pesto (a great addition to pasta dishes). Some things freeze better than others, so experiment. Pasta and potatoes don't freeze well, but sauces, fish, soups, and leafy vegetables freeze beautifully.

For some families—such as those with single parents, both parents working outside the home, or kids involved in activities most evenings of the week—finding time to eat together can be tough as well. If you don't routinely have family dinners, start on a weekend night and then gradually add them on one or more weekdays. Older kids may resist having to gather around the table because they want to hang with friends. They may try all kinds of ways to get out of family dinnertime—everything from "I'm not hungry" to "I have to study." Make family dinner an appointment everyone is expected to keep. Let them know that hunger is not a requirement to come to the table, and since the meal may last only twenty minutes, there will be plenty of time to study afterward.

If you are worried you won't have enough time to cook, especially on weeknights, set aside time, just as you would for a medical appointment. Pick a night that is not too jam-packed with events. Don't book anything within the hour before the meal if possible—this will protect the fringes of time needed to prepare the meal. Encourage others in your house to share the work—either by purchasing groceries, prepping, cooking the meal, or cleaning up. Many hands make light work! You might even take turns on cooking duty with other nearby friends or family members. One night one family makes the meal—doubling the amount—and either delivers it to the other family or has them over for dinner—and then the families switch.

Not used to eating at home? Start with one meal a week and then build from there. In the end, instead of eating out six days a week and one day at home, try working up to eating six days at home and one day out as a treat. You'll not only spend more time with your family, but you'll also save money!

If you tend to view food preparation as a chore or busywork, think of it as a gift of time to your family—with all the health benefits from the food itself.

Create meal plans. The third step is deciding what meals to make and what foods to select. It's important to simplify foods, options, and tastes and to select food that is as close to the garden and as little processed as possible—choose fruits, berries, vegetables, legumes, whole grains, nuts, and seeds. Foods that will rot are actually some of your best choices because they are in the most natural state and low in preservatives—and you know you have to serve them soon. Even if you have great food skills, take a look at the ingredients you are cooking with. Are your dishes calorie laden—high in meat and carbohydrates but low in fruits and vegetables? Are they high in salt—which ultimately makes them less healthy? Make sure the ingredients you select promote health. Minimize the fat—especially animal fats and trans fats such as vegetable oil or margarine containing partially hydrogenated oil in the ingredient list, as these can elevate cholesterol and contribute to coronary heart disease.

And be sure your meal is high in fiber. Select whole breads, rice, legumes, and pasta with higher fiber content. Some great bread choices are seven grain, dark rye, cracked wheat, and pumpernickel. Kids may be more open to eating whole grain breads than whole grain pasta. If your kids don't like its taste, consider adding more vegetables and using less pasta. Don't overlook beans and nuts. The centenarians ate lots of legumes, which include all kinds of beans, nuts, peas, and lentils. When selecting rice, brown or wild rice is best. If you enjoy white rice, try mixing brown and white rice together.

Can't read labels and aren't sure of how healthy a product might be? Not to worry! (And take it from me, even with a doctoral degree in a health field, labels can be confusing!) Along the way to encouraging us to eat healthier, some health enthusiasts attempted to teach consumers how to decipher the labels so they could select food that was only semi-processed, not ultra-processed. That way we'd all be able to eat food that was fast to prepare but still a healthier option.

I believe that attempt was misguided because most of your food should come *without* a label. I recommend embracing the concept of "no label,

Foods High in Fiber

- **Vegetables:** Dark-colored vegetables such as carrots, kale, spinach, beets, broccoli, and artichokes. In general, the darker the color, the higher the fiber content.

- **Fruits:** Raspberries have the most fiber; apples, bananas, and strawberries are also good sources. Don't forget to eat the apple peel; that's where most of the fiber is. (But wash it first—the peel is also where pesticides settle, so if you aren't eating organic foods, be sure to wash them well.)

- **Beans:** Particularly navy and white beans.

- **Legumes:** Peas, soybeans, and lentils.

- **Nuts and Seeds:** Sunflower seeds, chia seeds, flax seeds, pumpkin seeds, pistachios, almonds, walnuts, and pecans.

then it's good for my table." Stick to the food aisles requiring the least amount of label reading, your fresh fruit and vegetables. At least start your shopping with the fresh food aisles; that way your cart will have less room for the more processed food items.

One word of caution as you move toward eating fewer processed foods—something I wish someone had told me. While purchasing, storing, and eating more nuts and grains is a great habit to develop, invest in some good secure containers as well. If you don't, you'll end up like I did—battling Indian meal moths that take up residence in your pantry.

The reason these little buggers go bonkers for the stuff is because it's real food. They don't really want the other junk. So make the necessary investments to ward off pantry critters. And keep your nuts in the freezer, where they won't attract bugs and won't go rancid.

2. No food on the fly

Food should not be consumed in a hurried manner or while multitasking. Instead, sit down and spend time enjoying food with friends and

When going to the grocery store, take your imaginary "great-great-grandma"— or helpful centenarian— shopping with you. When selecting items, ask her, "Do you know what this product is? Would you recommend it for my family to eat? Does this food item rot?" If you answer no to any of these questions, then rethink that item.

family—your body, mind, and soul will thank you. Most Americans are eating more and bigger meals—typically outside the home—and consuming them as quickly as possible, all while multitasking. Once my husband told me, "Honey, when our kids come home from school, they drop their backpacks and head straight for the kitchen. They are like ants in the Amazon rain forest, devouring anything in their path." He was right. And I knew that had to change because the faster we eat, the more we eat—and the less we taste and enjoy food.

Dining with family and friends brings many positive benefits. Of course, refusing to eat food on the fly means you'll need to prepare food at home. Cooking is the great connector—not only does it gather family and friends together, it brings the outdoors in. Why not make cooking a family affair and have your kids—and your spouse—join you in washing, chopping, stirring, and otherwise preparing the food? Once the Blue Apron meals began arriving weekly on my doorstep, my kids and I started cooking together. You can also encourage your kids to consider cooking with friends. Centenarian Jane Pihl told me that during the Great Depression, she and her girlfriends made fudge together. They came up with this activity as a way to get together that didn't cost much money.

I liked her idea and decided to give it a try. I had my daughter invite her friends over from school one Friday afternoon and let them create, consume, and clean up. I called it "Cooking Up Friendship," and it was a hit! Who would have thought cooking involved dancing, music, and improv? I now have a standing appointment for my daughter and her friends to

Cookware Basics

After hearing about my research, Niklas Ekstedt, a famous Swedish chef who owns a Michelin star–rated restaurant, interviewed me about centenarian food practices for a documentary film on the simpler cooking methods of our ancestors.

Ekstedt embraces his own culture's cooking practices—some of which mirror those of many of the senior citizens I spoke to. For instance, like the centenarians who grew up using cast iron, Ekstedt prefers this type of cookware. A cast-iron Dutch oven (a large pot for cooking soup or casseroles, or for roasting meat) and a cast-iron skillet or two were the standard fare in many kitchens in the early twentieth century. Properly cleaned with nothing more than a little salt and a rag, the cast iron builds up a lovely patina over time, making it as nonstick as any contemporary cookware.

It can also be healthier. Not only is contemporary nonstick cookware often made with toxic carcinogens that scrape off and into our food, the iron from a cast-iron pan may help us get more iron in our diet, which is particularly helpful for pregnant women.

As we finished our interview, Ekstedt ran his fingers through his hair and told me with a smile, "Cook more like your centenarians—get your open fire, cast iron, and go!" Of course, you can use cast iron on the stove or in the oven, or even on the grill. But there's nothing wrong with learning to cook over an open fire. The more rustic skills you have, the more prepared you will be if you lose power to your home. With increasing wildfires, storms, and floods, the ability to cook without power can transform a week of cold food into a week of adventure by grilling and cooking food over an open flame!

How to season and use cast iron

Because you can use it in the oven, on the stovetop, or over an open flame, a cast-iron skillet's versatility is hard to beat. Before using it, however, you need to season it to keep it in good working order. Unseasoned, your food will stick like napalm to the pan. When your cast iron is seasoned and cared for properly, your food will glide off it like Teflon. First, scrub the skillet with hot water only, no soap. Next, completely dry it. Then spread a thin layer of vegetable oil over the surface, including the sides, bottom, and handle. Finally, place the skillet, cooking side down, on a piece of foil or a baking sheet. Then place it in an oven heated to 350 degrees for one hour. Repeat the seasoning occasionally to keep it in good shape.

What to look for in nonstick pots and pans
DaTerra Cucina, developed by a family in Portland, Oregon, is a line of lightweight nonstick pans with a beautiful modern design. Best of all, they don't contain harmful chemicals like the Teflon or cadmium found on many nonstick pans.

Simple cooking products
Overall, your cookware should be as simple as your food. There is no need for fancy gadgets; all you need are basic pots, pans, and utensils. But some electric cookware, such as slow cookers or sous vides, can be helpful for busy cooks. Despite its French name, a sous vide is easy to use—just plunge the machine (which resembles an immersion blender) into a pot of water, set the time and temperature, place your food in a freezer bag, and then plunge it into the water. The sous vide will heat up the water and maintain the temperature to prevent food from overcooking. You can even set it to cook while you're at work. One of my friends loves her Instant Pot—a pressure cooker that is easy to use and great for making beans quickly. On busy days, one of these appliances can ease your dinner preparation so that all you have to do when you come home is serve the dinner that's already been prepared! A food processor and blender can come in handy, helping you prepare homemade sauces, chop nuts, and puree soups.

I also recommend that you invest in a good set of knives. (One of my favorites is the Spyderco 4.5-inch utility serrated knife.) To keep your knife blades in good shape, wash them by hand and store them in a knife block. Sharpen them every three to four months. A sharp knife is a safe knife because you don't have to apply additional force when cutting foods. Along with your knife set, I also suggest that you get a set of plastic cutting boards in various sizes. I prefer plastic to wood because they can be placed in the dishwasher for deep cleaning.

gather after school to practice cooking and communing in the kitchen. I often encourage them to try out recipes that have been handed down over the generations in their own families.

When I asked centenarian Lidia Reichel, one of five children, to describe food preparation when she was growing up, she reminded me, "You had to make everything yourself, because there wasn't any store. All us kids had a lot of work around the house; we even had to bake our own bread if we wanted bread. We learned from our mom while we helped her in the kitchen." Sadly, home cooking has been on the decline not just in the US, but also in other parts of the world.

Until March 2020, home meal preparation in the US was on a downward spiral, according to a research firm that has monitored our eating habits for decades.[8] Eating out also appeared to be the way of life for many folks around the world, with people in places like Germany and Hong Kong routinely eating away from home. However, the arrival of the COVID-19 pandemic immediately changed our habits—globally we went into survival mode. With restaurants closed and shelter-in-place mandates imposed, we were forced to eat at home. Food flew off the shelves at grocery stores, and we rediscovered cookbooks. As the pandemic subsides, I am concerned that the United States and other countries will jump back into our old patterns of eating on the fly and away from home. I'm concerned that advertisers and the food industry will be quick to tell us once again—with greater emphasis because of lost profit margins—that we don't have enough time and/or the necessary skills to prepare meals. But the truth is, in the time it takes for a pizza to be delivered or to run to the nearest take-out joint to pick up dinner, you

Kick It Up with Flavor

A great way to spice up your dressings, marinades, and sauces is to experiment with different flavored vinegars, which you can find in grocery and specialty stores or online. Citrus-flavored vinegars, turmeric vinegar, and sherry vinegar all add great flavor to soups and salads. You can even drizzle some of these vinegars, such as chocolate or blueberry vinegar, over fruit for a healthy dessert.

Great Stockpiles for Health, Resilience, and Pandemic Planning

Stock your pantry:

- ☐ Canned beans
- ☐ Low-sodium canned vegetables
- ☐ Potatoes
- ☐ Dried beans
- ☐ Canned fruits
- ☐ Onions
- ☐ Nuts
- ☐ Dried fruits
- ☐ Vegetable broths
- ☐ Oatmeal
- ☐ Whole-grain cereals with fiber (such as Grape-Nuts) that you can top with fruit to entice kids to eat them

Though fresh fruit and vegetables are always better tasting and healthier, keep canned (low sodium) or frozen vegetables and fruits on hand to serve when fresh options are unavailable.

Stock your refrigerator:

- ☐ Salad bar (see below)
- ☐ Eggs
- ☐ Bell peppers
- ☐ Spinach
- ☐ Garlic
- ☐ Broccoli
- ☐ Avocados
- ☐ Zucchini
- ☐ Low-fat cheese
- ☐ Almond, soy, or skim milk
- ☐ Water
- ☐ Strawberries
- ☐ Blueberries
- ☐ Lots of frozen fruits/veggies

Prepare and keep items in your refrigerator that can quickly be made into a salad:

- ☐ Chopped lettuce*
- ☐ Olives
- ☐ Garbanzo beans
- ☐ Shredded carrots
- ☐ Cucumbers
- ☐ Tomatoes
- ☐ Chives/herbs
- ☐ Corn
- ☐ Salad dressing

*Don't chop your salad greens with a knife or they will brown. Tear them apart or buy a large plastic chef's knife, which will make it easy to chop large batches without discoloring the greens.

In addition to prepping produce for salads, you can pre-chop or pre-shred vegetables to use for cooking throughout the week. Fresh vegetables to keep on hand for quick and easy steaming include asparagus, green beans, and sugar snap peas. Also stock your refrigerator with a large amount of yeast, which can be difficult to find during an epidemic when you may want to make your own bread.

Stock your counter:
Keep fruit in plain sight on your counter so that when you or your kids feel hungry between meals, you can grab a quick snack from your fruit bar. Want a snack other than fruit? Then reach for a handful of nuts to curb your hunger.

could make a healthy, delicious meal—one that costs less than anything you could buy prepared.

In short, one of the first steps toward living a more balanced life like the centenarians do is choosing to create a meal at home. According to the *American Journal of Clinical Nutrition*, research shows home-cooked meals actually make you feel better—so even if the kids don't like the taste of the food and pronounce you "Chopped!" they reap other benefits by coming together.[9]

Dining in. This tip should come as no surprise. Food should not be consumed in a hurry or while multitasking. We have become so accustomed to the feeling of eating on the fly that it seems second nature for most of us. Both my daughter and son try to stuff bagels in their mouths on the way to school each morning. Worried they might get cream cheese on themselves, they usually wipe their grubby hands on the seats in our car. But I must confess, before I adopted the centenarians' dietary habits, I was responsible for aiding and abetting them. The evidence was everywhere in my car, from straws of various sizes to the array of plastic cutlery and napkins. I also kept giant-size wet wipes, just in case my kids had sticky fingers.

Food should not be eaten while driving, but food should also not be eaten while multitasking at home. How many of us have eaten while performing other tasks? I recently heard of a company that makes it their business to deliver you food while you sit at your computer so you can work while you eat. No longer is there time even to take a break.

It's important to focus on our food when we eat. Otherwise, we tend to consume more calories, and our minds don't get the chance to rest, relax, and connect with friends and family. So the next time you or your family sit down in front of the TV with a plate of food, ask yourself what benefits you are missing. Time with your family? Learning about each other's days? The delicious taste of the food you prepared as it is wolfed down with eyes focused on the screen? Chances are, you're missing a lot if dinnertime means TV time!

3. Choose water

The third rule of the centenarians is to drink water. Simply choose water—it's the best choice all around. It doesn't come in dynamic packaging or with fancy-colored dyes that are cause for parental concern; instead, it is virtually free or inexpensive. Invest in a durable water bottle so you can carry water with you wherever you go. No need to pair dinner with a glass of wine; go for water with a slice of lemon. Keep in mind that the Resiliency Capital centenarians didn't drink alcohol. Backed by scientific studies, the CDC warns of excessive alcohol consumption linked with short-term harms (like car crashes, drownings, and burns) and long-term health consequences (like mental health conditions, stroke, and various cancers, including breast, colon, throat, esophagus, and liver).[10] In addition, since children tend to imitate behavior they see in their parents, you can reduce the risk that your children will drink alcohol if you avoid it.

One of my colleagues at Loma Linda University, Dr. Jackie Chan (not the famed martial artist, but an epidemiologist), studied the health benefits of water. Using the large Adventist Health Study (AHS) cohort of over ninety thousand people, she found that drinking more water (not any other beverage, including tea) provides a strong protective effect against heart disease.[11]

When I asked my husband's great-aunt, centenarian Mulan Tsai, what she likes to drink, she answered with a smile: "Water."

"What about tea?" I replied. "Don't you like to drink tea sometimes?"

She shook her head and said, "No, just plain water." Throughout our interview, in fact, she sipped on a glass of clear water as if it were the elixir of life—which it is.

Curiously, none of the government food guides really promote water consumption. The latest USDA guide, My Plate, includes sections for proteins, grains, fruits, vegetables, and dairy. Where's the water?[12] After all, the adult body is made up of 60 percent water (a newborn is made of even more—78 percent), and water is so critical to life that we would die within a few days without it. It also has no calories, making it the perfect drink for kids and adults.[13] Why then isn't water included? It should be, particularly because we aren't getting enough.

In America approximately 75 percent of adults and 54 percent of children are chronically dehydrated, hindering our bodies from functioning properly and setting us up for a number of chronic diseases.[14] The latest edition of the American Dietary Guidelines (2015–2020), released by the USDA, indicates not only what we should eat, but for the first time what to drink to stay healthy. It recommends drinking "beverages that are calorie free—especially water."[15] This statement is a step in the right direction in encouraging us to consume water.

We are bombarded with all kinds of drink options in every color of the rainbow and for every activity, whether we need a boost in the morning or play a specific sport. Among the popular sugary drinks for kids are Gatorade, Hi-C, Hawaiian Punch, SunnyD, Capri Sun, and Dannon Danimals. All contain lots of sugar (usually in the form of high-fructose corn syrup), lots of calories, and potentially harmful dyes.

For the centenarians, who had limited incomes and limited access to well-stocked grocery stores, these unhealthy drink choices just weren't available—and thankfully so. In living more like the centenarians, I've cleaned up my own pantry and fridge, getting rid of the sodas and juice boxes I once routinely kept on hand. My children don't even ask for them anymore. A few times I've observed both my daughter and son looking in the pantry, then looking in the fridge, like they were on a search for the Holy Grail. They inevitably gave up and decided to quench their thirst with ice water. My liquid flaw was once a cup of creamer filled with a hint of coffee. I, too, have made the switch, though not as cold turkey as my kids. I now opt for one cup of tea in the morning, with only a small splash of milk and honey. It hasn't been too difficult for me; I only crave coffee when I walk by a colleague's office where she secretly brews her own cup. The smell still causes my eyes to close and my nostrils to inhale that heavenly scent.

IN A PINCH, IT'S A CINCH: SIMPLE FOOD TIPS

- If you don't have much experience with cooking, order vegetarian meals to make at home (like HelloFresh or other meal preparation services) and use this strategy to gain skills. We get two meals a week from one of these services. My daughter likes helping out with the meals, and I enjoy the time we spend together.

- Explore lunchtime finger foods. Send a sack lunch to school with your child at least once or twice a week. Include a variety of healthy food items (apple, tangerine, carrots and hummus, sliced cucumber or celery, peanut butter and jelly sandwich [if no peanut allergies] or veggie burrito) in fun sandwich bags. Bento box lunches contain many small compartments for a wide variety of food. Include a thermos with water.

- Want a quick idea to ward off hunger pangs? Have snacks in the pantry and fridge readily available that can satisfy your need for crispy or sugary sweet delights. Nuts, dried fruit, and vegetables can give you variety of texture and tastes and are far healthier than chips, crackers, or chocolate bars. After grocery shopping, chop veggies and put them into baggies so they are ready to use throughout the week.

- Looking for a simple way to encourage young kids to eat veggies? Light candles at each meal (not just dinner) to make the environment fun. Then let those who eat the most vegetables blow out the candles.

- Make an oatmeal bar with ingredients from your pantry. Include toppings like dried cranberries and blueberries and a range of nuts. Want sweeter oatmeal? Provide a little honey, cinnamon, or fresh fruit.

- Go meatless at least once a week. If your taste buds find that difficult, try a meatless meat product available at the grocery store. Substitute these for meat occasionally, but remember that fake meat in a can is still processed food. You can also substitute beans or legumes for meat in chili and soups two to three times per week.

- Get outdoors at breakfast, lunch, dinner, or snack times! Build on your active movement principles and take your food fare outside. Have a picnic in your own backyard or at a local park. Pack simple, healthy snacks for your picnic. Choose foods with brain-building omega-3 fatty acids such as chia seeds (fun and yummy to dip fruit into), edamame, salmon, and trail mix with walnuts. Your child's brain—and behavior—will benefit. Don't worry about planning all day; even spontaneous picnics (ready in fifteen minutes) can be fun!

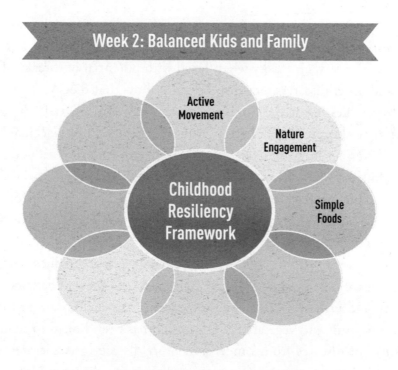

Week 2: Balanced Kids and Family

Active Movement

Nature Engagement

Childhood Resiliency Framework

Simple Foods

Third Resiliency Principle—**Simple Foods**

Want to learn from the centenarians so your family can enjoy improved resilience and whole health? Then begin to find balance for the body with a simplified, healthy plant-based diet.

GET YOUR FAMILY'S TRIPLE BOOST

Putting the simple foods principle into practice can help you and your family kick into high gear by:

Promoting happiness: A growing body of research shows that an increase in fruits and vegetables can reduce fatigue and boost feelings of happiness.[16] Consume more produce and eat your way to happiness! Staying hydrated can also help improve your mood.[17] So drink up the water!

Increasing resilience: Let's face it; we could all benefit from stronger immune systems, especially when faced with potential outbreaks of disease and other disasters. Scientific studies show that diets rich in fruits and vegetables boost the immune system.[18] A clinical trial has found these diets also promote a better antibody response after vaccination.[19] Even better, an increase in fruit and veggie consumption reduces children's likelihood of developing obesity and diabetes.

Vegetables and fruits have great hidden benefits not only for children but also for adults. Want to turn back the hands of time and ward off disease yourself? By eating more vegetables, most of which are 85 to 95 percent water, you will help moisturize your skin and reduce wrinkles. Vegetables also contain phytonutrients, which help prevent damage from the sun and protect against environmental toxins such as air pollution. Increasing fruit and vegetable consumption has been linked to reducing all kinds of diseases from cancer and heart disease to Alzheimer's and dementia. It may even reverse some conditions like diabetes. Not only is a plant-based diet great for humans, growing plants and vegetables is also healthier for the earth than raising animal-based foods, which take more energy and emit more greenhouse gases while growing. Remembering to stay hydrated is important, too, since so many of our bodies' systems—especially those providing protection from foreign particles, pathogens, and viruses—require large amounts of water.

Enhancing performance: Scientific studies show that diets with a higher vegetable intake are linked to improved cognitive function in children. A Norwegian study finds that kids who eat more fruits and vegetables have higher academic achievement.[20] However, decreasing the consumption of fruits and vegetables and increasing the consumption of processed foods high in fats and sugars by age three has been linked to a lower IQ by the time they turn eight.[21] It's important to stay hydrated by drinking water as well. Even a 2 percent dehydration has been found to disrupt our ability to perform in many settings from the classroom to the sports field.[22]

CONQUERING RESISTANCE

Picky eaters. You might encounter some resistance from your kids as you try to change their diet plans and habits, especially those who don't want to try anything new. One approach that has helped in my house is a rule requiring our kids to take two "no, thank you" bites of food. They can't just outright reject something without taking two bites. In fact, when the centenarians were children, it would have been unheard of to reject the food their parents gave them. They not only worked hard and were hungry, but they knew that whatever was set before them was their only option. Like the centenarians, the more children are exposed to new fruits and vegetables, the more their palates will adapt and accept them. So don't give up. If you feel as if you make multiple meals in a single evening because your family members have different tastes, simplify your approach. Make just one dinner, which can consist of many vegetable and fruit side dishes. That will increase the likelihood that everyone finds something they like.

Snack attacks. Your children may come to you right before dinnertime, complaining they are hungry. If you want them to have something, offer the fruits and nuts you've set out on the counter, or provide them with a vegetable tray with hummus for dipping. If they don't want to eat the veggies, they likely aren't too hungry. Reduce their dependence on snacks to encourage them to be hungrier at mealtimes.

Packed schedules. After the turbulent start to this decade, watch out for that pesky feeling that you need to make up for lost time. Feeling this way may increase the likelihood of overscheduling activities like sports or music lessons. Resist the urge to add extra activities too.

OVERLAP OF THE PRINCIPLES

As you focus on increasing the simplicity and health of the foods in your diet, consider how to build upon the foundation you created with an Active cornerstone by finding ways to incorporate being active and engaging the great outdoors in your new eating habits.

From preparing and collecting the ingredients, to cooking and even eating the food, the more you can do outdoors, the better. Walk to the store or harvest crops from your own garden. Bringing fresh fruit, vegetables, and herbs into the home is a great way to bring the outdoors inside. Once the meal is prepared, consider heading back outside and dining on the patio. Eating this way is a great way to connect with your Active cornerstone principles (nature engagement and active movement). You'll also reap more health benefits. A multinational study of over six thousand children found that more time spent outdoors was associated with a healthier dietary pattern.[23]

HOMEWORK TIME

It's time to roll up your sleeves and dive right in with your simple foods principle. Week 2 builds on the foundation set in the previous weeks.

1. **Set up your Balanced goals for simple foods.** This week you will be adapting or adding to your previous goals to include a Balanced lifestyle focused on food planning and mealtimes. Take time on the weekend to plan your meals for the upcoming week. What simple

meals do you want to make? (You can find easy recipes in appendix D.) When are you going to shop? What items are you going to purchase for meals and quick, healthy snacks? (Hint: Think fresh fruit or ready-to-go veggies.)

Select nights when you can carve out time to prepare a home-cooked meal for your family and note them on your calendar. When starting this process, it's best not to pick days when you will be slammed with events in the evening.

Remember to look for opportunities to overlap your Balanced lifestyle practices with your Active lifestyle ones. Try walking to the farmers market or grocery store to pick up in-season vegetables or plan to eat a meal outdoors on the patio or at the park.

Use the goals below or develop new ones:

NEW BASE GOAL

- **Simple foods principle:** Eat a meal made at home (using simple foods) with family and/or friends at least three times this week and ask a conversation-provoking question at each meal. (See appendix D for recipes and appendix E for some ideas on questions to start discussion at a meal.) If you are not serving a vegetarian dinner, choose leaner, healthier meats and offer at least two vegetable side dishes. If you can eat together outdoors, that is even better since you are practicing the nature engagement principle too!

    Overlapping principles include simple foods, nurturing relationships, and nature engagement if the meal is outdoors.

- **Optional new goal 1:** Prepare simple food lunches at home at least two times this week for your family to take to school or work.

- **Optional new goal 2:** Drink eight glasses (maybe more or less depending on your physical needs) of water each day and reduce your consumption of other drinks (like juice or soda).

EXISTING BASE GOALS

- Continue or adapt the goals you set for active movement and nature engagement.

2. **Implement and track your success.** Next, track your progress. Spend a few minutes each night before bedtime recording how you practiced the simple foods principle. Did your family eat any meals at home together? Did your family make any meals from scratch? Were you able to achieve the weekly goal you set for yourself? At the end of the week, review what you achieved over the past seven days. Remember you can repeat this week if you feel you have not met your goals. Use the Weekly Evaluation guide (see appendix B) to help you evaluate your progress.

 **Great Job!**

Congratulations on completing the second week of the program! You've taken another step toward a transformative life—building upon your Active foundation to find Balance through food preparation and dining habits. Take a moment to reward yourself. When you are ready, jump into the next chapter and keep your momentum going by engaging in the fourth principle—resting reset.

CHAPTER 5

WEEK 3:
RARING TO GO REBOOT

It's all about finding the calm in the chaos.

DONNA KARAN

"JUST FIVE MORE MINUTES, Mom, I promise. I'm gaming, and I'm good!" Jayden hollered. The clock showed exactly 9:30 p.m., and I didn't sense any rush on his part to stop.

"I'm taking your computer power cord if you don't turn it off right now," I yelled back. Joe was catching up on his work downstairs, but we both barked out commands to Jayden.

No one else in our house appeared ready to turn in for the night either. I walked around my bedroom like a seasoned warrior maneuvering a minefield. Stepping over lesson plans scattered across the floor and a handful of LEGOs strewn about, I walked past our small sleeping dog lying on the futon. Sadly, only Mr. Beans turned in early.

Joelle lounged in the master bathtub, imagining a spa day for her and her Barbie doll. Jumping up and down on my bed, Julia exclaimed, "I wanna book! I wanna story!" The dog opened one eye, making sure no one would dare crush him.

"Speed it along, Joelle," I instructed.

I picked up *The Day Jimmy's Boa Ate the Wash* from the two-foot pile of picture books covering my nightstand and began reading to Julia. After that, I said prayers with her and lay down beside her on my bed, hoping she'd fall asleep. To occupy my time, I donned my headphones, held my cell phone close to my face, and switched on Netflix.

When the house finally quieted, I relaxed, anxious for some rest. While rolling on my side trying to get comfortable, I was jolted wide awake by the cold sensation of a wet bedsheet. "Ugh," I groaned. I'd forgotten Julia's pull-up. Again.

Just another typical night in our harried household. Every morning Joe and I, each with a set of matching baggage under our eyes, would drag ourselves around the house trying to get the kids ready. Perhaps you and your family have your own hectic bedtime rituals. Once again, I learned how different things had been for my century-old friends and got some ideas on how to remedy my own situation.

When the centenarians were children, they stayed busy. They were up at dawn, worked on the farm or did household chores, walked to school—often miles—studied and played with their classmates, walked all the way home, did more chores, ate dinner, helped with the dishes, and did their homework. By then, they were ready for a deep sleep so they could repeat the whole cycle the next day.

Though chores, family time, and schooling took up most of their hours, they lived at a nonfrenetic pace, and their daily routines included time for rest and relaxation. Hulda Crooks (101-year-old Resiliency Capital member) recalled spending time relaxing while appreciating nature. "I grew up beneath its [the aurora borealis or northern lights] spectacular playground. During my childhood and youth in Western Canada its varied displays from mere wisps and veils of light to lively pageants that covered the heavens were familiar sights."[1] Because she learned early to include rest and relaxation in her days, it is no wonder Hulda writes in her memoir, "Take time for those regular hours of sleep, rest, and relaxation. Even a powerful draft horse must have hours of freedom from the whip. It is an error to overdraw your vital resources when you are young and then expect full strength and vitality at your disposal later in life."[2]

The story is different today. Most parents drive their kids to school—and more often than not, instead of being educated together with siblings in a single one-room schoolhouse or small building, each child goes to a different school. Increasingly, mothers work outside the home, and even stay-at-home moms work from sunup to way past sundown managing the household and caring for the kids. On average, families must care for homes three to four times the size of those the centenarians grew up in. Add homeschooling, and it's a wonder moms get any sleep.

Dads have it hard, too, even if they aren't pitching in with the housework (though hopefully they are). They are increasingly expected to work long hours, take home more work, and answer emails, texts, and phone calls at night and on the weekends.

But this extra effort on behalf of the family doesn't make it easier on kids. Homework often adds several hours to their academic day nearly every evening. Extracurricular activities—necessary to get into a good college these days, but also important to compensate for the more sedentary lifestyle we lead—take up even more time. Sports, clubs, fundraising and community activities, art classes, theater—you name it, chances are one or all of your children are constantly negotiating their schedules as if they were running for office and every minute had to be prearranged. And the first activity cut from our busy schedules is almost always one of the most important—sleep.

> *The key to keeping your balance is knowing when you've lost it.*
>
> ANONYMOUS

Our frenetic pace has resulted in a sleep deprivation epidemic, and not just in the US, but around the world. Surprisingly, human beings are the only mammals on earth willing to forgo sleep, and we pay the price. Poor health, distracted driving, quick tempers—all these and more come from not getting enough sleep. Sleep deprivation negatively affects the body's ability to overcome catastrophe when it strikes—like the COVID-19 outbreak.

Have you considered whether you or your family might be suffering from sleep deprivation? Are you ready to find out about the healing power of rest? Do you want to draw on the wisdom of the centenarians to increase resilience and wellness within your own family? Then this is your wake-up call.

WEEK 3: BUILDING BALANCED KIDS AND FAMILY

The third week of the program continues to focus on the letter *B*—for balanced kids and family. Along with the principle of simple foods, the fourth resiliency principle—resting reset—promotes balance in the body through restoration and rest, pausing to allow the body, mind, and soul time to rejuvenate.

PRINCIPLE #4—RESTING RESET

The centenarians we interviewed were from farming families whose waking and sleeping habits were tied to their work. Almost one hundred years ago, it was easier to rise and go to bed according to daylight hours, and people slept an average of nine hours each night.[3] One centenarian I interviewed, 101-year-old Dr. Ellsworth Wareham, recalled his childhood mornings: "I'd routinely rise between four and five thirty in the morning every day to go out to find and then milk the cows before eating breakfast and then heading off on the two-mile walk to school." As a heart surgeon, he remained disciplined, working well into his nineties.

In contrast to Dr. Wareham's experience, today we're more likely to sit for most of the day, whether that's in the car, at our desks, in meetings, or in front of the TV. As a result, our bodies aren't expending the energy that the centenarians did, which made it easy for them to fall asleep. In addition, the light, noise, and air pollution of our modern world increase the likelihood of our sleep being interrupted. Have you ever been jolted awake in the middle of the night by a loud noise going off in your house or outside? Do you find it difficult to keep your room dark from the time you go to bed until you get up the next morning? The internet and other technology make it harder and harder for us to shut our minds off before bed. The light from computer screens and smartphones also disrupts the production of melatonin, the hormone that regulates our sleep/wake cycle.

In one 2013 study, researchers found that a week of summer camping—with no smartphones—reset people's internal clocks to be in rhythm with nature's. Saliva samples showed that melatonin levels shifted when compared with a typical week at home, when the study participants typically went to bed around midnight. While camping, the levels started to rise around sunset, and the camper's "biological night" kicked in about two hours earlier. As a result, the campers turned in much earlier than their usual bedtime. They also woke up earlier, closer to sunrise.[4]

When I consider the prevalence of sleep deprivation and the rise in insomnia and other sleep disorders, I wonder whether all the sleep products and aids available are just treating the symptoms rather than getting to the heart of the problem. Even the passage of legislation in California, which delays the start time of classes in middle school and high school, may simply lead to other issues.[5] Does this change mean less time for youth to be active outdoors with natural light exposure? Now that school starts later, will bedtimes be pushed back too? If so, teens may experience even greater sleep difficulties.

We now sleep an average of less than seven hours a night,[6] and many people either struggle to fall asleep or drift off the instant their heads hit the pillow. (It should take five minutes or so for the brain to make the transition from wakefulness to sleep.) Our generation requires more help and planning to protect and encourage beneficial restorative sleep.

Just look at all the ads on TV for products guaranteed to improve sleep—ranging from mattresses to medications—and all the books and blogs with ideas to help you fall asleep quicker and sleep better. Consumers spent about $41 billion on all these products in 2015, and this number is only expected to increase.[7]

Not only do Americans sleep less than their elders did, many Americans no longer take much vacation time, if any, losing out on an opportunity for restoration. In 2018, 55 percent of Americans reported unused vacation time and a whopping 768 million unused vacation days.[8] Employees in other countries, including Japan, China, and South Africa, report taking even less vacation time.

From my perspective as an epidemiologist who studies social connections and their impact on health, one way I measure our society's values is through the advertising that targets our needs and desires. Based on that, I have to conclude that although we recognize our "unfortunate" need for sleep, we place greater value on staying busy. Sleep deprivation has become the new normal, but it comes with dire consequences we have yet to fully understand. If we continue on this path, what lies ahead for our families—for our mental, physical, and spiritual well-being? With sleep closely tied to our health and resilience, how will we fare in the face of future stresses and outbreaks of disease? It's time to change our view of rest by looking at the centenarians' practices and how we might implement them within our own families.

THREE FUNDAMENTALS FOR APPLYING THE RESTING RESET PRINCIPLE

1. Strengthen Your "R" (Rest)	2. Take a Moment (Relaxation)	3. Create Restful Space (Restoration)
Develop daytime and bedtime routines that will promote positive sleeping habits.	Take one day of the week away from work and school to experience rest, relaxation, and restoration.	Create space in your home, starting with your bedroom and extending throughout your house, to support rest and a restful state of mind.

Modern Times Call for Modern Methods

Though as children the centenarians lived in a very different world, we can still adopt some of their practices to promote resilience with our own families. Let's take a closer look at their three rules for applying the resting reset principle:

1. Strengthen your "R" (rest)

The first rule of thumb for experiencing the resting reset principle is to strengthen your "R"—referring to the longer, more restful sleep you need to experience each night. Sleep is extremely important for our physical, mental, and even spiritual health. Most of what we know about sleep has been discovered only in the past thirty years, coinciding with our declining practices of getting a good night's sleep.

According to the Centers for Disease Control and Prevention (CDC), one out of every three adults routinely doesn't get enough sleep, even though adequate sleep is critical to good health.[9] It's not only quantity (number of hours) but the *quality* of sleep that matters. Even those who get enough rest may suffer if their sleep quality is poor. They may spend eight hours in bed, but that doesn't necessarily mean they slept all eight hours. Waking often throughout the night disrupts people's sleep cycle, leaving them tired the next day. To maximize the health benefits, we should spend at least 90 percent of our time in bed asleep. With sleep deprivation such a widespread problem in the US, the CDC has declared it a national epidemic.[10] All this makes me wonder about the impact that sleep deprivation has had on our ability to fight the COVID-19 pandemic.

Unfortunately, children appear to be mirroring the habits of their parents; the American Academy of Pediatrics reports that 25 to 50 percent of preschoolers and up to 40 percent of adolescents experience sleep-related problems.[11] Depending on the age category and reporting source, the prevalence may be even higher.[12] Additionally, the CDC indicates more than two-thirds of US high school students report getting less than the recommended eight hours of sleep on school nights.[13] This practice isn't confined to the United States—sleep deprivation appears to be a global epidemic. The Canadian government has reported that 25 percent of Canadian children are not getting enough sleep; the UK has disclosed that upward of 57 percent of its children are not getting adequate sleep.[14] Many more developed and developing countries are following suit.[15]

Kids may show signs of sleep deprivation by becoming overly defiant or emotional (evident through temper tantrums, mood swings, or easily hurt feelings); developing hyperactivity or difficulty focusing; and experiencing sleep disturbances (trouble falling asleep even when overly tired, falling asleep the moment they crawl into bed, or difficulty waking up in the morning). These symptoms played out in the extreme in one little boy who couldn't sleep. Three-year-old Rhett Lamb was awake nearly twenty-four hours a day.[16] He would frequently lash out at his parents, and once even gave his mom a black eye. His body would wear out, but his mind would keep going and he simply couldn't fall asleep. Rhett displayed terrible irritability and had difficulty engaging and playing with kids his age. He was behind in school because he just couldn't focus. Doctors finally determined that a compression at the base of his skull was putting pressure on his brain and making it virtually impossible for him to fall asleep. After surgery, Rhett was finally able to sleep. His mood completely shifted. He was now calm and loving toward his parents. Within a month, he had caught up to what other kids his age were doing. Though Rhett's was a severe case, it gives us a frightening glimpse of the toll sleep deprivation takes on our bodies.

Though we often think of sleep deprivation as mainly an adult problem, research shows a link between chronic sleep deprivation and detrimental health conditions in children. Decreased sleep is linked to increased body weight, insulin resistance, and elevated stress levels. Scientists have uncovered a link between sleep loss and the risk of developing diabetes and obesity. A 2002 study of 8,274 Japanese children ages six and seven showed that fewer hours of sleep increased the risk of childhood obesity.[17] Researchers have hypothesized that sleep deprivation may permanently disrupt the hypothalamus—the region of the brain responsible for energy expenditure and appetite regulation. New research also shows children who lose on average just an hour per night in sleep may be at greater risk of developing diabetes.[18]

Another alarming trend among children is the increasing prevalence of high blood pressure—also called the invisible dragon because of the unseen damage it can cause inside the body. Almost twice as many children worldwide now may have high blood pressure as compared to a

Sleep Needs by Age Group[*]

Infant 4–12 months: 12–16 hours (including naps)
Child 1–2 years: 11–14 hours (including naps)
Child 3–5 years: 10–13 hours (including naps)
Child 6–12 years: 9–12 hours
Teenager: 8–10 hours
Adult: 7–9 hours

[*] According to the American Sleep Association; see https://www.sleepassociation.org/about-sleep/sleep-statistics/.

decade ago.[19] Not only do high-salt fast-food meals contribute to elevated blood pressure among children, a recent study of children ages two to ten found that sleep deprivation is linked to high blood pressure in kids.[20] Getting a good night's sleep can help restore blood pressure to normal. (Hypertension in kids can lead to even bigger health concerns, including blindness as well as kidney and heart problems.)[21]

Not only are chronic health conditions a concern, but skimping on sleep may be putting your family at risk for viral infections. Researchers discovered that poorer sleep habits, with less quality and quantity of sleep in the weeks before exposure to a virus, were associated with less resistance to the illness.[22] A small prospective study of fourteen- to nineteen-year-olds found that those reporting longer sleeping periods also reported fewer colds.[23] Furthermore, being sleep deprived may lower the ability of the body to respond to a flu vaccine.[24] Since most pandemics are caused by viral illnesses (including COVID-19), it is critically important to be fully rested.

In addition to these adverse physical health conditions in kids, sleep deprivation can also hinder the mental and social aspects of everyday life. According to a recent research study led by a Harvard pediatrician, children in preschool and elementary school who don't get enough sleep are more likely to have problems with attention, emotional control, and peer relationships at around age seven.[25] Because sleep deprivation hinders the ability to pay attention and concentrate, it should come as no surprise that sleep is also tied to achievement in school. As children get older, staying up later to cram for exams doesn't necessarily produce the desired outcome. Too many late nights can lead to excessive sleepiness and hinder academic performance—not to mention performance in extracurriculars like sports and music.

Learning more from Mohr

I was eager to find out about the childhood sleep patterns of the centenarians in my community when I met Salma Mohr. My research assistant, Alicia Torres, and I met her at her home inside an assisted living facility in Loma Linda. Her small room was pleasant and tidy, with her bed neatly made and pictures of her family all around. At 101, Salma was a bright, articulate woman with a witty sense of humor. She told us that she was one of the youngest among the ten children in her family, and they were terribly poor. Her father didn't work, so her mother and all the siblings pitched in to do housekeeping and odd jobs around the community so they could afford basic necessities like food. When I asked her about her childhood sleep habits, she quickly replied, "We got the average amount of sleep, eight hours, and we were always in bed by 9:00 p.m. Mother started shooing us off to bed after 7:00 p.m. since this was around the time our kerosene lamp would go out. We didn't have electricity in the house, a fact we just accepted. We had to accept a lot. No fancy additions."

> *Sleep is that golden chain that ties health and our bodies together.*
>
> THOMAS DEKKER

Salma slept in a double bed in between her two older sisters. They slept on a mattress, and back then, there was no thought about how comfortable it was or wasn't; they were fortunate just to have something to sleep on. They had no bedspread or sheets, so they slept between a couple of blankets. "The blankets were probably washed once a year in the springtime because Mother was already doing so much washing [of] clothes to make money to buy food for the table. There was no special fussing about getting to bed. Each day was consistent, going to bed and rising at the same time."

The majority of centenarians I spoke to were from farming families, so their sleeping and waking habits were routine, even on weekends. Even those whose families weren't farmers, like Salma, rose early every day of the week.

Anita Johnson-Mackey (105-year-old Resiliency Capital member) said, "We were taught to go to bed at a certain time. And no staying in bed in the morning. If we said, 'But I'm tired,' I could hear Mama saying, 'Well, maybe you'll remember to go to bed earlier. But you're getting up now, young lady.' And that was that." A recent article in *Scientific Reports* explains the importance of maintaining a routine sleeping pattern. Getting up earlier on weekdays while sleeping in on weekends correlated with smaller gray-matter volume in several regions of the brain in early adolescents.[26] Later bedtimes on weekends were also associated with poorer grades.

We've come to feel that being sleep deprived is a way of life—everybody is tired, so suck it up and get busy. However, given the potential health problems linked to sleep deprivation, parents need to be aware of their family's sleep habits and intervene when necessary.

Daily habits toward rest

The first step toward developing a daily habit of resting reset is to recognize your family's current practices and experiences. Take a look at the daily journal you completed prior to starting this program. Did you note any habits that impede your ability to rest or relax? A resting reset may require that you change some lifestyle habits and establish a healthy atmosphere at home that allows a breather. Where you start and how you encourage rest, relaxation, and restoration is entirely under your control! What's most important is that you have a plan.

Start by assessing your family's evening and bedtime habits. Do you have rules you abide by to ensure everyone gets to bed at a decent time? For younger children, a good bedtime is usually between 7:00 p.m. and

*Take a rest;
a field that has
rested gives a
bountiful crop.*

OVID

8:00 p.m. (See the chart on page 105 to determine the hours needed based on your child's age. Some children need more sleep than others.) Keep in mind that children tend to fall asleep faster when they get to bed before 9:00 p.m. Once you set your bedtime limits, stick closely to them. Canadian researchers found that the children with parents who followed strict bedtime rules had better sleep.[27] Make sure older children are off their computers and cell phones at least an hour before bedtime. The Screen Time app, available for both Apple and Android users, will enable you to disable your internet at a certain time. Several other apps, such as Net Nanny, BreakFree, unGlue, and Spyzie parental control, also allow you to limit your kids' screen time and block their access to unsuitable content.

After you've set your sleep schedule, look at your own habits and make sure they support healthy sleep. Like your children, you should stop using your phone, computer, or electronic devices at least one hour before bedtime. If you usually bring work to bed, you will need to stop doing that to disassociate your bed and bedroom from work and stress.

During the day, do your best to be sure you and your family get outdoors and are more active. The natural lighting outside helps our bodies fall asleep more quickly in the evening. The sooner and the more often you get outdoors throughout the day, the better chance natural lighting has to improve your sleep.

Don't plan too many activities close to bedtime. Plan ahead to allow plenty of time for your kids to complete big school projects so none of you have to cram to finish them the night before they're due.

2. Take a moment (relaxation)

The next rule of thumb for the resting reset principle is to take a moment. Be sure that relaxation—time to find peace and downtime for the mind, body and spirit—happens throughout the day. It is crucial to take breaks and allow our minds and bodies a moment to decompress. We are bombarded by emails, phone calls, text messages, television, and commercials. We rarely have a moment to let our brains get bored or wander.

I asked 105-year-old Anita Johnson-Mackey how she took breaks when she was young. Her eyes lit up and she replied, "Reading!"

With so many adventures to choose from in books, reading gave her comfort and escape from daily life. As an African American, she faced unique challenges as a child. "We lived not in the black neighborhood, but in a white community, which was hard for my family," she told me. "So early in life I always had a library book to take a break. I liked to go to the library to relax and read too. That was the one place we could always go, and Father felt it was a respite from the world."

Allowing our minds to take breaks comes with so many benefits, especially for stirring creativity. All types of innovative people, from scientists to famous authors, have experienced "aha" moments during periods of relaxation. Albert Einstein and the surrealist painter Salvador Dali were known for taking walks in nature during the day to help relax their minds and come up with new ideas. In his memoir *On Writing*, Stephen King said his book *Misery* came to him while he was taking a nap on a plane.[28] Johannes Brahms wrote symphonies, and it is said that naps at the piano helped him write his most famous lullaby—ironically a song notable for putting many children to sleep. Even companies like Nike and Google are catching on to the idea of rest for the mind by encouraging workers to take naps during the workday to stir creativity.

Structuring kids' days so they have time for adequate rest and unstructured playtime will give their minds time to rest, wander, and daydream—increasing their creativity, whether they're interested in science, math, or the arts. Such downtime will decrease their stress levels and make it easier for them to fall asleep in the evening. In addition to enhancing creativity and promoting independence, restful periods during the day are linked to a variety of health benefits. In a study of elementary school children, midday napping (not too late in the evening) was associated with "higher happiness, grit, and self-control"; reduced behavior problems; higher verbal IQs; and better academic achievement.[29]

To promote relaxation and rest, learn to value the white space on your calendar. Leave it open for spontaneous activities or simply for relaxing with family and friends. Such time sometimes makes for the best memories.

Learning to take a break

Do you ever feel like you have so much to get done before the week ahead that you run around all weekend? By the time Monday morning rolls around, do you feel like you need another day to recover before the week begins? With so many factors competing for our attention—household chores, work left unfinished, kids' activities—it may seem we have to work hardest on weekends or our days off work. If you feel this way, you are not alone. In today's fast-paced society, it is more important than ever to take a full day for relaxation to allow ourselves time to recover mentally, physically, and spiritually.

> *Every now and then go away, have a little relaxation, for when you come back to your work, your judgment will be surer.*
>
> LEONARDO DA VINCI

One important practice of the centenarians is always taking one day of the week to relax. They often refer to this as observing the Sabbath or taking a Sabbath moment. The centenarians observe the Sabbath from Friday evening (sundown) until Saturday evening (sundown). It's important to take one day of the week for rest. Dr. Robert Bolton (105-year-old Resiliency Capital member) said that as a child growing up in Canada, he and his family often visited their neighbors, who had extended a standing invitation to come over on the Sabbath. There they would relax, read Scriptures, and spend unhurried time with family and friends. "They had no stained glass windows and proper pews, no beautiful felts on a flannel board in a tastefully decorated children's room," Robert said. "They had only a small home set into the side of a hill in the rolling grainfields in Saskatchewan and the help their imagination and ingenuity could supply. And they invited their neighbors in."

Your family may observe this Sabbath time by attending church, connecting with God along with friends and family, and then heading out into nature. Experiencing nature on the Sabbath could be as simple as gathering for a picnic in the backyard, or you might choose to hike in the mountains or spend a day at the beach. The day of rest is not intended for lazy behavior or goofing off, but rather a needed break for the body, mind, and soul. I remember one senior professor explaining that his blood pressure drastically lowered on the Sabbath. He discovered this when measuring his blood pressure on Wednesday evening and then again on Saturday evening. After taking time off for the Sabbath, his blood pressure would routinely come down to a healthier range.

I feel fortunate to live in the Loma Linda region, where the elementary school lets students out by noon on Fridays to help families prepare for the Sabbath. Since shifting from a modern to a premodern centenarian lifestyle, our family shuts off the electronics and attends church rather than spending Saturdays parked in front of the TV and computer. After the service, we often head out for some mountain biking or hiking in the south hills. The change has been so remarkable that now if ever we miss spending this quiet time together on the Sabbath, we really feel the weight of increased stress when we start a new workweek. If your family is feeling stressed, tired, and anxious, consider taking one day of the week for relaxation and restoration. Even when the COVID-19 pandemic prevented us from attending church in person, we still maintained our day of rest and getting outdoors.

Rest and relaxation enable us to better deal with the day-to-day stressors of life. When your body is allowed time to rest, it can use that time and energy for restoring itself. Research has shown us that the immune system works best when the body has adequately rested.

3. Create restful space (restoration)

The final rule of the resting reset principle is to organize your home to support a peaceful, relaxing state of mind. Your home can become a sanctuary

Six Simple Steps for Taking a Day Off in the Week

1. **Schedule a full day of rest on your calendar.** For most families, setting aside Saturday or Sunday is easiest.

2. **Protect the fringes.** The centenarians are strict about taking off from Friday sundown until Saturday sundown, avoiding busyness and work during this day of rest. Be diligent about not allowing the workweek to creep into your day off. If you start doing work-related tasks, you're likely to end up with a fifteen-minute break rather than a full day of rest.

3. **Put away all electronics.** Take a break from computers, televisions, apps, phones, and other devices. If you use your phone, do so sparingly to connect with family and friends, not to watch videos, surf the internet, or play games. Your children will probably complain initially, so you and your spouse need to stand firm as a united front. Joe will often remind me and our children to put our phones away or not to answer emails on our Sabbath. When heading out to church or nature, we remind our children to leave their phones at home.

   Though abruptly going "cold turkey" with your devices may sound difficult, it will be easier if you are outside and engaged in nature. When you ditch your electronics for a day, you will likely have more conversations in the car, more engagement during mealtimes, more laughter over spontaneous games, and more peace throughout the day.

4. **No household projects.** Take a minimalist approach. On your day of rest, refrain from starting a new project, such as cleaning out the garage or some other labor-intensive endeavor that is more work than fun. Enlist the whole family in preparing the meals so it becomes an enjoyable activity and not another chore. Take a break from homework, too!

5. **Enjoy time in nature or with a worship community or both.** There is a healing benefit that comes from connecting with God and embracing nature. Spending time outdoors also allows you to build on the principle of nature engagement.

6. **Spend your day of rest with family and friends.** Connecting with those close to you is an excellent way to spend your Sabbath. Plus, this sets you up for practicing the fifth resiliency principle—nurturing bonds. If you already consistently take one day off each week for a Sabbath observance, consider encouraging others to join you and start a revolution.

away from the hustle and bustle of the working world. Decluttering will increase the feeling of peace and restfulness as soon as you enter the front door. If you are pressed for time, consider cleaning the area you see first when walking into your home.

When we visited my husband's great-aunt, Mulan Tsai, one of the first things I noticed was how inviting her house was. The front entryway was filled with jade plants and potted orchids, which provided a sense of serenity and beauty. The sun shone through expansive windows, and the rooms were simply decorated with beautiful Asian furnishings. Her home was neat, tidy, and peacefully quiet, with no loud television blaring. It was similar to many of the other centenarians' dwellings I visited, which had entryways and living rooms furnished and organized to foster a relaxed state of mind.

If you find it hard to keep your home neat and clean, consider hiring a housekeeper to help out once a week—and if that's too big an expense, just once a month can make a huge difference. Better yet, do as the centenarians did with their kids—get them to pitch in and help clean up the house as a part of their regular chores! To foster rest, relaxation, and restoration, try some of these tips:

During the day:

- Avoid caffeinated beverages late in the day. Drinking caffeine may make it more difficult to fall asleep. And remember, many sodas and sports drinks contain caffeine—one reason children can be hyperactive.

- Limit simple sugars like candies, cookies, and sodas. Such foods will give you an immediate sugar high and then cause you to crash. Prevent these dives by eating less of these foods—or cutting them out altogether.

- Take breaks outdoors. Routine exposure to natural light during the day will help you fall asleep faster at night.

Before bedtime:

- Remove phones from your bedroom or turn them off.

- Avoid artificial screen light right before bedtime. If you want to unwind in bed, read a good book, but no more Netflix in bed.

- Put on relaxing music in the evening to set the stage for transitioning from the hectic day into bedtime.

- Work as a team. Involve your partner in helping children get ready for bed. This underscores that sleep is a family priority. One of you can read a book to your kids or make up a bedtime story. One of my friends told me that her ex-husband would call their five-year-old daughter just before her bedtime. He would then tell her a special story, one that grew more elaborate every night. The daughter couldn't wait for bedtime to hear the next chapter in this continuing saga—and it always helped put her to sleep (while keeping her close to her father, who lived in another state).

- Establish and stick to routines. Kids thrive on them. For young children, a bedtime between 7:00 and 8:00 p.m. is entirely normal if starting the day between 6:30 and 7:30 a.m.

In the bedroom:

- Turn on white noise. If you or your family members fall asleep more easily to the sound of the ocean, crickets chirping, or a steady rainfall, consider getting a white noise machine.

- Use blankets and coverings appropriate for the weather. Change them when the seasons change. According to the National Sleep Foundation, the best room temperature for a good night's sleep is around 65 degrees Fahrenheit.

- Keep water near the bed. Children often wake up in the middle of the night, wanting something to drink. Consider giving them a water bottle they can keep nearby. This is equally important for adults, since many people are dehydrated by the morning, which may put them at greater risk for a heart attack and many other medical issues. If you wake up during the night, reach for your water bottle and drink up.

- Make sure pets don't wake up your family at night. High-energy dogs and nocturnal pocket pets like hamsters or hedgehogs may be restless and noisy. If you have any of these furry party animals, keep them out of the bedroom. During the day, give your high-energy pooches plenty of exercise, such as a longer walk or jog, to tire them out.

- Keep things simple and consistent. As children, the centenarians didn't rely on products to help them sleep. Instead, they spent plenty of time outdoors being physically active, and they followed routine, with strict early bed- and waking times.

IN A PINCH, IT'S A CINCH: RESTING RESET PRACTICE TIPS

- Take a noonday break and head outdoors to sit or take a quick walk. While you're there, blow some bubbles, which helps the body relax. When you need a break at work or school, take a moment to look out the nearest window. Try to observe a grassy area, a tree, or other vegetation. Now imagine yourself outdoors experiencing that "secret garden" with all your senses. Imagine the sun on your face, or the blades of grass under your feet. Count to ten and then journey back from your secret garden to the present. I used this trick in eighth grade math class whenever I was overwhelmed and needed a quick break.

- Encourage your kids to grab a puzzle or a coloring book and sit quietly near a large window or—even better—head outdoors.

- Spread a blanket on the ground in your yard, lie on your back, and check out the clouds. Make a game with your kids pointing out all the different shapes, objects, and animals the clouds are making.

- Take one day off during the week—a Sabbath moment—and head outdoors for a family picnic, a hike at the park, or a stroll through a museum. Leave the electronics and stressful workweek behind to focus on relaxing and spending time together.

- When your children lie down for a nap and ask you to lie next to them, take the time to do so. Don't worry about all the dishes in the sink or the office work to attend to. Breaks are good for them and for you!

- Routinely combine a great book with a nighttime stuffed friend to help younger children transition into bedtime. One of my favorite books to read at bedtime is *Good Night, Gorilla*, accompanied by a stuffed monkey. When I'm done reading, I tuck the monkey in first, followed by my daughter.

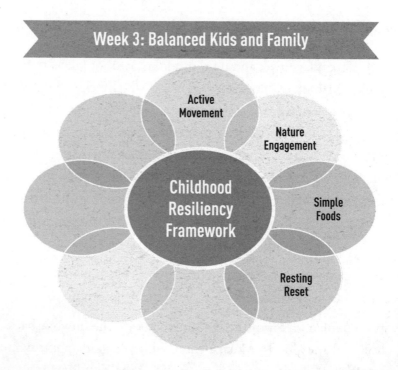

Fourth Resiliency Principle—**Resting Reset**

Want to learn from the centenarians so your family can enjoy improved resilience and whole health? Then take time for rest and relaxation each and every day.

GET YOUR FAMILY'S TRIPLE BOOST

Putting the resting reset principle into practice can help you and your family kick into high gear by:

Promoting happiness: Is anyone in your family often cranky and irritated? Researchers have found that sleep deprivation not only puts people in a grumpy mood but may prevent them from recognizing facial cues and feeling positive emotions.[30] A good night's sleep can put anyone on the path to positivity and happiness.

Increasing resilience: With better sleep, children are less likely to get colds.[31] Researchers have discovered that sleep is intricately linked with the immune system, which releases chemicals that promote sleep. When you don't get enough sleep, infection-fighting cells are reduced. In fact, a recent study found that a later bedtime was associated with an increased risk of developing the flu.[32] With adequate rest and relaxation, on the other hand, the body is better able to heal and be restored.[33] A recent study revealed that skin wounds healed significantly faster in people getting regular rest.[34]

Enhancing performance: Sleep plays an important role in cognitive skills and memory retention. Poor nighttime sleep, especially reduced sleep quality, can promote daytime sleepiness, which can hinder children's academic performance.[35] Researchers have found that when athletes get improved sleep, they are less prone to injury and illness and more likely to improve their performance and successfully compete.[36]

CONQUERING RESISTANCE

Be prepared to overcome the barriers you may encounter as you implement and maintain your relaxation and resting goals.

Holiday hustle. Holidays—particularly Christmas and Thanksgiving—can be a mad rush for the whole family. Make sure to build in downtime, especially for younger kids.

"Just one more." Kids are great negotiators. Be prepared for them to try stalling or derailing rest or relaxation habits. Be consistent and firm, particularly with your bedtime routines.

Pandemic times. Older children may be more reluctant to go to bed when routine schedules are thrown out the window—as was the case during the COVID-19 pandemic. My teenager began staying up later and later, trying to connect with his friends through any electronic device available. Be alert for this behavior and stick to your bedtime routines—it's best to be fully rested to help ward off infection.

OVERLAP OF THE PRINCIPLES

Restoration and resiliency can be enhanced by overlapping the resting reset principle with the first three principles (active movement, nature engagement, and simple foods). For example, increasing your time outdoors during the daylight hours will help improve your sleep at night. Exposure to natural lighting can help regulate your body's normal circadian rhythm, an internal system that tells your body when it is tired and ready for bed and when it is awake and ready to start the day. Exposure to natural light helps this rhythm function. A Finnish study found that young children who take naps outdoors in their strollers tend to nap longer than those inside.[37] Researchers from the UK supported the Finnish study and found that infants who spend more time outdoors during the day tend to sleep better.[38] Outdoor napping will more naturally lead to greater levels of vitamin D—which some researchers theorized may play a protective role against COVID-19 and other respiratory viral infections.[39] Outdoor naps are good for babies and parents, too! When our son, Jayden, was about six months old, Joe often took him outside in the evening to help him get settled and calm his fussiness. As an added bonus, Jayden slept more restfully at night after those evening strolls.

Researchers have discovered that what you eat or drink may also influence the quality of your sleep. Scientists studying the Mediterranean diet—one high in vegetables—found that those adhering to this diet had improved sleep quality.[40] In a study among school-aged children in China, researchers discovered that eating fish was associated not only with higher IQ scores, but also with better sleep.[41] Food intake near bedtime can also negatively influence sleeping patterns.[42] Drinking water and staying hydrated can also help you get a better night's sleep.[43]

These first four resiliency principles are intricately tied together. Having daily rhythms around sleep, diet, and outdoor activities helps the body function at its best.

HOMEWORK TIME

It's time to roll up your sleeves and dive right in with your resting reset principle. Week 3 builds on the foundation set in the previous weeks.

1. **Set up your Balanced goals for resting reset.** Add to or adapt your previous weekly goals to include the resting reset principle. Select from the following goals, or feel free to create your own.

NEW BASE GOAL

- **Resting reset principle:** My family and I will get eight hours of sleep each night (could be more or less, depending on individual needs) and will not use electronics for at least one hour before bed.

  Overlapping principles include resting reset and nurturing relationships if you spend time reading, praying, or doing any other quieting activities before bed with your family.

- **Optional new goal 1:** My family and I will take a complete day off during the week to experience a "Sabbath moment." We will kick it up a notch by spending much of that time in nature.

- **Optional new goal 2:** I will take a twenty-minute break each day with my children by spending time outdoors for relaxation and restoration.

EXISTING BASE GOALS

- Continue or adapt the goals you have set for active movement, nature engagement, and simple foods.

2. **Implement and track your success.** Carry out your plans and chart your progress. Spend a few minutes each night before bedtime recording the ways you and your family experienced rest, relaxation, and restoration. Were you able to achieve the weekly goal you set for yourself? Did you and your family achieve quality sleep and enough hours of sleep last night? Did you experience a Sabbath moment?

   At the end of the week, review your achievements throughout the week. Remember, you can repeat this week if you feel you have not met your goals. Use the Weekly Evaluation guide (found in appendix B) to help you evaluate your weekly progress.

   Remember that this is a personal journey, and every person has different needs. Your course of action will likely vary from other people's paths. Establishing a new habit means trial and error. Allow for adjustments and time to discover what works best for you.

———— Great Job! ————

Congratulations on completing the third week of the program! You've taken another step toward a transformative life—building upon the Active foundation you and your family established to find Balance through a restoring resting reset. Take a moment to reward yourself. When you are ready, jump into the next chapter and keep your momentum going by engaging the fifth principle—nurturing bonds.

CHAPTER 6

WEEK 4:
CULTIVATING LIFE-GIVING
RELATIONSHIPS

Ohana means family. Family means nobody gets left behind.

Lilo & Stitch

EAGER TO LEARN MORE ABOUT improving resiliency in my family, I headed north on the bustling LA freeway one morning to meet with Anita Johnson-Mackey (105-year-old Resiliency Capital member). It was rush hour, so traffic was stop-and-go. Fretting about being late, I weaved between and around other cars. That's when it hit me—many of the centenarians had not grown up with cars, much less rush hours, and I had yet to meet one who didn't take their time getting to where they were going.

I eased in behind a sedan going the speed limit and took a few deep breaths. The traffic slowed and stopped and started again, but I knew if I pushed it, I risked having a car accident—or at the very least, rudely cutting someone off and becoming the recipient of the "unhappy wave." I'd experienced this before, when I accidently cut off a man wearing ski goggles and lifting weights while driving a small truck. Apparently he was in a bigger hurry than I and taking multitasking to a whole new level. I turned on some soft music and reassured myself that even if I were late, I would be in a better frame of mind if I arrived relaxed and unhurried.

Slowing my pace calmed me and put me in a much better mood. And I arrived just in time, so my urgency had been unnecessary! In the lobby, a pleasant older woman, white hair piled and pinned atop her head, called to let Anita know I had arrived. "Now you just head on up and let yourself in," the woman said. "She'll leave the door ajar for you. She's not quite finished readying herself."

When I reached the apartment, I knocked on the door. "Hello, Ms. Mackey? It's me, Rhonda, from the university. Are you there?" I called out, stepping cautiously inside.

"Yes, yes," came a soft voice from another room. "Just make yourself comfortable in the living room. I'm still getting ready, but I won't be long."

Anita Johnson-Mackey had been born on New Year's Day 1914 in Riverside, California. She was one of the few African Americans in a largely white community. Her family was just a couple of generations removed from slavery. Who knew what she'd witnessed in her many years of life? I especially wondered about her childhood. My nerves started to get the better of me. She was one of the oldest people I had ever met and had been born in a time so different from my own. Would she like me? Would she judge me for not dressing better? My quick-dry wicking clothing kept me comfortable in the California heat but was not the most fashionable. I took a few more deep breaths—despite all the interviews I'd done, I felt as self-aware as an adolescent.

I seated myself on a comfortable yet elegant brown side chair. The shutters were open, allowing the light to gently filter in and brighten the tidy room. As I glanced around, taking in a century of life, the coffee table caught my attention. Its top sat on the back of two elephants, both a shade of mahogany except for prominent white tusks. I saw intricate African artwork everywhere, from a handmade pot holding a large green plant to hand-carved African statues on the table. Each piece looked like something straight out of a museum. I saw no television, but lots of books.

Then I overheard Ms. Mackey talking quietly to herself in the other room, as if she were looking for something.

"Can I help you with anything?" I quietly asked, walking toward her room. Her bed was neatly made, and pictures of her husband and family were on the side table.

Ms. Mackey was seated in a chair, looking elegant in a beautiful skirt and red sweater.

"What can I help you with, Ms. Mackey?" I softly asked.

"Just call me Anita, dear. You see that long shoehorn over there in the corner?" she asked, smiling at me.

"Yes, I think I see it, Anita." I made my way across the room and retrieved a blue plastic shoehorn with a long, thin silver handle from a basket in the corner.

"That's it!" she said. "You got it; thank you."

She was hard at work putting on her shiny black low-heeled shoes, adorned with bows and gold buckles.

I did my best to help her, but it took us about fifteen minutes to get her shoes on. I thought back to how hurried I'd been to get to the interview. Anita had welcomed me in right on time but showed no rush in getting down to business. Already I was learning from her.

She stood up and stamped her feet down into the shoes. "There, finally on," she declared. I followed her into the living room.

After some amiable chatter, we proceeded with the interview. I decided to jump right in with a tough question.

"What's the hardest thing you've ever had to endure?" I asked.

She quickly replied, "When I was ten years old, my mother passed away. After that I really had to step up and start taking care of the rest of the family. I was one of nine children, and four of the kids were younger than me, so there was always lots to do, but we did it together."

As she told me her story, I could tell that times weren't easy for Anita as she was growing up. They lived in the white community on about 6th Street in Riverside and walked each day to Lincoln School on 10th Street. "Where I went to school," Anita told me, "we were the only black children there." Once when her mother went to see the principal at the school, he shut the door in her mother's face. She and her family were often the recipients of angry stares and hushed whispers.

Anita turned quiet, and with her arms folded, recalled a close friend-ship. "Once an Asian family moved in next door to us. I liked playing with a little girl about my age. But when the girl's family realized how Caucasian folks treated us, they moved away."

I could sense how sad it had been to lose a good friend, not over a quarrel but because of the color of her skin.

Our conversation meandered, and then I asked my next interview question. "Did you have any pets that you were fond of or helped to care for?" I asked her.

"We had a pet dog. We really enjoyed having him, but a neighbor poi-soned and killed it," she said, her expression growing sad. "So my father said no more pets. He really supported us and wanted to make sure noth-ing bad would happen."

Next she told me about her family's strong ties to church and their community—they were always ready and willing to help one another. Her father ran his own business, Johnson's Carriage Company, and was well regarded.

"He was always teaching us 'what the real world is like,' as he called it. He encouraged us to stay calm and to think. 'He who loses his head loses his case. So don't get upset,' my father would say. Each evening over the dinner table, we would all sit together for quite some time and discuss the happenings of the day." Anita smiled a distant smile, as if lost in her memories, though very much in the present moment.

Today's children often miss out on rich family moments such as those Anita's family enjoyed around their dinner table. Many people feel a sense of great loneliness, even though we're more connected to others via tech-nology than ever before. Yet social media presents a skewed version of life, in which everyone seems to be happy and successful. Compared to those images, our lives may feel boring and messy. It's no wonder so many people feel lonely—they may have a thousand "friends" on social media, but no one to pour their heart out to or to help when the unthinkable happens.

Some studies say electronic media can help promote relationships; others claim online activity hinders deep relationships. No matter which side of the debate you fall on, if your electronic media doesn't result in a phone call or an in-person meeting, you are not getting the benefits available only from in-person relationships.

Another factor that contributes to loneliness is our mobility. We no longer remain in the communities we grew up in, as the centenarians tended to do. Instead, we relocate to wherever our jobs and spouses take us—only to have to move again a few years later. Neighbors once formed the backbone of a family's social network and safety net—they watched out for each other's children outside, they could be counted on to babysit in a pinch, they loaned each other tools or a cup of sugar. Almost everyone socialized with their neighbors over barbeques or games of cards. But that has changed. Many people wouldn't even recognize their neighbors if they saw them somewhere else.

We often measure our social success in terms of how many online "friends" we have or how many "likes" our comments generate. The problem is, those kinds of affirmation provide only fleeting joy. Lasting joy comes from real-life friendships and relationships. These strong relationships are especially needed when facing uncharted disasters, outbreaks, or hardships. Around the world today, many people feel more isolated, stressed out, and fearful than ever before, driven in part by the pandemic and uncertainty about life after COVID-19. We need strong, positive relationships now more than ever.

Want to find a way to truly reconnect with family and friends? The Resiliency Capital centenarians were skilled at developing and maintaining lifelong bonds that encouraged whole health. Want to learn their secrets? Want to strengthen your family's bonds, change your story, and rewrite your future? Let's learn how your family can strengthen life-giving relationships.

WEEK 4: CONNECTED KIDS AND FAMILY

In the previous chapters you learned about the first four resiliency principles. Now it's time for the fifth. The fourth and fifth weeks of the Resiliency Program focus on the letter *C*—for connectivity. Connectivity is such a critical cornerstone in keeping us safe, steadfast, and grounded—which is especially important when the storms hit. And the storms are hitting. *C* represents the fourth and fifth resiliency principles—nurturing relationships and faith foundation. Together, these principles promote connecting to friends and family and to a higher power—promoting health for the mind, body, and spirit. Let's take a closer look at how the centenarians cultivated these connections.

PRINCIPLE #5—NURTURING RELATIONSHIPS

Important to a thriving life are the deep connections with family and friends that sustain, protect, and encourage us. With time and careful attention, these bonds will strengthen and mature. Tending to a relationship makes me think of a skilled bonsai master planting a delicate seed and shaping it into a beautiful bonsai tree through regular watering, fertilizing, and pruning. Are you purposefully caring for the relationships in your life like a bonsai master?

We tend to think in terms of how others treat us, but the most important factor is not what others put into the relationship, but what *we* put into it—how we treat people, how much effort we make to spend time with them, and how we can give more to our relationships. Yet with the day-to-day busyness of jobs and kids, it is easy for life to pass by without our consciously thinking about investing in relationships.

Anita wasn't alone in treasuring the rich relationships of her childhood. All the centenarians I interviewed had strong social networks and nurturing, lasting relationships, many of which had started in early childhood. During my interview with Reynaldo Sanchez (100-year-old Resiliency Capital member), he picked up a picture of his special childhood friend and told me, "We've been friends since we were four years old. He is my friend from a long time, and I love him as [a] brother."

All the centenarians reported strong social ties, especially with their family members but also with neighbors and church members. As children, they spent time together helping with farm work, as well as community and church work. After their daily work was done, they played and socialized by reading together, telling stories, or playing cards or board games.

The centenarians came from various spiritual backgrounds, but each came from a family with a strong connection to a faith community, which provided a place for connection, belonging, rest, and entertainment. Their deep friendships provided emotional and physical support to help them navigate early adversity. These friendships and family connections were protective against many childhood ACEs, such as poverty, death of parents, environmental disasters, and financial ruin. We are facing similar situations today. The number of natural disasters around the globe is on the rise, tripling over the past thirty years,[1] from fires and earthquakes to floods, tornadoes, and hurricanes. Whatever might be the reason driving these changes, one thing is for sure: They take a heavy toll on our overall health and well-being. With the uncertain times we are facing worldwide—made worse in the face of the COVID-19 pandemic—we need the protection the centenarians experienced now more than ever.

It is well-known that our friendships can help protect and sustain us. Even the animal kingdom understands this concept. Take, for example, the penguins living in the harsh conditions of the South Pole, where temperatures reach 60 degrees below zero and the wind speed is up to 100 miles per hour. If you and I were placed in that environment, we would quickly freeze to death. The penguins, on the other hand, have a strategy that helps them thrive—they huddle together for warmth. The temperature at the center of their circle is about 70 degrees.[2] Like penguins, we can't make it on our own; we need to come together to thrive.

African elephants also demonstrate how to work together. The females don't raise their calves alone. The older elephants adjust the pace of the herd so the young can keep up. When a calf is injured or missing, several members of the herd assist in the search and rescue. Equally impressive is that elephants that haven't seen each other for years will recognize their

In nature we never see anything isolated, but everything in connection with something else which is before it, beside it, under it, and over it.

JOHANN WOLFGANG VON GOETHE

long-lost friend, even decades later, and act as if they'd never been apart. These rich relationships help them weather any storm. Take a lesson from the elephants, and remember your family and friends!

Researchers have theorized that family stories are an important part of shaping the emerging identity and well-being of the children.[3] To test their theory, they created the "Do You Know . . . ?" scale for kids to assess their family knowledge, including such questions as, Where did your parents meet? Do you know where your grandparents grew up? Do you know what high school your parents attended? My kids laughed when they learned my favorite toy was a doll that I named after the family car: "Babot Collada Chevrolet." Scientists have found that the more children know about their family history, the better connected they are, the higher their self-esteem, and the more control they feel they have. This deep connection makes stress feel more manageable.

THREE FUNDAMENTALS FOR APPLYING THE NURTURING RELATIONSHIPS PRINCIPLE

1. Make It a Priority	2. Show Up with Love	3. Use High-Level Connections
Set aside time to connect often with family and friends in good times and bad.	Practice thinking, speaking, and exhibiting loving behaviors on any and all occasions.	Connect through interactions that are the most effective and promote the greatest connectivity with others.

Modern Times Call for Modern Methods

Let's take a closer look at the three essentials of the nurturing relationships principle and discover how to apply this principle with our own families.

1. Make it a priority

One of your most important responsibilities to your children is teaching them to value meaningful relationships, as well as modeling the skills and time they require. The earlier in life these skills are learned, the better.

Prioritizing nurturing relationships means routinely connecting with others, being present in the moment, and actively listening. It means reaching out, not only in the good times but also when immense hardships hit and connection is needed most. Finally, we must be able to physically see or hear the other person. Being together in person is best, but if that is impossible (as it was during the pandemic or when living far apart), use electronics that promote hearing, seeing, or both (like Zoom or FaceTime). Though it's quick and easy to text and send emails, those messages often cause more confusion and put you at greater risk of miscommunication, especially when relationships are already strained. With our frenetic pace of life today, it's easy to put other pursuits before spending time with our family and friends, but positive relationships are worth the time.

When I asked centenarian Anita Johnson-Mackey if she sat with her family at dinnertime, she replied without hesitation, "Always. Always. No running into the kitchen, uh-uh. We sat down at the dinner table all together. And my father wanted to know what had happened during the day because we lived on the edge of an all-white neighborhood."

Her father knew that growing up African American in a predominately Caucasian community put them at great risk, especially after their mother's death. Her father was the son of slaves, so he knew gathering together provided both security and protection. When Anita's family sat down for dinner, they reflected on their experiences that day and discussed whether they'd faced any challenges that needed to be handled differently. This practice had likely been passed down through his family line—a powerful legacy.

You have to be present to invest in others, so make the people in your life a priority. A friend of mine sets a timer in her house to go off as a reminder to hug her daughter, who has special needs. The benefits of those hugs are immediate, as they calm her daughter and help maintain a sense of peace in her home. The busier your life, the more you need routines to ensure that connecting with others, especially your family, remains a priority.

Let's look at a couple of tangible benefits that come when we nurture our relationships.

Healing and better health. One story illustrating the power of close contact and connection led to major changes in the care of newborn twins. Kyrie and Brielle Jackson were born in October 1995, a full twelve weeks before their due date.[4] Each twin weighed only about two pounds. At that time, hospital regulations required that babies be kept separate to avoid the chance of one infecting the other, so each was placed in an individual incubator in the neonatal intensive care unit (NICU). After one week, Kyrie was clearly thriving, while her sister, Brielle, was not expected to live.

You never know the value of a moment until it becomes a memory.

DR. SEUSS

That November, Brielle's condition turned critical, and a NICU nurse decided to follow her intuition. With permission from the babies' parents, she placed the two babies together in one incubator. Within minutes, Brielle's blood-oxygen rate improved. Then the healthier twin placed her arm around her sicker sibling. Amazingly, Brielle's heart rate began to stabilize, and her temperature rose to a more normal range. A picture of Kyrie with her arm wrapped around her twin was appropriately captioned "The Rescuing Hug" and published in *Life* magazine and *Reader's Digest.* As a result of the twins' experience, the standard of care in most hospitals is to place twins together.

Though we can't say for sure that Kyrie's hug changed the prognosis for Brielle, we do know there is tremendous healing in the power of touch. Loving touch, like that from hugs, is critically important for infants and children to develop normally and thrive. Scientific studies confirm that hugging may boost the immune system and even reduce the risk of infections.[5] Researchers have discovered that hugging increases oxytocin in the body, the hormone linked to bonding with others.[6] Preliminary studies in animals even show that close social bonds can influence the diversity of positive gut bacteria, which is critical to overall health.[7] In light of all these positive benefits, prioritizing connections makes sense.

Collaboration. In addition to the health benefits, we simply accomplish more and greater things by working together. Think about the way geese fly in a V formation. Scientists have found that the birds position themselves this way and beat their wings in time with their neighbors to catch the preceding bird's updraft and save energy—using up to 40 percent less energy and reaching their destination sooner.

One Resiliency Capital centenarian, 101-year-old Belen Lopez, learned the value of working with others as a little girl. She grew up in a home that lacked running water, so every other day she and her siblings walked one kilometer to reach the nearby river. Rather than looking at their walk as a dreaded chore, she always looked forward to the outing. The river provided so much for the family—not only was it a place to wash clothes, but it also gave them the opportunity to hang out with friends, cousins, and neighbors. On the shore, some people boiled water and cleaned the clothes, while others took their makeshift fishing poles and worked at catching fish for a shared lunch. After collecting water for drinking, cooking, and bathing, they made the trek home. This communal way of life, of everyone helping each other, gave Belen a sense of security.

2. Show up with love

The second rule for practicing the nurturing relationships principle is to show up with love. Encourage your family (and yourself) to respond to every experience with kindness and tolerance. This rule means not only showing up with love for others, but offering love to yourself, too.

When centenarian Salma Mohr was a little girl, she loved going to school. Her older siblings had dropped out of school after seventh grade and gone to work to help provide for the family. They cleaned houses, and her older sister was known as one of the best housekeepers in their community. She got eight dollars a week to clean houses, a top salary for that work then.

If you want to go fast, go alone. If you want to go farther, go together.

AFRICAN PROVERB

> *Spread love everywhere you go. Let no one ever come to you without leaving happier.*
>
> MOTHER TERESA

"When I got up to the seventh grade," Salma said, "it was my turn to give up going to school and find a job. I just grieved. I must have shown it to my sisters. *Oh, if I could just go finish the eighth grade. Oh, if I could just finish the eighth grade.* And my two older sisters put their heads together, and they said, 'We've got to manage and let Salma finish the eighth grade.'

"Well, then I got to go to high school. But in my mind, I knew that this wasn't going to last very long, and I'd have to drop out before I could finish it. So I arranged with my teachers, and they helped me finish in three years; I was sixteen. And then the moping started all over again."

Fortunately, Salma's sisters came through again with love and support.

"And it was so funny because at that point I had to earn the money for books and pay for college. And of course I didn't have that. So the two older sisters and the two older brothers put their money together to buy my schoolbooks and helped pay my way."

Salma's siblings loved her so much that they worked hard to make her dream of education come true. Salma eventually became a teacher.

I think of that kind of love whenever I pass a prominent statue on my university's campus that depicts the biblical story of the Good Samaritan. Jesus told a parable about how a Jewish man was attacked, beaten, robbed, and left for dead while traveling from Jerusalem to Jericho. The first two men who passed by him were religious leaders. Neither stopped to help. Then along came a Samaritan. Because Samaritans and Jews were sworn enemies back then, hearing about the Samaritan's kindness would have shocked Jesus' listeners. The Samaritan scooped up the injured fellow, placed him on his donkey, took him to a nearby inn, and paid for his care.[8] Like the centenarians' experiences, this parable encourages each of us to lay down our judgment—whether against others or ourselves—and embrace one another with boundless compassion. Showing up with love begins by taking the initiative to connect with others, just as the Samaritan did.

Not everyone will look the same or believe the same. But we are all human and want to be heard and loved. Recently, my daughter Joelle confided that she had eaten alone at lunch for a while at her new school. Eventually, she made new friends, but it took many months. Knowing how sad it made her, she vowed to encourage other newbies and to be a smiling face they could connect with at lunch. As a mom this was hard for me to hear. Our inclination as parents is to jump in and solve things, especially when it comes to mealtimes—we are truly the knights of the lunch table. But if Joelle hadn't gone through this difficult time, she never would have expressed her passion for helping others—and purposefully showed up with love. Over the years her group of newbies has grown, and she has developed wonderful friendships. Now, whenever a new girl arrives at school, the administrator is quick to introduce her to Joelle and her friends.

Tolerance—the willingness to see others' opinions and expressions without reacting adversely, even if you don't agree with them—is another critically important aspect of showing up with love. As parents, we need to step back and ask ourselves, *Am I modeling tolerance and encouraging it in my children? Or am I quick to jump in with a furrowed brow and tell someone why their view is wrong and then try to convince them that my view is right?*

Centenarian Anita Johnson-Mackey's advice to parents is to "be slow to respond to something that may look offensive." It's better to respond by saying, "Why, I never thought of it that way" and then listen with respect for their point of view.

Grow and nurture your village. Do you find yourself feeling as if you don't have a village to turn to, either to give or receive support? If so, you are not the only one. Loneliness seems to be a growing phenomenon.[9] If you want to develop new friendships, take heart.

> *Resolve to be tender with the young, compassionate with the aged, sympathetic with the striving, and tolerant of the weak and the wrong. Sometime in life you will have been all of these.*
>
> GEORGE WASHINGTON CARVER

133

There are many ways to be the spark and grow your own village. An excellent strategy is taking the initiative and inviting a few people together for an impromptu potluck at your home or a nearby park. You can even tie it to a seasonal celebration, such as a fall harvest party or a spring fling, to make it easier to extend the invitations.

I met Erica, a young mom of five, through my health education program. She was a stay-at-home mom who felt immense loneliness. She wanted to put the resiliency principles into practice, including the development of nurturing relationships. However, her husband worked long hours and wasn't supportive in making any changes.

During one of our conversations, I asked her to list any opportunities she might have for meeting other moms. Erica realized she was surrounded by them—she met them every day while dropping off and picking up her kids from school. It took her a few weeks to get up the nerve, but she decided to "keep the stakes low and don't worry if they say no."

She finally asked the mom of a child in her daughter's class if they'd like to hang out after school one day. The other mom quickly agreed. After school, they walked over to the local playground and chatted while the kids ran around. Eventually the practice became a habit—the kids demanded it—and other moms joined in. As it turned out, the other moms were wanting to connect too. Slowly Erica began to open up and talk about her family's health journey. Four months later, she told me that the moms were working together to implement the resiliency principles in their families! Eventually the husbands got together during an outing and discovered they had much in common.

Another great way to grow your village is to connect with a local house of worship. More than likely, you'll meet many other families with kids of similar ages as your own. (As an added bonus, it will set you up for the sixth resiliency principle, faith foundation,

You can make more friends in two months by becoming interested in other people than you can in two years by trying to get people interested in you.

DALE CARNEGIE

which we'll explore in the next chapter.) If you aren't already attending church, find one in your community to join. If you already have a church home, become active as a volunteer. You may feel as if you don't have a moment to spare right now, but by investing time with others, you will reap health benefits and grow your social (and safety) network.

By worshiping together, you can create family bonds, as well as relationships between the adults and between the kids. Start by connecting with a few parents and their children before or after a service. I have a hard time remembering names, so after meeting a new family, I quickly pull out a little notebook from my purse in which I jot down their names along with where I met them, what they look like, and what they enjoy. That way, before heading to an event, I can check my notes. There is tremendous power in being able to greet someone by name. That family will be surprised and flattered that you remembered them. Already connected with a house of worship, but wanting to branch out? Consider trying different classes, sitting near different people, or joining a new volunteer service group. Make a point to introduce yourself to at least one new person each time you attend.

Strengthening bonds with family members may take the most work of all, but it also comes with great rewards. Routines can make it easier since everyone knows what to expect. For example, family dinners are a great way to stay connected and offer health benefits to boot. Research shows that families who eat together know more about their family history, are better connected to the family, have higher self-esteem, and are more resilient during difficult times.[10]

Connect with your kids! It's most important to nurture relationships within your family. If you feel as if your kids are driving you crazy and you never get a moment to yourself, chances are you are so tired that when you do spend time with them, you are not truly connecting. Ironically, the more we intentionally nurture those connected times, the less we'll feel as if we don't have enough time to ourselves. Furthermore, the more connected you are during the good times, the better prepared you will be to handle any turmoil and disasters.

Every evening, a friend of mine, Penelope, rushed around trying to prepare for the next day. Between her job and family, she had little time for herself. So Penelope cringed when her youngest son asked her to play boats and pirates with him as he took his nightly bath. Though it would take only fifteen minutes, Penelope had so much to do, and the last thing she felt like doing was crouch by a bathtub and play.

When she told me her dilemma, I suggested, "Why don't you throw yourself into character and become the pirate Captain Jack Snuffles and take along your coughing crew?"

Begrudgingly she agreed. After that first pirate-battling bath, she found that she had a little more energy and that her son went to bed more easily. The break was exactly what both her son and her brain needed.

If your younger children ask you to get down on the floor with them, sit down and play with them, even if for just five minutes. Playing a variety of games that everyone can participate in is a simple but effective way to connect. More than once, one of my kids or I have started an impromptu game simply by trying to keep a balloon off the floor. Even a simple round of bingo can provide a load of laughs: My favorite is dog bingo, which taught me about all the different breeds of dogs—who knew that Xoloitzcuintle was a type of dog or that it looks even stranger than its name?

One afternoon I decided to create a "Dinner Conversation Kick-Starter" box to engage my kids in more conversation over dinner. I wrote out a bunch of questions, each on an individual card. The questions included things like: What was your favorite trip ever and why? What do you like to do best on the weekend? What is the hardest challenge you've had, and how did you solve it? (You can find more questions listed in appendix E.) The children can answer however they like, but the grown-ups' answers have to be about our childhoods. I wanted to share stories from my youth with my kids—especially about my parents and grandparents—to help deepen our connections to family and to preserve traditions and history.

I also added a few challenge questions like: Who can make the funniest face? At first, my son, Jayden, made a fuss and didn't want to take part, but once he saw how excited Joelle was to share, he decided to do so too.

Tips for Nurturing Your Relationships

Want to care for and nurture the bonds you have with family and friends? To enhance your relationships, follow these tips and teach them to your children:

- **Listen and be present.** Are you an active listener? It's hard not to get distracted, so it's important to practice self-control and focus on actively listening to what is being shared. Try not to talk over or interrupt people when they are speaking. Resist the urge to interrupt. Ask follow-up questions: "Can you tell me more?" "How did that feel?" "In what way?" Ask "what" and "how" questions, and you'll be surprised by how much more people will tell you.

  Idea for you: One day this week, go for a short walk around the neighborhood (or any safe green space) with your family or spouse. Deliberately spend time listening to each other discuss your feelings and experiences of the day. Resiliency principles practiced: active movement, nature engagement, and nurturing relationships.

- **Be positive and supportive.** In all your interactions, practice goodness and doing the right thing—even if you think no one will ever notice. Be ready and willing to help one another.

  Idea for you: This week call a neighbor, a relative, or a friend and offer to bring over dinner one night. Perhaps you could double a pot of homemade soup or another recipe. That evening, take a stroll to deliver the meal. Resiliency principles practiced: active movement, nature engagement, nurturing relationships, and simple foods.

- **Let kind words flow.** Be quick with kind words and slow with criticism; avoid negative talk when using any form of social media. Be patient with yourself and with others. A key tip to building lasting relationships is learning the art of kind talk. The book *Simplicity Parenting* advises that we learn to think before we speak: "Before you say something, ask yourself these three questions: Is it true? Is it kind? Is it necessary?"[†] That is great advice for both children and adults.

Idea for you: This week find at least two people you don't routinely compliment and give them some words of encouragement. Resiliency principle practiced: nurturing relationships.

- **Enjoy the moment.** Not everything has to be about teaching a life lesson. Take a gentler approach. Sometimes just sit back, laugh, and enjoy the experience with your family and friends. Focus on being present in the moment; resist distractions.

  Idea for you: After your children get out of school, grab a blanket, a few snacks, and some bubbles. Then head out to the yard or sit on the patio and connect with your family for twenty minutes or so. Resiliency principles practiced: active movement, nature engagement, and nurturing relationships.

- **Share your stories and gifts.** Practice the art of kindness by going above and beyond what is needed. Offer help to others and don't be ashamed to ask for help either. And don't forget to share your stories; be vulnerable and connect. Take a lesson from the bonobo, a primate that looks much like a chimpanzee. These animals are known for their peaceful nature and their love of giving gifts (like fruit). Humans are unique in that gift-giving is practiced in every society, with specific cultural rules that define who we can and cannot give gifts to, what types of gifts are appropriate, and when and how the gifts should be given. Gift-giving helps us forge and nurture social bonds.

  Idea for you: Have a friend or relative who could use help? Maybe you could watch their kids while they run a quick errand, or perhaps you could help them with some yard work. If you have limited time, offer to help with a smaller project. Resiliency principles practiced: active movement and nurturing relationships.

- **Be loyal like the elephant.** Honor relationships by being faithful, supportive, and careful with your thoughts, words, and actions. Do

---

[†] Kim John Payne and Lisa M. Ross, *Simplicity Parenting: Using the Extraordinary Power of Less to Raise Calmer, Happier, and More Secure Kids* (New York: Ballantine Books, 2010), 193.

what you say and keep your word. Honesty is one mark of a true and loyal friend. I love how Horton the elephant models loyalty in Dr. Seuss's book *Horton Hatches the Egg*. After making a promise, he sits on a bird egg, keeping it warm through all kinds of terrible weather. "I meant what I said and I said what I meant. An elephant's faithful one hundred percent!"‡ We should follow Horton's example and keep our word.

Idea for you: This week when you make appointments with friends or family, work hard to keep them. This will demonstrate your loyalty and investment in your family member or friend. Resiliency principle practiced: nurturing relationships.

- **Acknowledge others' feelings and accomplishments.** Show empathy and compassion by remembering special dates, recognizing achievements, and sharing in people's joy or sorrow. Sending a thank-you card for a kind gesture or gift, a handwritten birthday card, or a note of sympathy seems like such a simple thing, but in this high-tech era, you will be a standout if you reach out in this way. Teach your family to be there for friends with supportive words and actions.

Idea for you: This week send a card—maybe even tuck in a drawing from your child—to someone. Take a quick break with your children to walk the letter to your post office. Resiliency principles practiced: active movement, nature engagement, and nurturing relationships.

- **Cultivate a heart of forgiveness.** Be flexible and the first one willing to mend a relationship through the bridge of forgiveness. As Martin Luther King Jr. said, "Forgiveness is not an occasional act, it is a constant attitude." When I asked centenarian Mulan Tsai her strategy for living a resilient life, she credited her forgiving heart, something she learned early in life.

Idea for you: Is there anyone in your life from whom you've drifted apart? Consider starting to rebuild the bridge between you by writing a letter of encouragement. Letting go of past hurts will not only grow your village but also bring peace to your heart and mind. Resiliency principle practiced: nurturing relationships.

---

‡ Dr. Seuss, *Horton Hatches the Egg* (New York: Random House, 1940).

- **Love lavishly.** A heart filled with love is the force of many of the nurturing behaviors above. So take time to care for others, showing unconditional love through words and actions. Remember that sometimes your actions speak louder than words.

  Idea for you: Each day this week hug one of your children, your partner, or all of them. They might think you are a little cuckoo, but they'll know you love them. Resiliency principle practiced: nurturing relationships.

Family story time. When I asked centenarian Salma Mohr what advice she had for parents with young children, she looked over at her grown daughter and smiled. Then she said, "Read with your little ones. Spend time holding them and telling them how much you love them." What a great way to "show up with love."

Salma told me that, as a small child, she didn't sit much and read with her mom or dad. "My mother was so busy trying to scrape by and earn a living for the family by washing clothes on an old washboard for a few cents' pay each day." Her father was not much of a provider or caretaker. When Salma adopted her first child, she recalls not holding him very often. Later, when Salma gave birth to her daughter, her mother-in-law encouraged her to cuddle and show more physical signs of love. I could sense in Salma a desire to go back in time and cuddle her children more.

Science uncovered the biological benefits of a few minutes of cuddling when researchers discovered that the brain releases the hormone oxytocin when people cuddle for twenty seconds or longer.[11] Even interacting with your dog can help you release oxytocin, according to a 2009 study.[12] The benefits of oxytocin are numerous—especially in protecting your body from the harmful effects of stress. Hugging has also been shown to reduce susceptibility to infectious diseases.[13] With the recent COVID-19 pandemic ravaging the world, we need to embrace (literally) all the risk-reduction opportunities we can and safely find or create new ways to connect. One of the safest ways to do that is to take more time with those in your own household. So take a break and cuddle with your little ones, either reading a good book or telling them a story. Don't worry if you aren't an expert storyteller; just make it up as you go along.

You can encourage story time in your home by creating spaces that will promote it. Older ones who read independently might appreciate an oversize beanbag chair, especially one that can accommodate a furry friend. Older children may not want to cuddle with a parent, but they may enjoy getting love from the family pet. Since our dog Mr. Beans enjoys the comfort of the couch, my children like lounging around on the oversize dog bed on the floor. Go figure.

3. Use high-level connections

The third rule for experiencing the nurturing relationships principle is to connect with one another using high-level forms of connection—those interactions in which you are with each other. By seeing or hearing additional verbal cues and responding with your own, you can be truly present.

The centenarians didn't have our technology. When they related to one another, it was usually face-to-face. The time we spend with friends and family, especially our children, has a tremendous impact on their present and future, but it takes concentrated investment. When a child asks you to sit on the floor and play, do you spare a moment to engage with them? When your teenager excitedly tells you about an accomplishment at school, do you stop what you're doing to listen and affirm them? When you do, you are making investments in their lives, creating stronger bonds with them, and giving them a sense of security. The earlier in their childhood you start connecting with them in this way, the better.

During the COVID-19 outbreak, many communities were ordered to "shelter in place"—a public health mandate to reduce the spread of the deadly virus. In such times it is especially important to connect and encourage one another because many feel isolated and alone. People found creative ways to reduce exposure but remain connected. Children used washable paints to write hopeful messages in their windows, or they hung signs encouraging those who passed by. Other people drove by loved ones' homes with birthday greetings. I heard of one couple who drove past friends' homes to do a gender reveal announcement, honking the horn of their car, which was decked out with a pink sign and balloons. Other people used Zoom to hold virtual dates. They played a board game, ate a meal, or baked together remotely. Some people dropped off notes on neighbors' doorsteps with their phone number and encouraging words. We learned it's possible to connect and practice social distancing; it just requires a little creativity.

We can create inviting spaces in our homes to promote connectivity too. My great-grandparents were Danish, and I appreciate their emphasis on *hygge* (pronounced "hue-guh"), or creating an atmosphere of coziness or comfort that promotes connectivity and friendship. Other countries, from China to the Netherlands, have their own words to describe this feeling. Each boils down to the desire to create inviting spaces that encourage people to spend time together enjoying the moment.

As I mentioned, when I stepped into centenarian Mulan Tsai's home, I immediately felt calmer. I also felt welcomed, from the front porch lined with jade plants to the warm sunlight flooding through all the windows inside. The seating in the living room was arranged to make conversation easier.

Centenarian Anita Johnson-Mackey's lovely home evoked similar feelings. She kept her shutters open to let in the sunlight, and her living room was arranged to foster conversations. Family pictures were displayed throughout her home. A small African dish—held aloft by her elephant table—held mixed nuts for Anita and her visitors to snack on. A vibrant green ivy in a large African pot livened up her kitchen table. Her cabinet of books was evidence of a lifetime of learning.

"Growing up, I learned if you take something off, put it where it belongs. Don't be messy. Everything has its own place," Anita said. Her childhood home was a large four-bedroom house, with many areas that encouraged getting together, from the family dinner table to the family living room— with a large piano that her brothers liked to play—to the screened-in front porch with a seating area that encouraged conversation and activity. Anita would often see her father and a friend deep in conversation on their porch.

Cozying up your own home can help set the stage for spending more time relaxing with family and friends. You don't need to remake your entire home; start simply by adapting one room. I made my living room more welcoming by moving in a rocking chair from another room, positioning the chairs and couch to encourage conversation, and adding a large basket to hide toys (baskets can hide a lot). Board and card games are tucked away but easily accessible when company arrives. I've also added soft, thick blankets and oversize pillows to encourage cuddling and relaxing.

Consider other areas of your home that could easily be made cozier. For instance, lighting candles at meals will help set a warm atmosphere. Setting out a swing and chairs on your patio will make it an inviting place for outdoor conversation. By making these small additions, you are encouraging slower, more relaxing activities with family and friends.

IN A PINCH, IT'S A CINCH: NURTURING RELATIONSHIPS PRACTICE TIPS

- Plan a backyard movie night with friends and family (to connect with each other and nature), complete with a few yard games. Invite acquaintances who are new to the neighborhood or parents you've met in passing at your child's school.

- Have a child celebrating a birthday? Consider throwing a centenarian-style birthday party. Host a smaller and more intimate party with family and a friend or two. Take a simpler DIY approach, perhaps holding it outdoors with a nature scavenger hunt.

- Keep compact card games stashed in your purse or glove box for a quick bonding game with kids or friends. You'll be prepared whenever you need to kill some time, remedy boredom, or distract the kids and get them to settle down!

- Send a friendship challenge card in your child's lunch box and encourage them to build positive friendships. One day a card might encourage them to say hello to a new person at recess, while the next day a card might encourage them to say something kind to a friend. If they can't read yet, simply draw pictures. Remember to ask them about their experiences after school.

- Dinnertainment, anyone? Keep a box with conversation-starting questions near your dinner table (see appendix E). My five-year-old niece likes this activity so much that when she sits down at my table, the first thing she asks is if we can start a conversation.

- Have your older kids carry a "friend in need" ziplock bag and be on the lookout for others needing help. Within the bag keep small useful items for helping in a pinch: Band-Aids, wet wipes, coins, a small amount of cash, tissues, rubber bands, and breath mints.

- Create a simple art project, perhaps using items from nature like leaves, flowers, or feathers, and present it to someone feeling down to show them your love.

- While driving your kids to and from school, why not strike up a conversation? Stash the cell phones, turn off the radio, and ask open-ended questions like "What was one of the best things that happened to you today?"

- Teach your children the value of connecting through handwritten letters. Or have them color pictures and mail them to their grandparents, relatives, or friends as a welcome and unexpected surprise. Get some stamps and send cards for birthdays.

- If you have older children, take part in an activity that interests them. If they like to play a strategy game, play it with them. If they enjoy biking, ride along with them. Conversation will flow more easily, and you may find an activity you can enjoy together for many years.

- Have a standing appointment for a potluck dinner or luncheon gathering with family and friends. Scheduling a recurring meal one day a week or a month is a great way to ensure you get together regularly. Don't worry so much about the menu; focus more on getting together.

- When visiting others, bring them flowers, coffee, or a bag of oranges to brighten their day. Be sure to ask about their children and family. Encourage your older children to ask questions and listen for answers too. When the visit is over, help tidy up, especially if you have children who have made a mess.

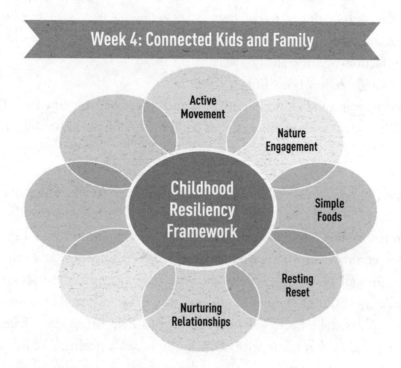

Fifth Resiliency Principle—**Nurturing Relationships**

Want to learn from the centenarians so your family can enjoy improved resilience and whole health? Then connect deeply every day with friends and family.

GET YOUR FAMILY'S TRIPLE BOOST

By putting the nurturing relationships principle into practice, you and your family will enjoy numerous benefits.

Promoting happiness: Need a quick pick-me-up? Spending time with those you care about can boost your joy while reducing stress and anxiety. When you get together with friends, you are thirty times more likely to engage in laughter.[14] Laughter has been linked with strengthening social bonds.[15] Laughing gives your mind a break and helps you deal with difficult situations. It reduces stress hormones and increases immune cells and infection-fighting antibodies.[16] Daily laughter has been linked to better sleep and the reduction of stress and risk of chronic disease.[17] Even the Bible documents the benefits of laughter: "A merry heart does good, like medicine" (Proverbs 17:22).

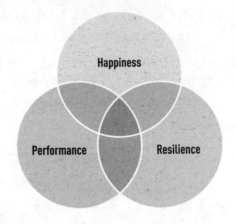

Increasing resilience: People with strong, positive relationships are less likely to become ill, and even when they get sick with colds, the illness is often less severe.[18] The developing field of psychoneuroimmunology has been shedding light on the link between close relationships and immune functioning.[19] Numerous studies show that social connections also lower chronic conditions like high blood pressure, heart rate, and cholesterol.[20] New parents, take heart—social connections help offset the challenges and depression that come with adapting to life as a parent. According to research from the Gottman Institute, the strength of a couple's relationship is key in reducing postpartum depression.[21]

Enhancing performance: Want to give a boost to your child's academic, musical, or athletic performances? Numerous scientific studies show the importance of relationships, especially among the family, to the academic success of the child, which likely extends to other areas.[22] Positive childhood relationships can buffer against stresses and influence healthy brain development.[23] Positive relationships may increase life satisfaction and help us get into the "flow" state, where we feel energized and entirely focused on an activity in which we are fully immersed. Flow is critical for all creative endeavors.[24] Research is also beginning to show a correlation between positive, loving relationships and improved athletic performance.[25]

CONQUERING RESISTANCE

As you work on connecting with friends and family, your family may experience a few challenges. Here are some helpful ideas to overcome such resistance.

Introvert challenges. Are you an introvert at heart? Do you find it difficult to branch out and meet new people? If so, take simple steps to increase and strengthen your social connections. Start small and seek out groups that interest you or reach out in places where you are already connected (like your child's school or a house of worship). Plan a playdate to get to know the parents of a child with whom your son or daughter has hit it off. When you meet new people, ask about their interests or family and then sit back and let them talk. Remember to be yourself and enjoy the moment of connecting.

Be wary of taking on additional responsibilities at work. Be careful of accepting new assignments that will require you to take home paperwork or stay later at the office. More often than not, it seems the people approached for "additional duties" are mothers with young children—others may see them as capable of juggling everything with ease. Before saying yes, consider how this decision might impact the time you have to spend on your family's journey toward resiliency.

HOMEWORK TIME

You have learned some ways to incorporate nurturing relationships into your life. Now it's your turn to put the centenarians' wisdom into practice and build on the foundation set in the first three weeks.

1. **Set up your Connected goals for nurturing relationships.** This week you will adapt your goals to include a Connected lifestyle focused

on nurturing relationships with family and friends. You will either adapt the goals you've already set around an Active and Balanced lifestyle, or create new ones to include the nurturing relationships principle. Use the following goals or create new ones:

NEW BASE GOAL

- **Nurturing relationships principle:** I will make dinnertime into family time by enjoying a homemade meal (with simple foods) together at least five times this week, and ask a conversation-provoking question at each meal. Weather permitting, we will eat outside!

  Overlapping principles include nurturing relationships, simple foods, and nature engagement (if you eat outdoors).

- **Optional new goal 1:** I will invite a new acquaintance/friend (and her children if it's a playdate) to my house for an outdoor picnic (with simple foods) this weekend.

- **Optional new goal 2:** I will practice speaking and/or writing words of encouragement to others and myself at least two times this week and encourage my family to do the same.

EXISTING BASE GOALS

- Continue or adapt the goals you have set for active movement, nature engagement, simple foods, and resting reset principles.

2. **Implement and track your success.** Each night, spend a few minutes before bedtime reviewing your goals. Use the Weekly Evaluation guide (found in appendix B) to help you evaluate your weekly progress. Remember, you can repeat this week if you have not met your goals.

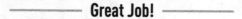

Great Job!

Congratulations on completing week 4 of the eight-week program. You are halfway there! As you go through each week, remember the value in a simple and slow approach to life. Feel free to repeat week 4 before moving to week 5.

CHAPTER 7

WEEK 5: FOLLOWING YOUR SPIRITUAL GPS

Live simply, love generously, care deeply,
speak kindly, leave the rest to God.

ATTRIBUTED TO RONALD REAGAN

I SAT TRANSFIXED AS CENTENARIAN Salma Mohr vividly described a scene from her childhood in the Great Plains. I could almost feel the dust on the road beneath the bare toes that six-year-old Salma danced on. It was a balmy Sunday in North Dakota, and she was headed to the small Pentecostal church in a nearby town. From an early age Salma loved to go there to worship every Sunday. She walked alone to get to the church, examining all the trees on the way, looking for good ones to climb.

"I was peppy and athletic minded," Salma said. As the fifth of ten children, she was also independent from an early age. Once she arrived at the church, Salma sat on the wooden floor right in the front row. She had no shoes on—she didn't get shoes until she was about thirteen—and she says she probably smelled bad from not bathing regularly. But her appearance didn't deter her; she just wanted to be there. Sometimes the preacher held vibrant revivals with loud spiritual music followed by a sermon from the pulpit about fire and brimstone raining down. Salma was mesmerized by his preaching—she listened to every word, soaking it all in. Nothing could have kept her away from that little church.

Back at her house, Salma would hold her own revivals for neighborhood friends. If she didn't have any friends at the time, she would simply preach to the rocks on the ground. Salma had a strong connection to her faith—and to the faith community. "It was my family of choice," she said. Sunday services were a respite from the constant challenges of her daily life, which included poverty, an often-absent father, and the death of her youngest sibling, whom she cared for immensely. As I listened to Salma recall her childhood, I had a sense that her faith was a protector—offering her momentary escape from her daily life and encouraging a spirit of peace and joy as she joined in the singing. Salma went on to become a teacher in a one-room schoolhouse, working with limited resources to instruct some tough children. But she was prepared and one of the best in her field, able to overcome any obstacle. Because of the seeds that had been planted early, she frequently came back to her faith connection throughout her 101 years.

Salma wasn't alone in her dedication to her faith. Each of the resilient centenarians I interviewed experienced a connection with a higher power, which started early in their childhood. God became an encouraging guide throughout their lives, providing comfort during challenging periods.

To develop resilience and maintain the health of the whole person—mind, body, and spirit—each part must be in balance and cared for. Spirit is the nonphysical part of you, the inner essence that is the foundation of your emotions and character. Just like your mind and body, your spirit needs rest, care, and comfort, especially during stressful times. Your faith connections can help provide for your spirit, enhancing the health of your whole body. You are hardwired to have this connectivity in your life; without it, you will probably feel the loss.

Do you want to empower your faith journey by connecting with God or a higher power? Do you want to help your family do the same? Are you looking for strength to help get your family through challenging times? Then read on as we start week 5.

WEEK 5: BUILDING CONNECTED KIDS AND FAMILY

During this fifth week, we will continue to focus on the letter *C*—for connectivity—building connected kids and family. Now that we've covered nurturing relationships, it's time to dive into the principle of faith foundation.

PRINCIPLE #6—FAITH FOUNDATION

The sixth principle—faith foundation—is about connecting with God and a faith community. Though the centenarians I interviewed came from different faith traditions, they all reported early exposure to and affiliations with faith-based communities, which provided them—and often their families—with support, stability, and strength in times of great adversity. They even supplied socialization and entertainment.

The centenarians mentioned several daily and weekly faith practices. They routinely prayed before each meal, thanking God for their food, as well as at bedtime. Their weekly practice included attending a house of worship, reading spiritual texts, and volunteering in church ministries and their community. Their faith seed was planted early in life, though as young children they didn't fully understand what it meant to have faith in God. As they grew older, however, they began to develop a deeper faith connection.

Dr. Mildred Stilson, a vibrant centenarian, described her life as being faith informed. "We are here to serve," she told me. Born to missionary parents, Mildred grew up in India, where her dad was a pastor and later became a physician. Watching her parents help others and take part in India's cultural activities helped Mildred understand faith as a form of service.

"I felt called to follow in the footsteps of Jesus and his ministry work, helping to heal people," Mildred explained. She was so inspired by her faith and her parents' service that she went on to medical school, where she was one of only seven women in her class. She became a pathologist, a physician who uses tissue and blood samples to diagnose a wide range of diseases. Feeling a higher calling, she became a missionary, just like her parents before her, and served in Africa. Mildred's early upbringing and experiences with her faith influenced all aspects of her life, a tradition that she passed on to her own children.

Cultures around the world experience strong faith connections through three main elements: belief in a higher power, affiliation with a house of worship, and the practice of prayer. Other activities that build bonds with God, family, and community include meditation, a day of rest or a Sabbath, personal sacrifice, religious rituals, spiritual and self-help books, fasting, and pilgrimages.

THREE FUNDAMENTALS FOR APPLYING THE FAITH FOUNDATION PRINCIPLE

1. Connect with the Higher Power	2. Connect with a House of Worship	3. Extend Your Connection
Acknowledge and routinely connect with God.	Develop a relationship with a house of worship.	Spend time praying powerful prayers.

Modern Times Call for Modern Methods

Let's take a closer look at the three essentials for applying the practices of the resilient centenarians to your own family.

1. Connect with the Higher Power

Some great ways to find guidance on your spiritual journey and grow closer to God are by developing and strengthening your relationship with a house of worship, reading spiritual texts (like the Bible) to gain new insight and knowledge, and praying out of a sense of need, repentance, thanksgiving, or even just to dialogue with God.

In the world the centenarians knew as children, all communities were tied together through faith. However, things are different today. As technology rapidly advanced and people became more mobile, regular worship often took a back seat to prosperity and other pursuits, and involvement in faith communities declined, just when society needed those connections most. Unfortunately, the number of Americans who claim no faith affiliation is rising. The global researcher World Values Survey determined that between 2007 and 2019, forty-three of forty-nine countries became less religious.[1] According to *National Geographic*, the newest major religion is in fact no religion at all.[2]

Nearly one-quarter of Americans questioned at the start of the COVID-19 pandemic said their faith had grown as a result[3]—though the strength of the impact and how long it will last has yet to be determined. With the increase in natural disasters, possible terrorist attacks, future global disease outbreaks, potential severe economic depressions, and the hectic pace of modern society, we need a connection with a faith community more than ever. Scientists have uncovered tremendous benefits from connecting with a faith community, especially for promoting lifelong resilience.[4] A number of studies have shown that youth and their families who regularly attend a house of worship have better coping skills and are more satisfied with their lives and more involved with their families—all of which helps them to endure challenging times.[5]

The centenarians know far too well the pain caused by significant hardships and loss, both as children and adults. Centenarian Salma Mohr described in great detail the loss she experienced as a young child. She prided herself on being the caretaker for the youngest sibling in her family—baby Maxine. One day, Salma's littlest sister became extremely sick. "She was very, very ill and had a terrible temperature," Salma told me. "But evening came, and her temperature rose even more. Mother made my other brothers and sisters go to bed. But I had refused. I couldn't go and leave little Maxine because I think I had the real genuine mother's heart for that child. I stayed till I got sleepy, I don't know what time. But way over in the middle of the night, I could hear my father crying with a horrible voice—he was heartbroken."

Salma crept out of her own bed and tiptoed down the hallway. "I listened for one minute and then I ran off to my bedroom because I knew what had happened. I started crying too. Little Maxine had died in the night." Salma's family, her faith, and her connection to a house of worship helped her cope with her immense loss.

When she was twelve, Jane Pihl (102-year-old Resiliency Capital member) got up one day in her Lincoln, Nebraska, neighborhood to learn that every bank in the US had closed—a horrific event that would long be remembered. That morning, the community's Union College Chapel became a gathering place for people in absolute shock. "I mean everybody came up to Union College Chapel. I'll never forget it," Jane explained, the memory of the comfort she found in her community of faith still palpable ninety years later. The people in her community didn't have much left, but they clung to their church, faith, and prayers to help ease their burdens and fears.

The start of the Great Depression was so devastating that "people were jumping out of windows," Jane recalled. People had lived through the Roaring Twenties, but now in 1929, they were panic-stricken. Many lost everything. Jane's dad was a landscape architect, and one of his customers went out into a field and ended her own life. Finances became tight for Jane's family, too, since no one hired a landscaper when they had no money. Their faith helped them to weather the storm. Perhaps you might be fearful today of the possibility of a new Great Depression following the COVID-19 pandemic, and a faith connection—just as for Jane and her family—could help your family weather the storm.

Whether you are already part of a faith community or aren't currently interested in connecting with one, I encourage you to read on. You may be surprised by the hidden benefits.

2. Connect with a house of worship

A house of worship is a place where people come together as a faith community.

As I explained in this chapter's opening story, centenarian Salma Mohr looked forward to attending her local church. She would head there every week, whether or not anyone went with her. "I was just five or six and lived close to the church and would go to the church every Sunday," she said.

The church was a place that called to Salma's soul. When her family moved, she began attending a new church with no thought to its denomination. "I didn't care, a church was a church."

For centenarian Anita Johnson-Mackey, connecting with her church meant crossing the railroad tracks and walking a long way. "I crossed the tracks and went to the black neighborhood to the wonderful, well-kept African Methodist Episcopal church." It was this church and its community that gave her family a feeling of connection and protection.

The key is to find a place that feels right for you and your family. One size does not necessarily fit all. Even if, for some reason, you are not ready to connect with a house of worship, I encourage you not to let that stop you from seeking a closer connection to God. In fact, one global organization (BSF International) grew out of several women coming together at a small house in 1959 in San Bernardino, California, not far from where I live. They had no idea they were starting a national movement; they were interested simply in connecting with one another and with God, as well as gaining a better understanding of the Bible. Today about 2,200 BSF groups meet in more than 120 countries, testifying to the hunger for a faith community worldwide.[6]

Despite the many benefits faith communities offer in a world filled with rapid technological advances and the resulting stress, far fewer families today connect with faith communities than when the centenarians were children. There are numerous possible reasons for the decline. Many families spend their weekends involved in the children's extracurricular activities, particularly sports teams, many of which now practice or compete on Saturday and Sunday mornings. Other families, especially those with young children, may not notice a direct benefit from attending church. Given all their other responsibilities, going to a house of worship every week becomes just another thing to do. Some may feel their kids just aren't that interested in attending, so why bother.

At the start of the pandemic in early 2020, many families that were attending adapted to worshiping online when houses of worship closed. In fact, many people relied on these streaming services to find hope and remain connected to their faith communities. Unfortunately, some of the health-related benefits of attending services are lost when the community moves totally online. If your family has never or rarely attended church, considering doing so. Following the pandemic, you will likely be in the company of many others who are reconnecting or who are newbies going to church for the first time.

If we don't become active with a faith community when our children are young, we are not caring for their spiritual health or planting and nurturing the spiritual seeds that will serve them as they grow. The amazing thing about seeds is that you don't notice the dramatic changes that are taking place beneath the surface once they're planted. But those hidden changes are necessary for the plant to produce fruit.

Tips for Connecting with a House of Worship

Need ideas on where to connect with a house of worship?

- Do a Google search for local houses of worship consistent with your faith.
- Ask family and friends.
- Just Yelp it.

Already involved with a house of worship but want to strengthen your connection?

- Volunteer to help set up or clean up, fundraise, or participate in outreach.
- Volunteer to teach a class or lead a group discussion.
- Volunteer to assist bringing people to and from the house of worship.
- Join a small group, whether for Bible study, fellowship, or support.
- Participate in family-centered activities, such as special events centered around holidays.

Not yet ready to connect with a house of worship?

- Gather with a group of friends or your family to read the Bible or another spiritual text together.
- Connect with friends and family and head out to nature to take a Sabbath moment.

Be open to how your family connects with a house of worship. What works for one family may not work for another. My husband and I chose our church initially because of the amazing Japanese vegetarian food served every Sabbath. We stayed because we found that the worship and preaching nourished our spirits, too.

If you already attend a house of worship, work on strengthening your connection. Do you show up for the forty-five-minute sermon just to check a box? Or are you there to learn and receive the blessing? It is far more powerful and strengthening for your spirit if you show up with an expectant outlook. Grab a notebook and pen and get ready to learn and be empowered.

3. *Extend your connection*

You can draw closer to God not only through involvement in a faith community, but also through prayer and reading spiritual texts. Many of the parents I interviewed agreed that one key benefit of being part of a faith community is the many people who come together to pray with them during challenging times. Prayer draws you closer to God and gives you guidance and strength.

After my youngest child, Julia, was born prematurely, she spent fifteen days in the hospital's neonatal intensive care unit (NICU). I was a complete wreck, crying and worrying all the time. Some days when I came to the NICU, I discovered little prayer notes—which included a Scripture passage offering hope—that the hospital chaplain had left on the side of my daughter's incubator. I immediately felt comforted, knowing that others were praying along with me for little Julia. Their prayers helped quiet my feelings of sorrow—giving me the emotional strength I needed to stay and connect with my child rather than flee the hospital in tears.

On the afternoon a nurse told my husband and me, "It's time for you to take your healthy baby home," I felt as if I had won the lottery. How much of her recovery was due to the miracle of prayer versus the miracle of Western medicine didn't matter. What mattered was the powerful, energizing support prayer had given me. And I knew that God's healing touch had pulled my newborn daughter out of danger and made her strong and healthy enough to come home.

The scientific community has done many studies on the health-related benefits of prayer.[7] They've uncovered its effectiveness at reducing feelings of stress and anxiety.[8] Taking a moment to pray in the morning will help you set the tone for the day. Do you or your family have difficulty going to bed because your mind is so busy that you can't sleep? Are you a multi-tasking worrier—concerned about your health, your kids, your work, or the many challenges impacting the world? Then bring your worries to God before going to bed each night and throughout the day to give your mind and soul needed rest. You might keep a prayer journal to record your requests and the way God answered. Reading back over it can renew your hope whenever you're faced with new difficulties.

Teach your children to pray and encourage them to turn to God, especially when faced with challenges that bring them to tears. Encourage them to pray before taking tests, before important events, and throughout the day. Once, my kids and I even prayed for a new dog. As we stood in the middle of the San Bernardino animal shelter, surrounded by a chorus of barks and whimpers, we said a quick prayer, asking God to help us choose a dog that would be a great fit for our family. Jayden added, "Please give us a dog that can do tricks."

My son then noticed a small, gray, dirty, poodle-looking dog at the back of a cage with three other pooches. Once the kennel assistant removed the disheveled dog from his cage, I gently lifted the mangy hair hanging over his face to make sure he had two eyes. He looked a hot mess and smelled much worse—a dingy old mop for sure. My son said to the man, "We'll take him!" And that was that.

Fast-forward a few years, and we realized we had a beautiful fluffy white bichon poodle mix we'd named Mr. Beans. He happened to be the smartest and friendliest dog we'd ever met. Best of all, he quickly learned to do tricks! So teach your children to be specific in their prayer requests. Also remind your children to thank God and express gratitude to him when they notice his blessing or experience his love and grace.

Whenever you clean up behind your kids or tuck them into bed, take a moment to say a quick prayer over them or ask for a blessing. These small prayers will shift your way of thinking—from focusing on the chores in front of you or your worries for your children to a mindset of gratitude and dependence on God. When my husband does the laundry, he says a prayer and asks for blessings as he gently places each child's clothes into the washer. (And I say a prayer that he doesn't mix the reds with the whites!)

The very day
I call for help,
the tide of
battle turns.

PSALM 56:9, TLB

A quick prayer doesn't require extra time, just a different thought. And when we shift our thought patterns by praying rather than fretting, we build new neural pathways in our brains that help us worry less and cope better in moments of stress or anxiety. Let's face it, we could all use less stress and worry. Why not give it a try?

For centenarian Jane Pihl, even the years before the Great Depression were extremely difficult. After her parents divorced, Jane's mother struggled to provide for her children. As a result, Jane lived with various relatives, friends, and members of their church throughout her childhood. Her siblings often lived elsewhere. Moving from home to home, Jane lived somewhat like a foster child before the foster care system was created.

By the time she was a teenager, Jane felt incredibly alone, without much direction or financial means to change her situation. Her friends were preparing to either marry or go off to college. Jane had nothing—neither a boyfriend nor the money to advance her education. One day, when the weight of severe depression felt like an elephant sitting on her chest, Jane cried out and prayed for divine intervention.

"I have to confess," she told me, "I wasn't praying, I wasn't studying; I had just given up. I thought, *It's not working.* I didn't have any roots or companions at that time. But something happened. The Lord was with me. And I remember I broke. One night I went to the Lord and I wept. I said, 'I have no future. I'm not with young people at college; I don't have any money to be in college. I'm sunk. No money at all. Dad's dead, and Mother's gone.'" Jane felt there was nothing more to do but to leave her situation with God.

Powerful Prayers Parents Can Pray over Their Children

By praying for your family, you are entrusting each of them to God, inviting him to provide for them in ways you cannot. You can literally pray about anything; I've provided a few examples below.

Prayer for Health

Dear heavenly Father, I thank you for the blessings in our lives. Please bless each and every one in my family with whole health—a renewed mind, body, and spirit. Give them energy to climb mountains, mental clarity to tackle problems with ease, and overflowing joy in their spirit. Thank you for providing a layer of protection around them, enabling them to thrive in the face of an epidemic or other major disaster. Amen.

Prayer for Academic Success

Dear heavenly Father, I humbly come before you and thank you for enriching our lives with the opportunity to gain knowledge. Please bless each of my children in their school endeavors. Grant them a spirit of perseverance to finish their work with excellence and abundant wisdom to help them pass exams with ease. Amen.

Prayer for the Future

Dear heavenly Father, thank you for guiding us in all our work. Please bless my children with an exceptional future, family, and career. Guide them in the journey to a career that will be both rewarding and fulfilling, and may their lives overflow with increasing abundance and a closer walk with you. Amen.

Prayer for Friendships

Dear heavenly Father, I come before you and thank you for all the friends you have brought into my children's lives. Please bless each of these relationships and help them to develop new friendships that are positive and uplifting. Teach my children how to relate to others in a spirit of increasing generosity, wisdom, and kindness. Amen.

Prayer for Stress Reduction

Dear heavenly Father, thank you for the many ways you provide for my family every day. You know about all the worries and demands that fill my mind and heart. Please help put my mind and heart at rest through your presence. Remove the stress from my body and give me and my family peace of mind. Amen.

Prayer for Safety
Dear heavenly Father, with so much that is going on in the world and even in our community today, I humbly come before you and ask for protection for our family, our friends, and those in need. Keep us safe from pandemics, forest fires, hurricanes, tornadoes, and any type of natural disaster headed our way. Amen.

She continued praying, and each time it felt as if a pressure valve inside her had been released. Within a month, her prayer had been answered. She received an acceptance letter to a local college—though she hadn't even applied. A friend of hers had submitted an application on her behalf, and her acceptance included a way to pay her tuition. Sometimes the help and guidance we so desperately seek are just a prayer away.

All the centenarians went through tremendously tough times, from childhood throughout their adult lives. Having reached a hundred years, they had lost many friends and family members along the way as well. Yet they are able to turn to their community and their faith—especially with twenty-four-hour access to prayer—for comfort and resilience.

In 2008, life hit Pat and Tammy McLeod hard when their son Zach collapsed on a high school football field; he had sustained a severe brain injury during a scrimmage game. Two emergency surgeries later, Zach began to slowly wake up. Despite their fervent prayers and some hopeful early progress, the McLeods soon realized that their beloved son was permanently disabled. Pat and Tammy had three other children, and they committed to keeping their family strong and helping Zach progress as far as he could. Without trying to pretend that their journey has been easy, they offer support and hope to other families who've faced unspeakable loss.[9]

The answers to our prayers aren't always what we want or expect; sometimes they are hard to accept and even shake us to the core. But God can use the bad experiences, as tragic and heartbreaking as they are, to help shape us

I know that when I pray, something wonderful happens. Not just to the person or persons whom I am praying for, but also something wonderful happens to me. I'm grateful that I'm heard.

MAYA ANGELOU

and get us to the point where we need to be in order to fulfill his purpose for our lives. God doesn't promise that he will keep us from the fire, but he does promise to walk through it with us. As the McLeods and my centenarian friends discovered, faith and prayer can give us resilience, help us weather storms, and lead to outcomes we may never even have imagined.

SCIENTIFIC REASONS FOR IMMEDIATE BENEFITS

Scientists can't understand and explain many aspects of faith. We are only in the infancy of grasping the potential benefits of belonging to a faith community. Research has shown that having a faith connection can reduce stress and anxiety and even boost happiness. A systematic review published in the *Journal of Religion and Health* looked at decades of published articles and confirmed the association between faith and happiness.[10] Studies have found that families with a regular connection to a faith community have better satisfaction with their lives, better problem-solving skills for health-related problems, and more family involvement than those who attended less regularly.[11] Additionally, praying frequently outside of formal religious services was linked with a reduction in the risk of depression and anxiety.[12] A faith connection has also been linked to decreased feelings of hopelessness and suicidal thoughts and behaviors.[13]

Not only does joining a faith community boost happiness and reduce the risk of depression in children, it's great for parents, too! A study of over 74,000 women who attend a religious service more than once per week found that they had significantly less cardiovascular- or cancer-related mortality compared with those who never attend.[14] A study of the same cohort discovered that women who attended Catholic mass more regularly were less likely to commit suicide.[15] A 2012 study of over 17,705 adolescents discovered that regular faith connection with a house of worship was associated with a decreased likelihood of substance use behaviors (like alcohol, drug, and tobacco use) as well as decreases in the likelihood of fighting, theft, and delinquency.[16]

Beyond the health benefits

In addition to these scientific studies detailing how faith communities impact our health, I wondered about their other benefits. I decided to do what I do best and began surveying moms and dads at church. Not only did they want their children to draw closer to God, they told me they regularly participated with church because they liked their children to connect with other kids outside of school. (The tiger mom side of me was quick to realize that when the children connected in this setting, it was so much more relaxing—for both mom, dad, and kids—with no scoreboards to monitor or loud, obnoxious cheering needed. What a relief!) The parents also appreciated meeting other parents with shared beliefs, helping their children learn better behavior and confidence by interacting with positive peers, helping their children learn valuable life skills through volunteering, and enjoying the singing and musical experience. One of the most common responses was the support their faith community provided—through faith, they found friendships that supported them in their successes, losses, and life challenges. The house of worship can provide enormous strength.

> *Faith is like Wi-Fi. It's invisible, but it has the power to connect you to what you need.*
>
> ANONYMOUS

IN A PINCH, IT'S A CINCH: FAITH FOUNDATION PRACTICE TIPS

- When you sit down for dinner, invite your family to pause for a moment and take turns saying a prayer, thanking God for your meal. You might also encourage your family to mention one good thing that happened to them that day. A vegan Mexican restaurant in Hollywood, Gracias Madre, takes being thankful to a whole new level. Before even ordering their meal, patrons must say, "I am thankful for . . . [whatever item they want to order]." The waiter then replies, "Yes, you are thankful for . . . [restates the items ordered]."

- Pray daily when rising in the morning or going to bed at night. Keep a prayer journal and jot down your requests and their answers.
- Practice a meditative prayer walk when heading outdoors for exercise. Pick a place a few blocks away and then walk or jog there. Begin praying on the way. When you reach the destination and turn around, meditate on your prayer and listen for God's response.
- Curl up with your children to read a spiritual text together, one that is age appropriate for them. Even better, take a blanket and the book outdoors to read together.
- Take a Sabbath moment and head outdoors to spend the day with family and friends in nature. Bring along some simple food snacks to eat as you share a simple devotional.

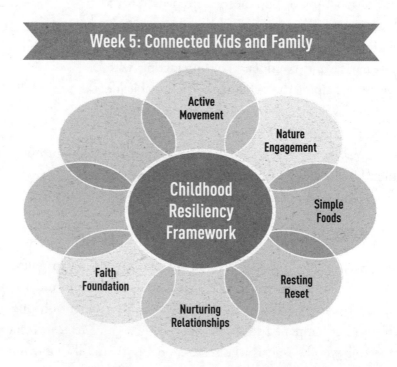

Sixth Resiliency Principle—**Faith Foundation**

Want to learn from the centenarians so your family can enjoy improved resilience and whole health? Then connect daily with God.

GET YOUR FAMILY'S TRIPLE BOOST

Putting the faith foundation principle into practice can help you and your family kick into high gear by:

Promoting happiness: By practicing the faith foundation principle, you can promote and strengthen your family's connection with God, decreasing the risk of depression. Researchers found that participating in a religious organization was associated with sustained happiness, unlike participation in political or other community organizations, which was linked to depressive symptoms.[17] Numerous other studies confirm that involvement with a house of worship can help keep depression at bay and provide encouragement, especially during challenging times. Connection with a higher power is commonly associated with improved family relationships and satisfaction.[18]

Increasing resilience: Scientific evidence points to immediate health benefits for both children and adults who practice their faith. These include a reduction in stress and anxiety, as well as a lower likelihood of risky behavior and a decreased risk of major chronic diseases. Studies have also uncovered links between church attendance and a boosted immune system, which is critically important given the threat of future outbreaks.[19] And as the centenarians have discovered, connecting with a house of worship even increases longevity. Finally, people who have a vibrant spiritual life can't help but feel a connection and passion for the natural world, as well as a desire to protect and preserve it.

Enhancing performance: Regular attendance at worship services is associated with improved academic performance.[20] One study found that children who attended a house of worship once a week had a GPA that was 0.144 higher than those who didn't.[21] Another study found that church attendance boosted math and reading scores. After surveying a group of high schoolers, researchers discovered that the scores for students who frequently attended religious services were significantly higher than those of their less religiously involved peers—all of this is likely music to any mom's ears.[22] This potential increase in academic performance probably translates to other areas of children's life, from music to sports and beyond.

CONQUERING RESISTANCE

As you work on strengthening your faith foundation, you may experience a few challenges. Consider these ideas to overcome the resistance.

Not a "spiritual" person. You don't have to feel spiritual to attend a house of worship. Every person is embodied with a spirit, and it is important to find ways to promote resilience for that part of you. If you don't feel ready to visit a house of worship, consider gathering outdoors with friends or family to read Scripture while connecting with nature.

Fear of the unknown. Going to a church for the first time reminds me of heading off for the first day at a new school and worrying that you'll be sitting alone at lunch. A great strategy for overcoming fear is to partner up and don't go alone. Get your spouse on board and go together as a united front. If you are a single parent, invite your own parents, another nearby relative, or a friend to come along. Keep in mind that if it doesn't feel like a good fit, you don't have to go back—but do keep looking for a worship house to connect with.

Too tired. Feeling exhausted after a long week of events that kept you on the go? Keep in mind that attending a house of worship will reenergize you and give you an emotional and spiritual boost.

Too many other activities. If you feel your family doesn't have time, reevaluate how loaded your schedule is. You and your family need to nourish and develop your spiritual—along with your physical and mental—well-being.

Kids aren't interested. To appeal to young children, try finding a church with an outdoor playground or indoor play space. To get older children interested, try suggesting they invite a friend along or go to a church where their friends already attend. With the allure of a playground or a meetup with friends, your kids may end up begging you to go to church each week.

OVERLAP OF THE PRINCIPLES

Having learned the sixth principle, it's good to pause for a moment and consider how the principle of faith foundation interacts with the others. All the other principles provide an opportunity to connect with God. By spending time in nature—either at rest or in active movement, with friends and family—you can connect with a higher power. Before meals, it's great to pray and show a thankful spirit for what you are about to receive. In one study, researchers discovered that regular attendance at church was positively correlated with improved sleep.[23] A study of Thai women with breast cancer showed that they did better if they had a sense of spiritual well-being and good family and social support, as well as connections with nature and a higher entity.[24] The more you can overlap the principles, the better.

HOMEWORK TIME

It's time to roll up your sleeves and dive right in with the faith foundation principle. Week 5 builds on the foundation set in the previous weeks.

1. **Set up your Connected goals for your faith foundation.** Adapt your goals to include a Connected lifestyle focused in part on building a faith foundation. After reflecting on your goals from previous weeks—focusing on an Active, Balanced, and Connected lifestyle— decide whether you will adapt them or create new goals to include the faith foundation principle.

NEW BASE GOAL

- **Faith foundation principle:** My family and I will attend a house of worship and/or take part in a "Sabbath moment" to connect with God at least one day during the week.

    Overlapping principles include faith foundation, nurturing relationships, and nature engagement if you spend your Sabbath moment outdoors.

- **Optional new goal 1:** I will pray at least once each day, focusing on each of my family members. I will record that prayer (or prayer list) in a journal.

- **Optional new goal 2:** I will read one spiritual text with my family for twenty minutes this week and engage in conversation on the topic.

EXISTING BASE GOALS

- Continue or adapt the goals you have set for active movement, nature engagement, simple foods, resting reset, and nurturing relationships principles.

2. **Implement and track your success.** Use the Weekly Evaluation guide to help you. Each night spend a few minutes before bedtime to record

- whether you worked on a faith foundation goal that day

- how you feel after practicing the principle

- how easy or difficult it was to stick with your goal

- whether you followed it closely or deviated from it, and if so, in what way

- any barriers that stopped you from working on your faith foundation and how you can address them

- how well the rewards are working and other possible rewards

At the end of the week, review what you achieved over the previous seven days. If you miss a day or two of achieving your goal, don't be discouraged. Remember, you can repeat this week if you feel you have not met your goals. Use the Weekly Evaluation (appendix B) to help you evaluate your weekly progress.

Great Job!

Congratulations on completing the fifth week of the eight-week Resiliency Program! As you continue, remember the value in a simple and slow approach to life. Feel free to repeat this week before moving to the next. If you are ready to go forward, get set to learn about the seventh resiliency principle—positive mindset.

CHAPTER 8

WEEK 6:
EMBRACING A
MOUNTAIN-MOVING MINDSET

It always seems impossible until it is done.

NELSON MANDELA

THE COLD WIND WHIPPED HIS FACE, but ten-year-old Ellsworth plodded on as he made his way across the grassy pasture. He shoved his hands into his coat pockets, hoping to warm them. It was only 5:30 a.m., but he was already trudging across the fields to bring his family's dairy cows back to the barn. The morning that Ellsworth Wareham, 101-year-old Resiliency Capital member, was describing to me was a typical one for him growing up.

Life in their Alberta, Canada, farming community was anything but easy for Ellsworth and his family. He'd been born in Texas, but his parents had moved north to the farm in Canada, thinking life would be better there. However, his father struggled to gain financial security for his family, which included six children. With an abundance of physically demanding work always needing to be done—from dairy farming to growing and harvesting grain—there was no time for disagreements or squabbles among family members.

So Ellsworth had gotten up early to gather those black-and-white beasts—the dairy cows—who often sought refuge in a distant group of bushes where they huddled together for warmth. Locating the cows and sending them to the barn was the easiest of his morning chores. Next he would milk the cows and separate the milk with a hand separator, a messy and difficult task. His family didn't have a fancy operation—they didn't even have electricity. Everything had to be done by hand.

After finishing his chores, Ellsworth would sit down to a simple breakfast. Then he'd head back out into the chilly air to walk two miles to the local school. Ellsworth's life on the farm was harsh and physically demanding, but he learned that hard work and responsibility were not a burden, but a blessing. That lesson would take him far in whatever he chose to do.

Early on, his mother had told him to get an education—so he set that as his primary goal. His father wondered how Ellsworth would ever be able to afford college. Nevertheless, while working hard for his parents, nineteen-year-old Ellsworth set his sights on improving his prospects. "You can't allow circumstances to shape what your ultimate goal is," he told me. "I remember very clearly, being out of school about one year or two—no money, no anything—and I was just walking alone one day [when] I got to thinking about if I really wanted to be a doctor. I didn't have any means, but I really wanted to be a doctor, and so I made up my mind to become one."

Grateful for the little he had, Ellsworth relied on hard work and drive to excel and fulfill his dream. He worked for two years, saving all his money for school. He graduated from college, went on to medical school, and then trained in cardiac surgery, a relatively new specialty back then. When asked about stresses in his life, Ellsworth said, "Experiences which are, let us say, demanding or challenging develop character and help you not think about the little minor irritations anymore."

Ellsworth became a world-renowned cardiac surgeon, one of the earliest to perform open-heart surgery—he literally held lives in the palms of his hands. He cofounded the Loma Linda University Overseas Heart Surgery Team and traveled the world performing open-heart surgery for adults and children in underdeveloped countries. He is believed to have performed the first open-heart surgery in Pakistan in the early 1960s. His team was praised for their work in Pakistan by US presidents Johnson and Nixon, as well as the king of Greece and Saudi Arabian royalty.

Ellsworth worked as a physician until age ninety-five and was still going strong at 101 when my team and I came to interview him. While walking into his home study, I noticed sitting next to his black-and-white wedding photo a framed quote with a motto he lived by: "Morning, noon, and night, let gratitude as a sweet perfume ascend to Heaven."

Based on his humble childhood beginnings, no one would have predicted that he would accomplish so much. However, Ellsworth was just one of many centenarians in the Resiliency Capital who overcame childhood adversity to live abundant and fulfilling lives. Want to learn more about how they beat the odds, despite tremendous barriers? Want your children to develop grit and perseverance as well? Read on to learn the centenarians' secrets and how you can put their wisdom into practice with your own family.

WEEK 6: DETERMINED KIDS AND FAMILY

The sixth week of the Resiliency Program is represented by the letter D—for Determined—building families and children who are determined to help themselves and others. This letter represents the seventh and eighth resiliency principles—positive mindset and helping hands. Tied closely together, these two principles focus on developing a positive mindset and learning how helping others will enable your family to achieve that goal.

PRINCIPLE #7—POSITIVE MINDSET

If I were to describe the centenarians in general, one feature that stands out is their tremendous focus and grit. Believing their actions would result in positive outcomes, they set goals and persevered to reach them, despite countless obstacles. Whenever I asked centenarians about challenges in their lives, they'd inevitably say something like "I didn't have any challenges or hardships." But their life stories are filled with all kinds of difficulties, both as children and adults. Yet they chose to focus on the good things rather than the hardships. They were grateful for simple experiences, blessings, and opportunities, seeing the positive in each situation.

THREE FUNDAMENTALS FOR APPLYING THE POSITIVE MINDSET PRINCIPLE

1. Focus Your Steps	2. Cultivate Positivity	3. Embrace Gratefulness
Focus your steps and set life-changing goals, remembering the positives, no matter how small, as you progress.	Practice positive thinking and speaking, and take actions to promote positivity in your life.	Have an attitude of gratitude.

Modern Times Call for Modern Methods

Let's take a closer look at the positive mindset principle and the three essentials—focus, positivity, and gratitude—so you can begin applying the principle with your own family.

1. Focus your steps

The centenarians didn't allow difficult circumstances to limit their mindsets or influence their behaviors. They chose not to settle. They focused on their goals, determined to achieve them. They persevered despite all the setbacks and doubting people who told them their ambitions were impossible. Many of them continued to set goals later in life, well into their seventies, eighties, and even nineties and beyond. Remember mountaineering Hulda Crooks? When she was in her fifties, Hulda began setting goals for mountain climbing. In her nineties, she set new climbing goals and became world renowned for summiting some of the highest mountain peaks on multiple continents.

Each one of us is more powerful than we give ourselves credit for, and the impact you and I can have on our own lives and those of others is unimaginable. But don't focus on the unimaginable—imagine all that you and your children might do. Find ways to tap into your mind and use it for good—doing so will encourage your children to do the same. Don't let major challenges, limited resources, or outbreaks stop you and your family from reaching your goals.

Life brings a series of dreams and goals; whenever you reach one, set an even bigger one. Ellsworth wanted to go to college. Then he decided to go to medical school. Then he chose to train in heart surgery when few training programs were available. Then he found a way to perform surgeries around the world. At each stage, he reached his objective and set another. When individuals set ambitious goals, not only will their lives change, they can literally save lives, as Ellsworth's career trajectory demonstrates.

Ellsworth was a teenager during the Great Depression and grew up in a community in which nobody went to college. But he saw going to college as his only option—it wasn't a matter of whether he could go or not; it was only a matter of what he had to do to get there. The same was true for mountaineer Hulda Crooks. With no formal training in mountain hiking, she decided to teach herself to climb mountains. By the time she was in

Going for the GOLD Strategy

You can go for the gold with my GOLD Strategy, created to help you develop and implement a positive, life-changing goal.

- Goal: Set a goal for yourself that has the power to promote positive life change or growth.
- Obstacles: Identify barriers that might derail you.
- Leap: Come up with strategies for overcoming the obstacles.
- Do it: Develop a plan and implement it.

Post your GOLD Strategy in a prominent place, and be sure you tell your family members you are determined to reach this goal. Additionally, place objects or pictures around your home to remind yourself daily of your objective.

As your family sees you reach your goal, they will feel inspired to do the same. Help each family member create their own GOLD Strategy, and reward each one when they achieve it. Read on to learn about cultivating positive self-talk to help you reach your goal!

her nineties, the list of mountains she was determined to summit included the highest peaks in the US and Japan. It wasn't a matter of whether she could or should hike these mountains; it was only a matter of what she had to do to reach the top.

2. Cultivate positivity

The second rule for practicing the positive mindset principle is engaging in positive thoughts, speech, and action. A positive mindset starts with positive thinking, which just means approaching difficulties more constructively, optimistically, and productively. You think the best is going to happen, not the worst. When things don't go according to plan, you see the setback as a temporary situation. In contrast, negative thinkers—those who are more pessimistic—are more likely to blame themselves or others when bad things happen. They tend to expect negative outcomes and assume the fallout will last for quite some time. Negative thinking may seem normal and harmless, but it actually works against people's ability to succeed. If you persistently think negatively about yourself and your abilities, you can actually increase the likelihood of a negative outcome.

Centenarian Belen Lopez was just twelve when she began working to help take care of her family. Her father had left the family years earlier, so her mother and her siblings began preparing and selling meals to nearby farmers and cattlemen to earn money to support themselves. Many of the workers did stop by for a meal; unfortunately, they had to sit on the dirt floor while eating. Belen decided to remedy the situation.

"One day, I noticed that we didn't have a table. Can you believe that! My parents didn't think of having a nice table where we—and all these men who were coming for meals—could sit. I told my sisters, 'Let's go get wood and make a table.' We cut down a tree and made it."

As a young physician, Dr. Mildred Stilson (100-year-old Resiliency Capital member) worked in an isolated clinic in Africa. She remembers running a medical clinic with her husband in a rural region with limited resources. They had to make do with any available support, including their young daughter, whom Mildred trained to hold the anesthesia bag.

"My husband had to be away a lot because he had to do all the shopping for the hospital, driving the long, long miles to do it," Mildred told me. "And so I took care of the hospital while he was away. And sometimes there wasn't even a nurse to help if I needed to give an anesthetic for surgery or for a miscarriage, for instance. I needed somebody to assist me." Mildred pretended to hold up a cylinder with the anesthetic, the tubing, and the release clasp, describing how she would instruct her daughter. "So I took my daughter and put a gown on her and said, 'Now, there's this and you drop it [the release clasp]. And watch the drugs go down and I'll do the math and when I tell you to stop, stop.'"

Examples of Negative and Positive Thinking

Negative-Focused Thinking	Positive-Reframed Thinking
"Bad things always happen to me."	"I've been blessed in so many areas of life."
"I'm never going to be successful."	"This time, I know I am prepared to succeed."
"I'm not talented enough."	"I have talents and skills, and I am capable. I will do the best I can."
"Nothing I do ever turns out right. Why should I even try?"	"I'm going to take a different approach to increase the likelihood of success."
"My kids don't have the smarts to be high achievers."	"My kids can achieve whatever they set their minds on and work for."
"I'm just not pretty or very good-looking."	"I am beautiful just the way I am. I am uniquely and wonderfully made."

Does positive thinking really make a difference? Absolutely! Even if you or your family members don't naturally look on the bright side, there are ways to cultivate positive thinking.

A great way to encourage positive thinking is to start by promoting positive self-talk. Even professional athletes know the importance of practicing a positive mindset, and they participate in training sessions on cultivating positive self-talk techniques. Scientific studies support the belief that how you think about your performance, before and during the event, will influence your outcome.

A pessimist sees the difficulty in every opportunity; an optimist sees the opportunity in every difficulty.

WINSTON CHURCHILL

A recent study of 117 athletes—across a wide variety of individual sports (like gymnastics, swimming, and wrestling) and team sports (like volleyball and ice hockey)—was conducted to assess the impact of positive self-talk on athletic performance. Athletes were assigned to either the control group with no special intervention or to groups who received one-week or eight-week self-talk intervention in addition to the usual training. Researchers discovered that those practicing positive self-talk performed better than those who did not and that the more self-talk they engaged in, the better they did.[1] Imagine that—thinking and speaking your way to victory!

The study concluded that self-talk is associated with greater self-confidence, less anxiety, greater self-optimization, improved self-efficacy, and better performance. Moreover, by participating in the study, the athletes learned to increase their attention on the thoughts running through their minds, promote positive self-talk dialogue, and reduce interfering thoughts. They learned to recognize their emotions as they engaged in self-talk and to focus during training and competition. Many other studies of sports ranging from soccer to swimming also support the benefits of positive self-talk.[2]

Positivity works across many disciplines. Have any budding artists in your family? A scientific study found that people with creativity and high self-efficacy—the belief that they can accomplish what they put their minds to—perform better and are even more creative than other people.[3] When children learn to practice positive self-talk early, they are more likely to have a growth mindset—the belief that their intellectual abilities are adaptable and that they can rise to the challenge.

By now you might be wondering how you can put positive self-talk to work in your own life and with your family. Read on to learn how you can achieve a positive mindset no matter how pessimistic, cynical, or dubious you might be. Even if it doesn't come naturally, there are ways you can cultivate positive self-talk.

Strategies for achieving a positive mindset

Begin by recognizing and categorizing the thoughts in your head. Do you tend to think about more positive things or to let your mind ruminate on the negative side? You only have so much room in your brain, and when you fill up the space with negative thoughts, you have little room for positive ones. You and your family members need to catch yourselves when you begin to focus on negative thoughts so you can make room for better ones. Pay attention to the frequency of your negative thoughts and when most of them occur—is it in the morning, afternoon, or evening?

The key is to break the cycle. When you catch yourself thinking negatively, shift the dialogue in your brain. Think of something positive or how you might view the challenge constructively—*just think about that!* As Anita Johnson-Mackey (105-year-old Resiliency Capital member) said, "Don't get angry at hardships; try to look at them as learning opportunities."

It may help to change your environment and head outdoors for a quick walk to help clear your mind. Centenarian Hulda Crooks wrote, "Sameness leads to madness. The ever-changing outdoor scenery is restful to our senses."[4]

While working as a professor and overseeing online schooling for my kids (the schools had mandated closures due to the pandemic), I received a telephone call. The local county health department needed more epidemiologists and asked me to come and help in the battle against COVID-19. Helping the county would truly test my ability to stay positive. At times the situation became overwhelming with cases rising—not just globally and nationally, but in my own community. Two thousand positive cases were identified in my county over just one weekend. The hospitals and ICUs were filling and the death toll rising. As I felt myself moving into a rut of despair, I knew I needed to get my mind together to keep up the good fight, so I took the advice of my centenarian friends and regularly headed outdoors with my kids. As we took a brief walk around the block,

Your Family's Powerful Personal Motto

A great way to replace the negative thoughts in your mind is to have a powerful motto—*just speak it*. The same way athletes are trained to practice positivity and focus, you can develop your own positive motto and practice visualizing and verbalizing it. As you make your positive statement, breathe out and focus on your breath and the words. This will help you focus your mind on the upside and release stress and anxiety. Remember, practice makes permanent.

1. **Create your motto statement.** You can go through this process as a family, or older kids may want to work on one independently. To get going, think up two different mottoes—one that fits a specific challenge you face and one that can be used anytime.

    Specific motto: "I will lose these extra pounds within three months through healthier eating and more exercise."

    General motto: "I am a wonderful person, filled with extraordinary potential to be successful at whatever I do."

2. **Visualize yourself using it and overcoming challenges.** Picture yourself practicing your motto and your performance improving over time. Imagine an event where you will perform or compete. Use all your senses to set the scene: the noises, the smells, the sights. See yourself saying your motto and then performing at your best.

3. **Repeat the motto throughout the day and in various settings.** Rehearse your motto frequently, especially before and during important events.

I'd say a quick prayer for health and healing for my family, for our community, and for our world. My mind and spirit immediately felt better, and my children were happier too.

Another great way to promote a positive mindset is to consciously let go of regret, anger, worry, and bitterness—*just release it*. Let go of the toxic feelings so the healing will come. If you made a mistake, someone hurt you, or life doesn't seem fair or isn't turning out the way you planned, don't dwell on it.

> *Positive mindset is like personal hygiene; you have to work on it every day.*
>
> ANONYMOUS

In Disney's *The Lion King*, the lion cub, warthog, and meerkat sing "Hakuna Matata," Swahili for "there are no troubles." No matter what happens, promote a positive mindset by shifting from a focus on your troubles to a focus on your opportunities. Don't fret. Centenarian Amy Sherrard (101-year-old Resiliency Capital member) was the child of missionary parents and often faced the unexpected. "You have to have a geographic spirit. You plan to the *n*th degree, and as soon as you press the start button, you go with the flow."

Turning to God in prayer can help you release negative feelings and shift your mental focus. Prayer can help ease your burden and lead to a sense of hope and support—and the very act of praying can help you articulate your problem and the solution you are seeking.

A third great way to promote a positive mindset is to allow yourself and your family time and space for positive learning experiences—*just learn it*. Take up a hobby, learn to play a new musical instrument, or enjoy the arts, which can all help relieve stress and build skills. The more you develop your abilities, the more confidence you will gain and the more you will realize that you can achieve what you set out to do. Positive learning experiences will shift your focus from hardships to a state of peace and relaxation.

Recognize your child's strengths and give them opportunities to develop them. Most of the centenarians had hobbies from early on, which brought them comfort and joy. Anita Johnson-Mackey (105) and Dr. Stilson (100) took to reading, and Jane Pihl (102) played piano.

As a child, Jane lived for several years with a woman who gave piano lessons. Jane had no way to pay for lessons, so she simply pretended to play as the woman taught her students in another room. "I was playing by ear probably at nine, ten years old. The way I learned piano was with these little games—play a few notes from a tune and see if my friend could recognize the song. Well, we started playing these games, and [I] kind of caught on how to do it." Throughout her life Jane often played piano for her own enjoyment. At the end of our interview, I got a kick out of sitting with Jane at her piano as she patiently tried to teach me a few chords.

"It's easy," she assured me. "Just play these three chords and you have yourself a little tune."

My hands, stiff and awkward, just wouldn't cooperate, but I enjoyed it anyway. In that moment, I was twelve again, playing piano and having fun with my good friend Jane. I realized that playing piano—or starting any hobby—generally takes patience, a willingness to make mistakes, and above all, a spirit of playfulness.

Finding your child's interests starts with conversation and observation to discover what they like. What activity have they told you they'd like to try? What do they naturally take to? Do they have artistic talents? Musical talents? Can they take things apart and put them back together? Are they physically gifted in a sport or dance? Once you have a good sense of their natural talents, look for local classes or training opportunities. The key is not to push them toward activities you want them to excel at but rather allow children to guide themselves toward their own interests.

A fourth idea for promoting a positive mindset is to look for signs or symbols to boost your mood and promote pleasant thoughts—*just see it*. What items or symbols in your life inspire you or give you comfort? Maybe you can find something in nature—like a butterfly or white bird—to serve as a signal that positive change is coming to help you and your family shift your thinking in the right direction. Literally, it could be anything that helps put you in a positive mood.

It might even be a collection of objects. A friend of mine had a great solution when her daughter was scared about beginning a new year of preschool. My friend made her little girl a Protector Pouch in which she placed a small stone to symbolize her strength, a feather to symbolize her ability to go far, and a little gem to symbolize her wisdom. Her daughter carried the pouch into preschool with her; not only did having this "magical" pouch to hold give her courage, it made her a hit with new friends who wanted to see what it was. What a smart mom!

Positivity Protector Pouch

Collect the items below and place them in a small drawstring pouch, one that is small enough to fit in your child's pocket:

- String: To represent their connection with friends, family, and God
- Feather: To represent the ability to go far
- Gem: To represent clarity of vision and wisdom
- Stone: To represent strength and the ability to defeat giant obstacles
- Stick: To represent bravery, like that of a brave leader
- Mustard seed: To represent courage, since the tiny black mustard seed can grow eight feet tall and help sustain the birds that eat its seeds

You might adapt and personalize the items to include such things as religious symbols or tiny handwritten notes from you. The pouch string can represent the uniting of your hearts, a reminder that you love them and your hearts are tied together. When you present this gift, teach your child about each item and what it represents.

3. Embrace gratefulness

Going hand in hand with positive self-talk and thinking is an attitude of gratitude. To be grateful is to notice your blessings, no matter how big or small, and to be thankful for them. Centenarian Salma Mohr didn't have much as a child, but early on she learned not to complain. Instead she expressed gratitude for even the smallest things. She recalls not owning a doll of her own, but rather than feel deprived, she treasured the thrill of just touching the hair and dress of a neighbor friend's doll. Then one day, she found her own treasure.

"On our way to school we had to go through an alley. And each day we would pass by everybody's garbage along our walk. And one day, of all things, I found in the neighbor's garbage can the most gorgeous pieces of broken glass. And I could tell by some of the larger pieces that it must have been a glass plate or bowl. And it was clear and blue."

Salma carefully scooped up the pieces and took them home, where she kept them in a special box. She would often take out her blue pieces of glass and shine them up with a cloth. "Oh, that was my first treasure I ever owned. On sunny days I would carefully take them outdoors and let the sun shine through them and put new spots everywhere. That was my toy." What one person had thought was a useless bowl, broken and without a purpose, became a young girl's prized possession. Despite how little her family had, Salma developed a grateful perspective.

Centenarian Anita Johnson-Mackey also remembers learning as a child not to complain. As an African American living in a white community in the early 1900s, she could have held on to a number of grievances. But she realized that though she didn't always have control over her situation, she did have control over her attitude.

"I learned early in life, if something came up, don't be complaining at all," Anita told me. "And ask yourself, *Did I have anything to do with this? What can I do about it now?*" This mindset and approach to hardships served her well. Later, while working for Veterans Affairs as a medical social worker, Anita encouraged her clients to change their inner dialogue from complaining and defeatism to one focused on gratitude, action, and positive change.

When I'm tempted to let all the difficulties I'm facing get me down (especially when I was caring for my family while helping to battle COVID in our community), I often think about Nick Vujicic. Nick is an international motivational speaker from Australia who is famous for his positive outlook on life and upbeat attitude despite his enormous challenges.[5] He is one of only seven individuals worldwide living with tetra-amelia syndrome, which is characterized by a lack of arms and legs. When he was born in 1982, his parents—Boris and Dushka—were heartbroken. After overcoming their emotional distress, Nick's parents were determined to give him the most normal childhood they could. From the beginning his parents instilled the impor-tance of always being thankful for what he had, no matter the situation. Nick grew and learned to do things most other children were doing, but in a slightly different way. He was a rough-and-tumble young boy, and one of his favorite activities was rid-ing a skateboard flat on his stomach, towed behind

Gratitude . . .
turns what
we have into
enough.

MELODY BEATTIE

the bicycle of his brother or a friend. Though his parents would worry he would injure himself, he typically replied, "It's not like I'm going to break an arm or a leg!"[6]

Though bullied as a child, Nick was determined to succeed in every-thing he put his mind to. Still, he spent his childhood and teen years feel-ing lonely and depressed. But as a young adult, Nick found faith through prayer, and his attitude turned from self-pity to self-actualization. He began speaking at schools spreading a message of hope, especially for those bullied or facing tremendous difficulties. In 2005, at the age of twenty-three, Nick founded Life Without Limbs, an evangelistic orga-nization. A few years later he developed the school curriculum Attitude Is Altitude to spark passion and hope around the world with a core mes-sage that our attitude determines our ability to succeed. Nick has since married, had children, and lives a life of true abundance. He uses his personal experience to inspire others to action. He proves that no matter your circumstances, you can make positive changes and be an overcomer.

Even when disappointments happen and life doesn't go exactly as planned, we can be encouraged when we remember that what may seem unfortunate initially may turn out to be a blessing in disguise. A traffic jam might have kept you from getting to your destination on time, but

Ten Activities to Encourage a Thankful Heart

1. **Forget the sheep; count your blessings.** Each night before bed think of ten things you are grateful for that day.
2. **Pray before each meal.** Express gratitude for the food you are about to eat.
3. **Take time for family experiences.** We gain more joy from experiences than from things, so take time and make a fun memory.
4. **Find a cause and volunteer.** You'll learn more about the helping hand resiliency principle in the upcoming chapter, but start thinking now about ways you can volunteer as a family.
5. **Just head outdoors.** Enjoy the natural world in different kinds of weather, and express thankfulness for the seasons.
6. **Send handwritten cards or drawings.** You and your kids will bring joy to others when you either thank a loved one or friend for something they've done for you or just let them know that you love them.
7. **Display gratitude reminders.** Hang up drawings, magnets, or pictures to remind yourself of what you have been thankful for. Create magnets for your own fridge and share them with others.
8. **Give a gift your family and friends can share.** You might select an old-fashioned board or card game or, better yet, come up with your own game (like Thankful Charades or Gratitude Pictionary).
9. **Start a thankful jar.** You might start this in January by decorating a container with your kids. Keep slips of paper and a pen next to it and encourage family members to jot down unexpected blessings; good things that happened to them; or simply people, places, and things they are grateful for. Then read the slips of paper on the following New Year's Day.
10. **Read books with your children to help them learn about gratitude and gain perspective.** *The Giving Tree* by Shel Silverstein, *The Thank You Book* by Mo Willems, and *Sylvester and the Magic Pebble* by William Steig can help teach the concept of thankfulness. Reading books about other countries and how people live can provide perspective. Books such as *A Life Like Mine: How Children Live Around the World* by DK and UNICEF, *The Barefoot Book of Children* by Kate DePalma and Tessa Strickland, and the *Friends around the World Atlas* developed by the child sponsorship and Christian aid nonprofit Compassion International offer glimpses of life around the globe and stir conversations.

that backup might have prevented you from a collision with a distracted or reckless driver. A job opportunity might have fallen through, but it could have been an unexpectedly bad fit, or a better opportunity could come along soon. Even a difficult "sheltering in place" mandate during the COVID-19 outbreak led to some positive benefits—within just a few months, some wildlife began making a comeback, and the air pollution was almost extinguished in many areas of the country.[7]

Many of life's failures are experienced by people who did not realize how close they were to success when they gave up.

THOMAS EDISON

When we stop focusing on our misfortunes, weaknesses, and faults and start acknowledging and being thankful for all the good things in our lives (including what we are doing right), our mindset will shift from dashed expectations and disappointment to appreciation and positive thinking.

A great way to start acknowledging your blessings is by keeping a gratitude journal. Studies have found that writing down our feelings of gratitude results in immediate health benefits and leads to a more positive mindset. In two university studies, two hundred undergraduates were split into three different groups, each with a different writing task.[8] One group was told to record their blessings; the second to record their hassles; and the third to record their experiences in general. Participants in the gratitude group felt better about their lives overall and even began looking forward to the upcoming week. Not only did they feel more positive emotions, they were more likely to help someone in need of emotional support or with a problem. A Polish researcher discovered that counting and recording our blessings each day can reduce feelings of stress.[9]

If journaling doesn't appeal to you, think of other strategies to document or notice the blessings your family experiences (like writing them on a chalkboard, jotting them down on sticky notes and placing them on the fridge, or reflecting on them over dinner or at the end of each day).

Recalling the positive events and blessing in our lives was especially useful during anxiety-ridden times like the COVID-19 outbreak. The news and social media focused on counting the numbers and discussing the tragedy. While it is good to be in the know, it's better to keep our central focus on the positives rather than concentrate on the uncontrollable variables around us.

> *When I started counting my blessings, my whole life turned around.*
>
> COUNTRY SINGER
> WILLIE NELSON

IN A PINCH, IT'S A CINCH: POSITIVE MINDSET PRACTICE TIPS

- Practice following up every negative thought with a happy one. Notice throughout the day when you have a negative thought. Then either state your motto to yourself or respond with a positive comment. You can also take a step outdoors to help change the negative dialogue loop in your mind.

- Take a moment and visualize yourself accomplishing a great feat. Imagine what the accomplishment feels like. What friends, family members, or other individuals surround you? What are they saying?

- Practice saying the general motto listed on page 182 or create your own. Post it in a location where you will see it each morning. Develop a family motto with your spouse and kids; encourage them to start off each day on the right foot by stating this motto.

- Keep a gratitude journal. Jot down daily all the blessings in your life that you are thankful for. Make it a family affair and encourage your kids to add their thoughts.

- Make gratitude into a fun game. During dinnertime, see who can come up with the longest list of things they are grateful for. Parents can even share things they were grateful for as a child. Have simple prizes handy for a few categories, like the longest list or the craziest or most interesting blessing.

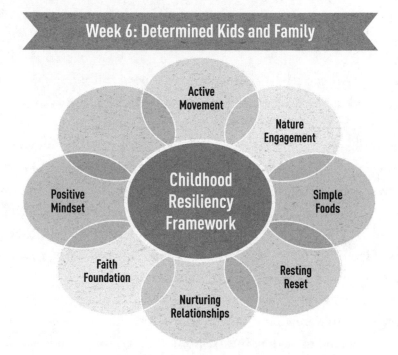

Seventh Resiliency Principle—**Positive Mindset**

Want to learn from the centenarians so your family can enjoy improved resilience and whole health? Then set a life-changing goal and engage in positive self-talk every day.

GET YOUR FAMILY'S TRIPLE BOOST

By now, it's probably obvious that learning to cultivate a positive mindset early in life has immediate and long-lasting benefits linked to performance, relationships, self-confidence, happiness, and health. Putting the positive mindset principle into practice can help you and your family kick into high gear by:

Promoting happiness: By practicing the positive mindset principle, you and your family can improve your mood and develop a happier outlook on life. Even better, according to an article by three psychologists, positive thinkers are likely to have more luck in love.[10]

Increasing resilience: Your mind can have a powerful influence on your body's health and resilience. According to researchers, a positive mindset has been linked with immediate health benefits such as increased resistance to the common cold, lower stress levels, greater confidence and self-esteem, and more energy. A group of scientists studied 334 people over two weeks, assessed their attitudes, and then gave them a squirt of rhinovirus, the germ that causes the common cold. After monitoring the participants, they discovered that those with a more positive attitude were less likely to come down with a cold.[11] There truly is a strong connection between your mindset and your immune system.

Ever hear of the "placebo effect"? Studies show that when people believe they are receiving a medication or treatment—even when they aren't—they tend to have a positive mindset that often provides healing.[12] Numerous studies have also uncovered a link between having an optimistic outlook and an enhanced tolerance to pain.[13]

Enhancing performance: A positive outlook will help you and your family to feel more confident, better rested, and more energetic, which can increase the likelihood of successful outcomes in academics, creative arts, athletics, business, and relationships. Barbara Fredrickson, a positive psychology researcher at the University of North Carolina, published a landmark paper on how a positive mindset impacts people's skills.[14] In one experiment, Fredrickson assigned college students to one of five different groups to watch a video. Each video was intended to ellicit one positive, negative, or neutral emotion. After watching the film, participants were instructed to list everything they would like to do at that moment. Upon analyzing the data, Fredrickson found that those who had watched the two films that elicited positive thoughts and emotions listed a significantly greater number of action items than the subjects who watched the negative or neutral videos.[15] Positive thoughts and emotions are more likely to broaden people's sense of possibility. Fredrickson calls this concept "broaden and build" because having a more positive mindset and being open to greater possibilities can encourage individuals to develop new skills useful in many aspects of life.

CONQUERING RESISTANCE

As you and your family work on strengthening your positive mindset, consider the following ideas if you face any of the challenges below:

Too many Eeyores. Eeyore, the donkey character in the *Winnie-the-Pooh* books by A. A. Milne, inevitably finds the bad in everything. He hangs his head, he moans and complains, and no matter how good things are, he finds a reason to be depressed. Let's face it, it's downright tough to be around someone who is an Eeyore. But that doesn't mean you need to abandon them. They need your positive attitude and words to encourage them to shift their outlook. Watch your own thoughts and emotions when you are around these people, but continue to take up the challenge to try bringing them back to a positive place.

Consecutive setbacks. If you feel like you have gotten stuck in a rut and nothing you are doing is working, take a time-out. Give your mind a break and recharge your batteries. Once you do, you can reapproach the problem through prayer or by developing a specific motto to repeat and focus your mind as you tackle the challenge again.

Worry about what other people might think or say. When others begin to observe all your benefits with practicing a positive mindset, they may want to join you.

OVERLAP OF THE PRINCIPLES

The positive mindset principle overlaps with each of the other principles. Scientific studies have even shown that a positive mindset is directly linked with experiencing better sleep and building better relationships. A recent study found that people who are sleep deprived have more difficulty remaining positive, which is an even more compelling reason to fully experience the resting reset principle and fulfill the sleep needs of your body.[16]

Spending time being active outdoors in nature not only helps you get better sleep, it also immediately influences your mental health by promoting self-esteem and a positive mood and decreasing stress and anxiety, all of which support a positive mindset. In addition, studies have found that the foods you consume can influence the functioning of your brain, promoting the ability to think positively.[17] Foods like spinach, tofu, nuts and seeds, and salmon can help boost serotonin. Serotonin is a neurotransmitter and is important in regulating anxiety, happiness, mood, and focus—and it doesn't stop there. Serotonin also helps regulate sleep, appetite, wound healing, and bone health, and almost 95 percent of it is created in the gut.[18] That's right, a chemical needed to help positively influence things in your brain comes from your stomach! Only recently have scientists begun to study and understand this amazing connection between your tummy and your mind. Though more research is needed, it is becoming clearer that eating a more plant-based diet is important for promoting a positive mindset.

HOMEWORK TIME

It's time to roll up your sleeves and dive right in with your positive mindset principle. Week 6 builds on the foundation set in the previous weeks.

1. **Set up your Determined goals for a positive mindset.** Add to or adapt your previous weekly goals to include the positive mindset principle. Use the following goals or feel free to create new ones:

NEW BASE GOAL

- **Positive mindset principle:** Spend five minutes each night before bed recording your blessings for the day—both those you personally received and those your family members experienced. At family dinners, give thanks for the specific blessings your family received over the past week.

Overlapping principles include positive mindset and nurturing relationships.

- **Optional new goal 1:** Identify, schedule, and train for an outdoor event (like a mountain climb or a 5K walk or run) to complete, either individually or with family members.

- **Optional new goal 2:** At least once during the week, have your children tell you two things they were thankful for that day before bedtime. Then pray with them and give thanks for specific blessings they have received.

EXISTING BASE GOALS

- Continue working on the goals you have set for active movement, nature engagement, simple foods, resting reset, nurturing relationships, and faith foundation principles.

2. **Implement and track your success.** Activate your plans and chart your progress using the Weekly Evaluation in appendix B. Each night, spend a few minutes before bedtime to record:

   - whether you worked on the positive mindset principle that day
   - how you feel after practicing the positive mindset principle
   - how easy or difficult it was to stick with your goals
   - whether you followed it closely or deviated and if so, in what way
   - any barriers that stopped you from experiencing a positive mindset or positive self-talk and how you can address them
   - how well the rewards are working and other possible rewards

At the end of the week, review what you achieved throughout the week. Remember you can repeat this week if you feel you have not met your goals.

Great Job!

Congratulations on completing the sixth week of the eight-week program! As you go through each week, remember the value in a simple and slow approach to life. Feel free to repeat this week before moving to the next. If you are ready to move on, get set to learn about the powerful mind plan and the eighth resiliency principle—helping hands.

CHAPTER 9

WEEK 7: BECOMING THE SOLUTION

The best way to find yourself is to lose yourself in the service of others.

MAHATMA GANDHI

I COULD PICTURE FEATHERS AND chicken feed everywhere. Lidia Reichel (100-year-old Resiliency Capital member) was describing her childhood on a farm in rural Argentina, where she helped feed three thousand clucking hens each day. But that was just part of her daily tasks—she did everything from milking cows to making cheese, from planting and tending crops to watching younger siblings. The third of nine children, Lidia pitched in and helped out wherever she could from a young age.

"As soon as we learned how to walk and talk," Lidia told me, "we'd have to work on the farm. My mom would dig into the soil to plant, and I'd help her." The family ate whatever they planted—including onions, garlic, cabbage, carrots, lettuce, potatoes, cucumbers, and watermelon. If they wanted bread, Lidia and her mom had to prepare the dough. There was no supermarket nearby.

Lidia's work didn't end when the farmwork had been completed;

instead, she and her family would head into town to help at the community church, which also served as the local schoolhouse and needed to be cleaned every day. Lidia attended school there as a child, making the one-hour walk each way. Eventually, her grandfather purchased a home near the church for the students and teachers who lived far from the school. As she got older, Lidia took on more duties alongside her family, helping with cooking and cleaning for the students and teachers. In her spare time, Lidia knit blankets to keep the children warm at night.

Rather than being resentful at having to work so hard as a child, Lidia continued to serve others with a happy heart throughout her life. She moved closer to the city around age seventy and invited students to live with her. She enjoyed their company, and in return, she tended to their daily needs. Eventually, in her nineties, Lidia left Argentina and settled in Loma Linda, California, to be closer to her grown kids and their families.

Lidia told me she never had much, but she was always willing to share with others what little she had. In fact, as we talked, Lidia was knitting a blue baby hat. I learned that she knits eight hundred hats each year for newborns and donates them to a hospital that serves the underserved. Imagine that—she makes at least two hats a day!

I asked Lidia her advice for parents who want to raise resilient children. "Encourage them to always help others!" she replied. In fact, every centenarian I spoke with was driven to help others. Hulda Crooks shared her love of nature, encouraging others to get moving and hiking to stay physically fit. Sales of her book continue to fund a university scholarship in her name. I also benefited from her help in the form of a grant to support my research on how the environment influences health.

Ellsworth Wareham, a heart surgeon, traveled across the globe to provide surgery for those without money or access to Western medicine. Anita Johnson-Mackey was never able to have children of her own, but that didn't stop her from donating funds to help send children to school. "I was reared with the thought that you're giving with the wrong spirit if everybody's got to know what you've done. You give quietly," she said.

Their simple acts of kindness have touched the lives of countless people and helped guide their lives, giving them extraordinary resilience. Want to learn the centenarians' secrets and put them into practice with your family? Want to help your children discover purpose in their lives? Want to help your family build resilience in the face of hardships? Then read on and put their wisdom into practice.

WEEK 7: DETERMINED KIDS AND FAMILY

The seventh week of the Resiliency Program is represented by the letter *D*—Determine to do for others. More specifically, week 7 represents the eighth resiliency principle—helping hands.

PRINCIPLE #8—HELPING HANDS

This week you will learn about the eighth and final resiliency principle, which involves your family helping out in your household and the community. From as young as age three, the centenarians often had chores around the house and on the farm. Farming was a physically tough way of life that required everyone to pitch in, from planting seeds and harvesting crops to tending to livestock. Children's work was real and valued. Young children often helped prepare the food and tend to even younger siblings. More than half the centenarians reported that as children they were responsible for cooking, cleaning, and sewing clothing for church members, students, teachers, and community members who temporarily stayed in their homes. Their families were also engaged in church activities and ministries, which they viewed as opportunities to help others, especially the poor—even if they themselves didn't have much. Family members were always ready to jump in and act whenever someone called for help, even at the last minute. The drive and willingness to help others was a seed planted early in the centenarians' childhood, and it matured and bloomed throughout their lives.

THREE FUNDAMENTALS FOR APPLYING THE HELPING HANDS PRINCIPLE

1. Connect with Your *What*	2. Connect with Your *Where*	3. Connect with Your *Why*
Everyone has gifts and resources that can be shared to make a positive impact. What gifts can your family share with others?	You can make a positive impact around your household, your community, and even the world. Where can you and your family share your gifts?	Through helping others, you can create cherished memories, find a sense of purpose, and build your life story. Why do you serve others?

Modern Times Call for Modern Methods

Have you or your family seen recent opportunities, possibly because of disasters like the pandemic or devastating forest fires in the western US, to jump in and offer help to the community? Let's take a closer look at the helping hands principle and the three essentials—connect with your *what*, your *where*, and your *why*—for applying the principle with your own family.

1. Connect with your what

The first important step in practicing the helping hands principle is identifying and sharing your talents and resources with those in need. Have you ever thought about what special gifts you or your family members might have? A special gift can be just about anything that is unique or creative about you. Even time and a willingness to help are gifts that can be shared with others.

I like the story of one boy who shared his time and passion to promote positive change. In the seventh grade, Craig Kielburger read about Iqbal Masih, a child slave who'd worked in a carpet factory in Pakistan. After learning that bonded labor was declared illegal by the Supreme Court of Pakistan, ten-year-old Iqbal escaped from the factory where he'd been forced to work and led a campaign against childhood slavery. Tragically, however, he was killed two years later.

Craig shared the story with his class, and many were moved to act. Along with eleven of his friends, Craig started a charity called Free the

Children. Without money or financial backing, they got right down to business by bringing awareness to the public and government officials about indentured children around the globe.

"Kids are looking to get involved. They're searching for it," Craig said.[1] He felt that something as important as making the world a better place, especially for children, would take everyone pitching in, not just grown-ups, and he was determined to do his part.

Remember centenarian Dr. Mildred Stilson? During our interview Mildred told me about her early life as a child living at an altitude of seven thousand feet in a remote little village nestled in the Himalayan mountains. When her parents moved there as missionaries in 1916, they were the only Caucasian residents. They had arrived at a chaotic time. The First World War was already raging in India, and the man who was supposed to meet them to tell them what to do and where to go had died unexpectedly when the ship he was on was torpedoed in the Mediterranean Sea.

Without his guidance, her parents first learned the language and then worked many years not fully knowing what they were doing in India. Mildred's dad had always been interested in science and providing basic medical care, beginning with bandaging his own pets' wounds. Once he was able to talk in their own language to the village schoolboys with whom he worked, they started coming to him with medical needs. He was the only one around who had any knowledge of what to do when someone had been hurt badly. Once more villagers realized that her dad could help take care of sick people, many sought him out. He once estimated that he devoted only half his time in India to his work as an ordained minister; he spent the other half at the dispensary tending to the sick.

"When my sister and I got to be about six, seven years old," Mildred told me, "he started inviting us to come help him." The girls rolled up their sleeves and made cotton balls and bandages to assist their dad in his care for the sick. This instilled in Mildred a desire to help others.

"I think the biggest thing it did to me as a child was make me realize how very, very fortunate I was. And it made me realize that what I really want to do is something that will help reach people wherever they

*If your gift is to
encourage others,
be encouraging.
If it is giving,
give generously.
. . . And if you
have a gift for
showing kindness
to others,
do it gladly.*

ROMANS 12:8, NLT

are on the earth, whether it's South America, India, Indonesia, wherever," she said. "They have a life that is so hard compared to the joy and privilege that I have, that I couldn't possibly think of just living the rest of my life doing only for myself."

Mildred went on to complete medical school and then returned to the mission field as a physician. Imagine if everyone—adults and children—shared their gifts, talents, time, and compassion with the world. Doing for others can positively change life for yourself, your family, your community, and even the world.

2. Connect with your where

The second element of the helping hands principle is identifying opportunities for getting involved and then taking initiative to do so. Your family can take action at three levels: your household, your local community, and the global community.

Home sweet home. One of the first places children can learn about leaning in and lending a helping hand is in and around the home. By taking part in chores, children begin to focus less on themselves and more on others. However, in today's society most housework is done by one or both parents (usually the mom) or even a professional housekeeper. Research conducted by Dr. Richard Rende, a developmental psychologist, found that though 82 percent of US adults had to do family household chores when they were young, only 28 percent have their own children help out with chores.[2] Other countries like Canada, China, and the UK are also experiencing a similar shift in decreasing help from children with chores.[3] Gone are the days when children were referred to as "Mommy's little helper." Many parents today don't see the need or the benefit of having children take part in chores. Often, they don't feel they have the time or the energy to supervise their children or to make sure they do their chores.

Inventory of Your Family's Talents and Resources

Take time as a family to discuss your particular talents and interests. You might be surprised by the wheels you set in motion. Keep in mind that you don't have to be an expert to help others; you just have to be willing to share your passions, talents, and time. This is especially true for children. Consider the list of talents below and take inventory of your family's strengths:

- Art (like drawing, painting, sculpting)
- Music (like singing or playing the piano or violin)
- Sports
- Math or other academics
- Animal care
- Gardening
- Cooking

- Friendship
- Babysitting
- Writing or storytelling
- Woodworking and/or repair skills
- Fundraising
- Specialty training or skills (like medicine, dentistry, architecture, photography)

One of the most important gifts you can share is the gift of time and having a willing spirit to help others—especially during times of adversity.

Kids' whining and complaining only increases the reluctance of many parents to expect them to help keep the household running:

"Do I really need to do it?"
"But she doesn't have to do it, so why do I?"
"I *can't!*"

As a result, moms and dads may decide it's just easier to take care of the housework themselves rather than tackle the chore of household chore negotiation itself. By excusing children from helping, we may finish the cleaning more quickly; however, our children will miss out on the hidden benefits that come from contributing to the household. In his book

Raising Can-Do Kids, psychologist Richard Rende says the tendency to assign kids fewer chores is troubling, given its importance to social and behavioral development.[4] The extra effort by parents is well worth it— even if it's a daily challenge.

After studying various indigenous communities in Mexico and Central America, psychology researchers from the University of California, Santa Cruz reported on a division of housework in these rural communities that was similar to what the centenarians experienced in their childhoods.[5] They observed children three or four years of age helping out alongside adults and older siblings. They coined the term "learning by observing and pitching in" to describe the young children who took the initiative to help after watching others around them. These kids were already collaborating with their families and communities in a range of complex activities, such as cooking, running errands, or tending to younger children. Their parents' goal was for the children to become responsible contributors to their family.

Working alongside family members was an important feature of the centenarians' upbringing as well. Tasks were focused on "family care" rather than "self-care." For example, when it was time to fold the laundry, one or more children were tasked with folding all the clothes, not just their own. During the pandemic, I began wondering how many parents reading this book had to do double duty when it came to household chores, given the stress and increased time families spent at home. It was definitely a great time for us to implement a "family care" approach.

Centenarian Mulan Tsai explained that her father died when she was only seven, so she had to help her mother and younger siblings with all the household chores. In addition, Mulan began sewing to help her mother provide for their family. Reynaldo Sanchez (Resiliency Capital member) also lost his dad early—in fact, he told me he never really knew him. "I used to get up very early to help around," he said. "My mother was older and by herself." One hundred years ago, epidemics and tragedies were more commonplace. When family members became severely ill or even died, everyone pitched in to make it through. Because young children were trained to help around the house, they were prepared when calamity struck.

In earlier times and even in developing countries today, toddlers learn to help out. In rural areas of Africa and Asia, it isn't at all unusual to see toddlers bringing sticks to the fire to help their mothers or grandmothers cook, hauling small pails of water from the river, or tying dolls on their backs to prepare them for carrying younger siblings when they're older.

While taking on such responsibilities is not as common in the West, it's wise to remember that even very young children can help. We often assume they aren't capable, but by giving them small tasks, we are planting the seed that tells them they can. In fact, they usually want to help—we just discourage them because more often than not their help leads to more work for us! But do give them a chance—the extra effort now will pay off as they grow older. Toddlers who practice mixing cake batter may be able to make pancakes for the family when they are six or seven. Preschoolers who learn to put their toys away before bed are likelier to develop a habit of picking up after themselves.

When my son was four, he could deadhead my rosebushes and trim back other plants with blunt-tip scissors. He even cut one of my loveliest bushes into the shape of a cartoon character—unfortunately, I had no prior knowledge of his detailed plan. By the time he went to kindergarten, he had some of the best scissor skills in his class.

One way to make household chores more fun for younger kids is to play music and tie it to the completion of the task. For example, clean one room in the time it takes to play a song or vacuum the house in just five songs. Mary Poppins—the nanny in Disney's musical film—understood the value of reframing a child's approach to household chores. "In every job that must be done, there is an element of fun. You find the fun and—snap!—the job's a game." As they tidy their nursery, Mary sings along with the children, "Just a spoonful of sugar helps the medicine go down in a most delightful way."[6] Why not put on some Mary Poppins and clean along with her delightful, energizing songs?

Older children who haven't been assigned many chores in the past may need time to get into the habit, but continue encouraging them and give them more complex tasks that are age appropriate. They may be able to help with mowing the lawn, cooking a meal, sewing worn clothing, washing the dishes, and even buying the groceries (supervised, of course).

To encourage older kids, let them know they can earn rewards such as that beloved computer time or a special activity. While working together, you might tell them about the chores you did at their age—and how they differ from today. You might also take a trip to a local heritage center or historical museum to get a taste of what chores were like back in the nineteenth century.

Not only does completing chores help build strong family connections, it also provides physical activity. The centenarians stayed active and strong in part through household chores. Moving, bending, stretching, and lifting are all part of keeping a home and yard in order—and are just what you need to keep your body limber.

According to the Center for Parenting Education, another important benefit to chores is that they teach life skills, like doing laundry or making dinner.[7] Children who don't learn these simple tasks grow up to be dependent on others to do them for them. Everyone—males and females—should know how to cook their own meals, clean their own homes, and wash their own laundry. Of course, teaching these tasks can be time-consuming—for both you and your children. I was once concerned that if my kids helped with chores, it would take away from the time they needed for homework and other activities. But once I made clear that helping out at home was expected, they got on board (despite the moans and groans). I quickly discovered that many chores can be done in twenty minutes or less. More importantly, children who learn to complete tasks at an early age are much more likely to be focused and productive later in life.

Before assigning chores to family members, get their input. Also, ask yourself if anyone is ready to learn a particular life skill (like cooking, buying groceries, doing the laundry, or mowing the lawn). Don't expect them to do chores that are beyond their cognitive or developmental abilities, but do give them a chance to be challenged. If they screw up—and they will—don't scold them; encourage them. Point out what they did right, praise them, and let them know they are going to get even better the more they do it. And avoid gender stereotyping—girls need to learn to mow the lawn and repair things, and boys need to learn how to fix a meal and do their own dishes.

If you or your spouse currently do most of the work in your house and yard, you may need a mindset change just as much as your kids do. Let go of the standard of perfection, especially with toddlers, knowing that the experience of helping others is more important than a flawless outcome.

You might also look for ways to give and get support from other households. Again, the centenarians show us the way. As you may recall from chapter 6, Belen Lopez worked alongside her family, cousins, and neighbors as they came together at the river to wash their clothes and fetch water for household use. They all pitched in to help one another. During her childhood, centenarian Salma Mohr and her family received loving support from a neighbor. When the work overwhelmed Salma's mom, the children maintained the home. "Our neighbors next door were the loveliest people on earth," Salma told me. "On one occasion my mother had a mental breakdown and Mrs. Brown said, 'Now, you're going to come over to my house. I'll take care of you.' So this lady took my mother into her home and nursed her back to health."

Banding together with neighbors or friends is still a good practice today. Could you and another family take turns preparing meals or share grocery shopping duties? Depending on your skills and talents, maybe your friends would take care of your yard in exchange for your help with childcare. Sharing responsibility in this way can minimize the burden on both of you. Connecting with others will also help you strengthen your relationships and grow your village, which is especially important when hard times hit. When you help others, you help yourself, too.

> *Everyone helped his neighbor, and said to his brother, "Be of good courage!"*
>
> ISAIAH 41:6, NKJV

Tips for Getting Children Involved Helping around the House

- Use the natural curious and helpful nature of younger children to get them in the habit of helping out. Start them with just one responsibility at first, such as setting out the napkins or salt and pepper shakers, and then gradually increase their responsibilities. They can help you with all kinds of kitchen duties, from washing fruits and vegetables to setting and clearing the table or stirring ingredients in a mixing bowl. They can help with the dishes by placing them in the dishwasher or on the drying rack, folding the family laundry, sweeping the floor, or dusting.

- As children grow, allow them greater autonomy with chores and give them a variety of challenging tasks, like vacuuming, washing the laundry, putting the groceries away, and mowing the lawn (when age appropriate or with an old-fashioned push mower). You can even have them help with the grocery shopping by giving them your list and teaching them how to choose the best product for the best price.

- Pets are a great way to teach children responsibility and empathy. They can walk the dog, feed the hamsters, and when they're older, clean and change the litter box.

Your local community. Next look outside your home and consider how you might help others in your community. A way to start is by talking with your children about what it means to volunteer and help those in need. When your area faces a community-wide disaster—such as devastation from tornadoes, hurricanes, pandemics, or other disasters—be ready to offer a helping hand.

Centenarian Dr. Robert Bolton told me, "One of the most exciting times in my memory came when the hay harvest was on at the academy [school]. A beautiful hayfield along the Battle River had been obtained from which to cut acres of rich grass for the livestock. The mowing, raking, and stacking of the hay would require several days." His dad supervised the operation, and Robert and other willing students helped. Not only did the hay feed the livestock, it generated critical income to keep the school running.

No matter how big or small, children still do amazing things to help others! As Anita Johnson-Mackey (105-year-old Resiliency Capital member) said, "Ask yourself, *What's the problem? What needs to be done? What can I do about it? When can I get started?*" She might have had Roman McConn of Augusta, Georgia, in mind. He was just four when he asked for donations to a local animal shelter instead of birthday presents. His family had just adopted a dog from a shelter, and his mother had become a committed volunteer there. Soon they wanted to do even more. What started as a small donation to help out led to the founding of the charity organization Project Freedom Ride, which transports dogs from animal shelters with high kill rates to forever homes across the nation.[8] In addition, Roman began featuring dogs that needed new homes in brief videos, many of which went viral. In recognition of his good work, the American Society for the Prevention of Cruelty to Animals (ASPCA) named him 2018 Kid of the Year. He and Project Freedom Ride have now saved more than 1,800 dogs.

Your global community. Your family may also decide to lend a helping hand at the global level. Dr. Ellsworth Wareham and his wife have a fond memory of traveling to Mexico after learning of a very sick little girl who needed heart surgery. Her family did not have the resources for or even access to the medical care she needed, but Dr. Wareham was able to go and perform life-saving surgery. Today child sponsorship programs like World Vision and Compassion International enable families in first-world countries to provide monthly financial support so kids around the globe can get access to education, medical care, and other forms of support in their own communities. Sponsoring families receive letters from and can write to the child they support.

You might be surprised with the ideas your kids come up with as well. While sitting in his classroom, six-year-old Ryan Hreljac learned that millions of people around the world don't have safe water to drink. He went home and begged his parents to help. They offered to let Ryan raise money doing chores around the house. In a couple of months, he had earned $70 to build a well in Uganda, only to find out a well would cost over $2,000. Rather than giving up, Ryan began speaking to schools and service clubs to garner support. Wanting to do even more, in 2001 he founded Ryan's Well Foundation, which has brought drinking water to over one million people in seventeen countries.[9]

Where to Find Volunteer Opportunities for Your Family

Many places in your community may offer your family the opportunity to start lending a helping hand. Check their websites for a list of volunteer positions or the name of the volunteer coordinator.

1. **Local museums** (great for older children and teens)
2. **Churches** (great for all ages)
3. **Public libraries** (great for older children)
4. **Animal shelters or rescue organizations** (great for older children)
5. **International projects with volunteer organizations** (great for all ages). Some helpful websites to check out are VolunteerMatch (VolunteerMatch .org), All for Good (AllforGood.org), and Youth Service America (YSA.org, which also offers toolkits for starting a volunteer initiative).
6. **Friends and family** (great for all ages). Ask your family or friends if they need a hand with anything. Or simply invite them over for a simple dinner you and your family prepare.
7. **Neighbors** (great for all ages). A good way to meet your neighbors, especially those who are elderly, is by offering your help. Even a simple drawing by a child and a note of encouragement left on a doorstep can lift the spirits of a lonely senior.
8. **Local nursing homes** (great for all ages). You can help with a wide range of activities, such as caroling at Christmas, playing the piano, or dropping off children's artwork.
9. **Your own family's initiative** (great for all ages). Is your family passionate about a specific cause? Perhaps you'd like to clean the debris along a local beach or bike path. Why not call a family meeting and brainstorm ways you could help out? Then pick the top one or two strategies and put them into action.

Before volunteering with your kids, be sure to ask questions so you have a good idea of what to expect. Keep in mind that volunteering doesn't mean a lengthy commitment to a particular place or person. Volunteering shouldn't be overwhelming and all-consuming; if it is, you will lose energy and incentive. Be realistic with your schedule and what will work for you. Don't feel you have to change the world. The key is to find what feels right and inspires your family to take action and make an impact.

3. *Connect with your* why

The third element of the helping hands principle is identifying your family's reason and motivation for leaning in and lending a helping hand. Helping around the house and volunteering in communities should come from an internal desire to do good. God calls us to help and encourage one another. When we engage in acts of kindness, we benefit along with those we help. When it comes to assisting others, once you've connected with your *why*, you'll be more motivated to succeed at this resiliency principle.

Find your purpose. One great reason for lending a helping hand is to gain a new sense of purpose. Want to change things up in your family in a positive way? Then volunteer. Want to stop focusing on your own worries and shift your focus to others in need? Then volunteer. Want to develop cherished family memories by doing something meaningful together? Then volunteer.

Look to donate your time to something you and your family are passionate about. The seed you plant and nurture in your children for helping others will take root and grow. Don't be surprised if this seed begins bearing fruit at a young age. It may even give your child a new sense of purpose and help direct them toward their life's calling.

When the COVID-19 pandemic hit, I began sharing each evening with my family about the hardships other families were facing. I knew firsthand because I was working with a local county health department fighting back against the rising numbers. With the second wave descending upon the nation, I couldn't help but recognize the exponential growth in positive cases, the rising number of people hospitalized, and worst of all, the increase in death of loved ones. I even received an email from a grandfather in Brazil begging for help as they faced the pandemic ravaging his country. At the dinner table one evening, my family asked what they could do to help. While discussing the hardships, my daughter suggested we pray for the families. We paused for a minute and realized she was onto something. Right then and there we decided each evening before bed, we would pray specifically for families to protect them from getting COVID-19 and for those that already have it, that they would experience immediate healing. Not many may have known that we were praying—but we felt called to rally as a family and to stand in the gap to help support those in need. So now we pray for resiliency and healing from the pandemic for families around the world, and we encourage all moms (and dads, grandparents, and other relatives too!) to join in praying with us!

At the intersection where your gifts, talents, and abilities meet a human need; therein you will discover your purpose.

ARISTOTLE

One woman who began her life with nothing became world-renowned for helping the poor. This desire to help others began as a seed planted by her family during her childhood. Agnes Gonxha Bojaxhiu was born on August 26, 1910, in Skopje, Macedonia, the youngest of three children. Throughout her childhood, she was influenced by her family to take part in the church and to care about helping those in need. When she was only eight, however, her father died unexpectedly. Her mother, who often took food and clothing to the destitute and sick, became a powerful and positive influence on Agnes. She knew by age twelve that she wanted to help the poor. At eighteen, Agnes left her family and became a missionary in India.[10] She believed that works of love are works of peace.[11] For her selfless and tremendous efforts, she was awarded the Nobel Peace Prize in 1979. We know her better by the name Mother Teresa.

Not everyone who gives as selflessly as Mother Teresa becomes famous, of course. Yet they reap many other benefits. "When you assist people," Marjorie Joseph told me, "you feel good yourself that you are making other people feel good." Marjorie—or "Sis," as she is known by her family and friends—speaks from personal experience. And Marjorie has had so much experience; at ninety-one, she's almost a Resiliency Capital centenarian. Born in Montserrat, a Caribbean island, Marjorie was one of nine children. She grew up helping her parents and her grandparents with their farm duties—from growing sweet potatoes, plantains, rice, and peas to tending to the goats, chickens, and cattle. As a teenager, Marjorie knew she wanted to help others, so she enrolled in the local nursing school. After graduation, she became one of the first public health nurses in her region. Her work was hard, strenuous, and gratifying—she helped restore many starving infants and children to full health.[12]

Marjorie especially enjoyed delivering what folks in the community knew as KLIM. "Help is on the way," Marjorie would often tell a resident in passing. "A KLIM shipment is due anytime." (Marjorie's daughter told me that KLIM was just *MILK* spelled backward. The recipients often opened the boxes of milk upside down, so that's the way the word looked to them.)

Though hers isn't a household name, Marjorie was honored by the queen of England herself when the governor of Montserrat presented the honor of Member of the British Empire (MBE) and the British Empire Medal to Marjorie on Elizabeth II's behalf. Marjorie has continued to help and support her local church even into her nineties. What a wonderful experience for Marjorie and for all those families she has helped.

Opportunity knocks. The seeds for helping others were planted in the childhoods of Mother Teresa, Marjorie Joseph, and each of the centenarians I interviewed, and those seeds were nurtured throughout their lives. A daughter of a friend of mine often volunteered throughout her middle and high school years. She did everything from "seal sitting"— watching over baby seals to protect them from prying humans who might scare away the mama seal—to volunteering as a state representative for Special

The unselfish effort to bring cheer to others will be the beginning of a happier life for ourselves.

HELEN KELLER

Olympics. As a result, she received a full scholarship to a prominent college in the Northwest. That isn't unusual. Recently I had a meeting with a higher-up who is connected to the board of admissions for Loma Linda University Medical School. She said they look for applicants with a clear mission who have been actively making a difference in others' lives. Volunteering is like knocking on a hidden door; you never know what opportunities might present themselves as a result.

> *Life's most persistent and urgent question is, "What are you doing for others?"*
>
> DR. MARTIN LUTHER KING JR.

Going through this resiliency journey has changed my own perspective on my other volunteering activities. Before developing this program, I was stuck in the monotony of checking boxes and getting things done. Now I look to see how I truly can be a greater positive force for joy, and doing so often requires only a small change in my approach. I'm now bringing the KLIM!

IN A PINCH, IT'S A CINCH: HELPING HANDS PRACTICE TIPS

IDEAS FOR HELPING AROUND THE HOUSE:

- **Meal prep.** Have your children pitch in and help you with the dinnertime meal. Toddlers can help wash fruits and vegetables, while older children can cut up items and assist with directing the younger children.
- **Laundry time!** Everyone can pitch in and help with the family laundry. Older children can collect clothes and towels from around the house, place them in the washing machine, add detergent, and turn it on. Younger children can help older ones with the folding. Any of your clothes need mending? If so, encourage older children to sew up the hole—and that goes for boys, too! If a sock has a hole, place an ordinary light bulb—one you can hold in your hand—inside to stretch out the sock, making it easier to mend.
- **Scrub a dub.** Washing the car is especially fun in the summer for children of all ages. Kids can also help pick up items inside the car and

clean up any food debris they might have dropped. Who knows—picking up after themselves a few times may make them a little tidier in the future!

- **Yard duties.** Children of all ages can help with maintaining the yard. Older children can help with mowing and weeding. Younger children can help by using safety scissors to cut back plants, raking leaves, or picking up sticks.
- **Pet care.** If you have pets like guinea pigs, rabbits, or hamsters that have cages, or a cat with a litter box, have older children clean those while younger children help watch the critter or gather cleaning supplies. Enlist your children in feeding their pets to teach them the importance of responsibility and caring for others.

IDEAS FOR HELPING LOCAL AND GLOBAL COMMUNITIES:

- **Trash cleanup.** When your family takes a walk around the neighborhood, bring along a small bag to pick up any debris that needs to be thrown away or recycled.
- **Suppertime.** Invite a family over for dinner. Better yet, make it a standing invitation! Once each week or month, have them over to your home to share your meal.
- **Neighborly love.** Do elderly neighbors need help around their home? Perhaps you could pull weeds in their yard, paint their fence, help bring out their trash cans, or deliver their groceries.
- **Coins for a cause.** Raise funds and donate them for a special charity. Children are great at coming up with ideas and implementing them. Start a lemonade stand, collect soda cans, mow yards, sell arts and crafts, or create an "-athon" event (like a walkathon, skipathon, danceathon, or skateathon) or a GoFundMe page (gofundme.com) to raise money for a good cause or for someone in need. Spread the word to family, friends, and neighbors; post notices on local bulletin boards, newspapers, radio stations, or online videos.
- **International support.** Join a group doing volunteer work around the globe. Your entire worldview might change after this trip of a

lifetime! Check with your school or church to see if they are sponsoring any international trips. Or research organizations that organize international mission trips.[13]

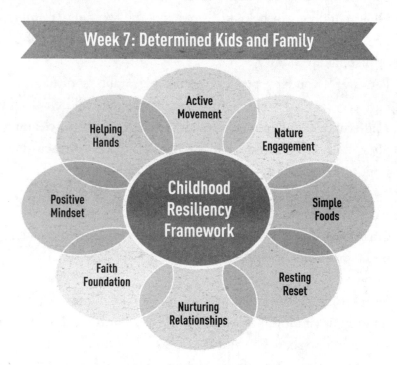

Eighth Resiliency Principle—**Helping Hands**

Want to learn from the centenarians so your family can enjoy improved resilience and whole health? Then encourage your family to take the initiative to pitch in and help at home and in the wider community.

GET YOUR FAMILY'S TRIPLE BOOST

Putting the helping hands principle into practice can help you and your family kick into high gear by:

Promoting happiness: Lending a helping hand and volunteering can be just plain fun for you and your family. Volunteering can also create and strengthen bonds between family and friends as you work together. You might even make new friends along the way. Scientific studies show that not only does volunteering reduce the risk of depression, it improves overall self-esteem.[14] In a study of toddlers, researchers discovered that the act of giving a treat to another child, rather than receiving it, was associated with increased happiness in the giver.[15] The bottom line: Encourage your family to share their time, talents, and gifts, and enjoy the positivity and happiness that follow.

Increasing resilience: Not only does volunteering promote happiness, it also decreases stress and boosts the immune system. A clinical trial of high school students—some assigned to a weekly volunteering assignment and others put on a waiting list—revealed a significant boost in immune cells and reduction in the stress-related hormone cortisol in those who volunteered.[16] Research conducted by the Harvard School of Public Health indicates that "volunteers spent 38 percent fewer nights in the hospital" than non-volunteers.[17] Lending a helping hand also reduces the risk of chronic diseases—like dementia or heart disease—and slows down the aging process.[18] Those who volunteer to help clean up and protect our environment not only reap benefits themselves, but they also promote resilience for our entire planet.

Enhancing performance: A great side benefit of volunteering is the exposure to new experiences, new ideas, and new ways of thinking. Volunteering is also a great way to increase creativity since it often requires coming up with solutions in the absence of many financial or other resources. As we've seen, high school and college students who volunteer learn important life skills and have an advantage when applying to college or graduate school.

CONQUERING RESISTANCE

As you begin encouraging your family to work on lending a helping hand, you may encounter a few challenges. Here are some helpful ideas to keep in mind for overcoming resistance:

No time to volunteer. Researchers have found that those who give away their time actually end up feeling as if they have more time than those who don't help others.[19] So pitch in and lend a hand! Don't wait for the right conditions, or you might never get started.

No place to go. Practicing the helping hands principle doesn't have to mean leaving your community. All you need is a different perspective. Why not invite over neighbors, family, or friends—especially those going through a hard time—to enjoy a movie or game night? Or your family could raise funds for a cause you're interested in, and donate the money.

No luck on first try. If you decide a volunteer assignment wasn't a great fit, try another. Be sure to look for environments or events your family is interested in. If you enjoy spending time in nature, find a way to volunteer in the outdoors. If your family enjoys singing or playing instruments, incorporate your musical talents in your outreach (like performing at a nursing home).

Nothing to offer. Don't assume you don't have needed skills or talents. Take the initiative to offer someone a helping hand or an encouraging word. Create your own Meetup group (Meetup.com) to meet other families in your community who want to pool their talents and help each other or another local group. Or post on Nextdoor.com, a website geared to keep members of local communities informed and connected.

OVERLAP OF THE PRINCIPLES

Whether helping in and around your friends' homes, cooking meals, or driving friends to church, the helping hands principle easily dovetails with other resiliency principles. If you want to grow your village, lending a helping hand is a great way to increase and strengthen your connections. It's even a way to model these resiliency principles to other people.

Health benefits can be magnified when the resiliency principles overlap, which can be especially beneficial when a pandemic strikes. One study found that people who volunteered and got an adequate amount of sleep (six or more hours) reduced the systemic inflammation in their bodies.[20] Clearly, that is an immediate benefit of stress reduction for the whole body.

HOMEWORK TIME

It's time to roll up your sleeves and dive right in with the helping hands principle. Week 7 builds on the foundation set in the previous weeks.

1. **Set up your Determined goals for helping hands.** Add to or adapt your previous week's goals to include the helping hands principle. Use the following goals or feel free to create new ones:

NEW BASE GOAL

- **Helping hands principle:** My family and I will spend one hour during the week or weekend pitching in at the same time on household tasks.

  Overlapping principles include helping hands and nurturing relationships as well as nature engagement if chores extend to the yard.

- **Optional new goal 1:** My family and I will help one other person or family to experience at least one of the resiliency principles this week. We will volunteer to help watch the children of a family friend so that grown-ups can have some free time. While watching the children, we can take them outside to play in the backyard and get some sunshine.

- **Optional new goal 2:** My family and I will identify and sign up for one international volunteer trip the whole family can take part in.

EXISTING BASE GOALS

- Continue or adapt the goals you have set for the active movement, nature engagement, simple foods, resting reset, nurturing relationships, faith foundation, and positive mindset principles.

2. **Implement and track your success.** Use the Weekly Evaluation guide to help you track your progress. Spend a few minutes each night recording the ways you and your family helped others. Did you do something special for someone else? Did any of your family pitch in and help with household chores? Were you able to connect with and support anyone in your community? At the end of the week, review what you achieved throughout the week. Were you able to achieve the weekly goal you set for yourself?

———— Great Job! ————

Congratulations on completing the seventh week of the program! Feel free to repeat if needed. In the final chapter, we'll look at how to thrive as you sustain all of the resiliency practices and even build your family's legacy.

CHAPTER 10

WEEK 8:
BUILDING A LEGACY OF HEALTH
(AND HAPPINESS!)

If you are going to live, leave a legacy.
Make a mark on the world that can't be erased.

MAYA ANGELOU

THE WINTER'S DAY WHEN I SAT on our patio watching Julia dig in the dirt seems so long ago—as does my family's harried, junk-food-fueled life. It hasn't always been easy, and we still have a lot of work to do. The day before I started on this chapter, for example, my husband pulled a coupon for a fast-food burger out of his wallet, waving it around like it was a Willy Wonka Golden Ticket.

"Go ahead if you really need to," I told him, but now my family's "need to" is a rare occasion.

After all, my family and I have benefited tremendously from this journey. We are more aware of the impact our daily choices have on our health, resilience, and ability to thrive in the face of adversity. My children no longer get terribly upset over the changes we make in pursuit of resilience or declare me "chopped" if I encourage them to try a new food.

I measure my family's progress in several ways: Cholesterol is down, weight is down, headaches are fewer, happiness is up (though sibling rivalry is still a common theme), communication is better, my children's initiative is slightly up, our pace of life is slowing, and our contentment is growing.

The other day, I went to visit centenarian Salma Mohr. After I updated her on my family, she told me, "You're getting it! Keep going!" As a retired teacher, she couldn't help but assign me a grade, which I'm happy to report was an A. Then she asked, "Are you using the knitted cloth I gave you to clean your kitchen?" Almost one hundred years ago, when her siblings did housekeeping to provide for their family and put Salma through college, they thought she might never learn to clean well. Now she is teaching and inspiring so many, not only to clean our kitchens but to clean up our lives.

"Thank you so much, Salma, for teaching me a better way!" I whispered to her as Julia and I gave her an affectionate hug before packing up to leave.

And I am grateful for the many centenarians who shared their wisdom, which I've been able to put into practice with my own family. This focus on resiliency for health came at an opportune time—it helped our family become more resilient just before the world was throttled by COVID-19. We're better prepared for whatever might come next as well.

Setbacks have occurred—like the time my son crushed his nose during a school basketball game. In the middle of that crisis, our resiliency principles were flung aside while fast food flew in. (There's a reason the Golden Arches are located near hospitals.) Challenges will occur. Life happens. But unexpected difficulties can make you stronger and help you rely on some of your resiliency principles—such as nurturing relationships and faith foundation—even more.

KEEP GOING!

Congratulations on completing the eight-week Resiliency Program. By now you should be well on your way to practicing the eight resiliency principles:

Active (*active movement* and *nature engagement*). Remember that these two principles are the keystone habits for a more resilient life. By getting outdoors and moving each day, you set the foundation for incorporating the other principles.

Balanced (*simple foods* and *resting reset*). Consume a more plant-based diet and prioritize sleep and rest to regularly allow your body time to recover.

Connected (*nurturing relationships* and *faith foundation*). Spend time with friends, family, and God. We weren't meant to go through life alone, so build your strength and resiliency through your relationships.

Determined (*positive mindset* and *helping hands*). When you think, relate, and reach out to others in constructive ways, you help yourself and others.

By practicing each of these principles, your family will grow more resilient and offset the damage that the stresses of daily life can cause. Use the Resiliency Program Maintenance Scorecard (appendix C) as a tool to help you maintain your new habits.

When you invest time and energy in practicing these resiliency principles, you give yourself and your family a gift, one with both immediate and long-lasting benefits. In addition to better health, you are likely to see an increase in their happiness and their ability to perform at all their endeavors, including school, work, sports, music, and much more. And some of these practices will improve the resilience of those around you and the planet as a whole.

Remember, too, that the more you practice these principles in tandem, the greater the boost to your immune system and your whole health because they have a synergistic impact on one another. Finding ways that the principles overlap will also make you more likely to continue practicing them.

In fact, at this point in your journey, that may be the biggest question you are pondering: *How in the world am I and my family going to maintain these resiliency principles?* I believe the answer lies in four steps: Stay connected to your *why*, defeat three major challenges, teach and encourage others, and build a lasting legacy by promoting healthy resilience for future generations.

1. STAY CONNECTED TO YOUR *WHY*

One of the most important ways to keep the momentum going is by connecting with your *why*. Almost anything is possible if you have a motivation that maintains your focus and your passion—especially when challenges arise. Picture what success looks like for you and your family, and speak your positive mindset motto. Don't get discouraged and give up when the inevitable setbacks occur. As you continue pressing on with your *why* in mind, you'll be amazed at how much stronger and more resilient you become.

Tools to Remind You of Your Motivation

- **Vision board.** Get a small poster board and cover it with pictures and quotes to keep you going. Place your vision board in a spot you will see daily.
- **Daily motto.** Look in the mirror each morning or night and recite your daily motto for living a healthy, whole, and resilient lifestyle.
- **Green ribbon.** Remember to wear a green ribbon or string to remind yourself of your motivation for healthier living.
- **Calendar.** Use your calendar to help you set goals and track your progress.
- **Prayerful mindset.** Spend time each day praying for guidance, strength, and perseverance.
- **Encouraging relationships.** Connect often with friends and family who can share in your resiliency journey and encourage you onward—and vice versa.

2. DEFEAT THREE MAJOR CHALLENGES

Be attuned to the major threats to practicing the resiliency principles long-term and develop strategies to overcome them. The three ever-present obstacles that may deter us from our journey are time constraints, the allure of modern society, and ourselves. Let's take a closer look at each, along with some ideas for overcoming them.

Time constraints

We each have only twenty-four hours in the day, though we often wish we had an extra hour or two to accomplish everything we need to get done. It may seem as if we are running late to everything and that everyday life is like flying on an airline that overbooks every flight. Learning to live within the twenty-four-hour time limit we all have is possible, but it takes intention.

> *Success is the sum of small efforts, repeated day-in and day-out.*
>
> ROBERT COLLIER

First, don't overschedule your days. Remember that whenever you say yes to something, you are inherently saying no to something else. Take a look at your calendar and determine your nonnegotiables (like work hours, transporting kids to and from school, church, and sleep), which are set items on your calendar. Your negotiable time is the remaining time on your calendar; use these hours to build your family's resiliency.

Prioritize and set aside time for your resiliency journey. Before making another commitment to your schedule, ask, Is it a nonnegotiable? Is it necessary that day? Is it promoting my or my family's resilience? You might also leave some white space on your calendar, which you can use to promote your family's resiliency. Many of my cherished family memories are of spontaneous activities like an impromptu outdoor picnic on our own front lawn that included story time and a game of "soccer" (using a random ball, random rules, and a couple of goalposts).

The allure of modern society

A second challenge to our resiliency journey may be the desire for (or pressure from others to get) the latest, greatest technology, house, car, or experience. Acquiring any of these typically brings multiple costs, from having to work more to cover the expense to devoting more free time to use or maintain the item.

Before moving ahead with any major purchase or technology upgrade, remind yourself that you now make decisions for the good of your family's health and resiliency. You don't need the most expensive vacation, the latest model of car, the biggest house, or the best clothes. These items are ultimately distractions that can pull you away from this wholeness journey. Learn to appreciate a more simplified life.

Ourselves

We are often our own worst enemy. For one thing, we each have an inner critic that fights for control of our thoughts and outlook. Sometimes this inner critic speaks more harshly to us than we would ever speak to a good friend who made a mistake. The goal is to tame the inner critic and learn to speak kindly to ourselves when we slip up.

We also tend to seek immediate results or magnificent changes overnight. The inner critic might tell us, *See, things aren't working quickly enough. I told you this wouldn't work.* We need to tune out our inner critics so we don't become discouraged and give up. We often aim for perfection, assuming anything less is unacceptable or a reason to give up trying. (We moms who want to give our families the very best are especially vulnerable to this.)

Sometimes even well-meaning friends and family members may fuel that inner negative critic as you become more focused on spending time in nature than on spending time "being productive." Perhaps an observer will say, "I don't have time to take a walk with my family every night," implying, *Don't you have better ways to spend your time?* They might not even say it aloud but through their body language—rolling their eyes or shaking their head when you mention one of your resiliency exercises. You could either invite them to join you or ignore the comment and quietly recite your personal motto (like "I am healthy and whole and striving for resilience").

Keep in mind that you are forming new habits, and just like any new skill, these things will take time, patience, and practice to develop. Look to relationships and systems that will protect you from yourself. What people in your life encourage you? Having an accountability partner—perhaps a friend or your spouse—may be helpful. What systems or spiritual practices do you have in place to help support your desire to change? You can also pray for wisdom and perseverance. Having supportive connections in place is important to be successful at whatever you set your mind to accomplish.

> *You're braver than you believe, and stronger than you seem, and smarter than you think.*
>
> CHRISTOPHER ROBIN TO WINNIE-THE-POOH

3. TEACH AND ENCOURAGE OTHERS

An excellent way to sustain your practice of the resiliency principles is to teach them to others. When you do, you can't help but have them become more embedded in your own life. Don't worry if you don't feel you are trained or have completely mastered each of the principles; just jump in and share.

While at the home of a close friend who had invited several families to come over and hang out, I began talking about the Resiliency Program with a mom I didn't know very well. She became animated as we began discussing places where her family could volunteer. Her kids were young— eight and five—and she wanted to plant the seed for helping others. I had thought because she and her husband are both specialty-trained physicians, they would already know this information inside and out. But that was just my own misconception. The reality was that this mom was excited to find safe ways to get her children involved in helping others. I was happy to search for new opportunities to share with her. Something similar happens whenever I talk with people about how to begin practicing a specific resiliency principle.

In the end, find your passion among the resiliency principles (are you an excellent cook or experienced hiker?) and share it with others. Your enthusiasm will be contagious. You might even discover better ways to

While we teach,
we learn.

ROMAN PHILOSOPHER
SENECA

accomplish the resiliency principles. Studies show that when you teach something to others, you grasp it better yourself. This is often referred to as the protégé effect.[1] So go on—empower yourself through empowering others. You just might grow your own village too.

Going hand in hand with teaching is encouraging others, not only through supportive words but sometimes more powerfully by sharing your story with others. Explaining your own journey promotes connection and healing. If I've learned one thing from the centenarians, it is the importance of connecting with one another through compassion and love as we share our stories and life experiences. Listening—really listening—while others share their stories is a powerful way to connect.

In the beginning of this book, I shared my personal story and struggle with resiliency. I work in a field—public health—that expects its practitioners to have it all together when it comes to health. I know I'm far from perfect; like many others, I often struggle to maintain healthy practices. But each day I am thankful for the opportunity to continue building resiliency in my own family and encourage other families as well. Some days I do better than others, but I'm in it for the long haul.

To love ourselves
and support
each other in
the process of
becoming real
is perhaps the
greatest single act
of daring greatly.

BRENÉ BROWN

Leave your inherent pursuit of perfectionism at the door and step inside and connect. Author and researcher Brené Brown has spent years studying courage, vulnerability, shame, and empathy. In her book *Daring Greatly*, she describes how the courage to be vulnerable can transform the way we live and is the starting point for love, empathy, and belonging. From a resiliency and public health perspective, along with my perspective as a parent, I believe we need to create a new social norm that promotes healing through sharing our stories. Our nation and our world need this desperately.

4. BUILD A LASTING LEGACY

A final reason to keep practicing these principles is the desire to build your family's legacy. Use your resources and your ingenuity wisely to come up with strategies that work for you. Be nimble and adaptable. Fortify yourself for future setbacks by always keeping your eyes on the goal. As a parent, you are in the seed-planting business, laying the groundwork for health, happiness, and even higher performance.

With the thousands of choices you make each day, you are creating your own legacy. You impact not just yourself and your family by your decisions; you also touch those around you and even the wider world. Connecting and sharing your stories with others may create a synergistic resiliency movement. Just as a tiny snowflake alone isn't much, when enough snowflakes gather together, they have the strength to move the mountainside. Bring as many moms and dads as you can along with you. Big things often have small beginnings.

No matter what your family history may be, the steps you take can bring you closer to a legacy of health and wholeness. This is the bigger story that you are creating, connecting with a previous generation to discover their resiliency secrets and carrying the lessons forward in your generation and those to come.

> *The best legacy we leave is not for our children but in our children.*
>
> DEBORAH ROBERTS

GET READY, GET SET . . . KEEP GOING!

As you come to the end of this book, take a moment to evaluate your progress. Retake the Resiliency Survey you took at the start of this book to identify your strengths and opportunities for improvement. Because some principles will be easier than others to maintain during certain seasons, use the Resiliency Survey from time to time as your guide to help your family gain resiliency. After identifying which principle(s) could use more work, reread the chapter devoted to it and look for ways to better incorporate that principle.

Though I call this an eight-week program, it is really a launching pad for a continuous journey to resiliency and wholeness. Now that you have started the work and invested in your family, continue to care for your initial investment. When you don't see immediate results, remind yourself that you are in the seed-planting and caring business. Those resiliency seeds may take time to mature and sprout. Sometimes the sweetest fruit doesn't look like much on the outside and may take the longest to mature. Carry on the work, my resilient friend. Have faith as you wait for the harvest to come.

ACKNOWLEDGMENTS

WRITING A BOOK IS SO MUCH HARDER than I ever imagined, and it wouldn't have been possible without many kind and helpful people, especially my loving family. I would like to express my deepest gratitude to my husband, Joe, for encouraging and supporting me over this long book journey. I am grateful for the countless sacrifices he made, especially for all he did around the house to keep the moving parts moving so I would have time to write. I'm so grateful for his belief in me. I am also thankful to my children, Jayden, Joelle, and Julia, for being my champions and cheering me on.

I would like to thank my parents for their unconditional love and for encouraging me to be uplifting to others wherever I go. I am grateful to my mother-in-law and father-in-law for helping me with the centenarian interviews, especially with Auntie Mulan Tsai, who is now an amazing 107 years in age, and for expressing interest in and excitement about my manuscript.

I'd like to send an enormous thank-you to all my mom friends, especially Yvette Lee, for all her help, excellent ideas, time spent reading my manuscript, spot-on advice, and amazing friendship.

Deep gratitude goes to my friend Molly Dougherty for always encouraging me and for the countless conversations as we pored over my early chapters. I'm also grateful to Krystal Gheen for her support and for the recipes she shared that are included in this book. I'd also like to thank my colleagues and friends across the Loma Linda University Health (LLUH) campus for their words of encouragement and advice.

I would like to express my sincere appreciation to my good friend Johanny Valladares and her family for assisting with the centenarian research. Additionally, Johanny helped document the centenarian research by taking beautiful pictures of those I interviewed. She took the photo that appears on the back cover as well. I am also grateful to Alicia Torres, Marco Pasco-Rubio, Celia Chen, and the students who volunteered to help me with the interviews and so much more.

I have deepest appreciation for Lisa Tener, the best book coach ever! Thank you for truly helping me bring my book to life. I'm also grateful for Joshua Edwards and Janice Harper, who assisted me with my book ideas and writing efforts.

I am extremely grateful for Linda Konner, my highly talented agent, who could see the potential in this book even when I didn't see it myself. Thank you for connecting me with an outstanding and highly supportive publishing house!

If acknowledgments were given as hugs, this would be a huge one for the team at Tyndale House Publishers. I would like to thank the Tyndale team for all their support, but especially Jan Long Harris and Kim Miller!

My special thanks go to the centenarians and their families who graciously shared their time and wisdom cheering me on. We need your advice now more than ever! I'm also grateful to the younger parents who took time to talk and share ideas with me.

Finally, and most importantly, I thank my heavenly Father for answering my prayers and sending me on the journey of a lifetime.

QUESTIONS FOR DISCUSSION GROUPS

1. What made you decide to read this book?

2. What do you think of the book's title? How does it relate to the book's contents? What other title might you give to the book?

3. In what ways did the book change your approach to the ways you support your family?

4. What feelings did this book evoke in you?

5. What are some of the stressors facing families today? Which of these stressors do you think are the most common or the most challenging and why?

6. In what way does stress affect the body? And are there any particular stressors that are especially worrisome to you?

7. Which of the resiliency principles resonate most with you and why? What other creative strategies have you considered for practicing any of the principles?

8. Which of the principles do you think might be the most difficult to practice consistently? Why? Do you have any special strategies for overcoming these challenges?

9. What do you think is meant by the idea that, when it comes to following the Resiliency Program, the ease is in the overlap and the power is in the synergy (see page 62)?

10. Have you been able to apply any of the principles in an overlapping manner? Which ones and how?

11. How might you encourage extended family or friends to put these principles into practice?

12. If you had the chance to ask the author one question, what would it be?

RESILIENCY PROGRAM ASSESSMENT SURVEY

PLEASE TAKE A FEW MOMENTS TO answer these questions about your current lifestyle practices. Complete the survey according to your own habits, or replace the word *I* in the statements below with *My family* if you want to assess your family's habits. Circle the number that best describes how you feel each statement corresponds to your current lifestyle practices using the following scale:

1 = Strongly disagree
2 = Disagree
3 = Neutral, neither disagree nor agree
4 = Agree
5 = Strongly agree

This survey is designed to help you discover your own or your family's resiliency strengths and opportunities for growth. Therefore, it is important to answer each question openly and honestly, but not to worry—you are the only one who will see your answers.

Once you complete a section, calculate your score by tallying your total points and then multiplying that number by four—this will give you your percentage out of 100 percent. Sections 1 through 8 are about the resiliency principles, and section S is about your overall approach to a simplified lifestyle, similar to the way the centenarians approach living. The category with the highest total score is your or your family's resiliency strength, and the lowest shows an opportunity for improvement.

1. Active Movement					
1. Each day I am moderately active for at least 60 minutes.	1	2	3	4	5
2. I primarily walk, bicycle, or use other physically active forms of transportation rather than a car, public transit, or other motorized vehicles.	1	2	3	4	5
3. I have a pet that I routinely take for a walk each day.	1	2	3	4	5
4. I rarely sit for eight hours or more each day.	1	2	3	4	5
5. My overall lifestyle is more active than sedentary in nature.	1	2	3	4	5

Total = _____ x 4 = _____ out of 100 = _____%

2. Nature Engagement					
1. I (or my family) routinely get outdoors each and every day for at least 60 minutes.	1	2	3	4	5
2. While outdoors I am physically active.	1	2	3	4	5
3. I get outdoors even when the weather is poor.	1	2	3	4	5
4. I participate in activities that require me to get outdoors each day (e.g., gardening, going on hikes, etc.).	1	2	3	4	5
5. I enjoy spending time outdoors.	1	2	3	4	5

Total = _____ x 4 = _____ out of 100 = _____%

3. Simple Foods					
1. I routinely eat dinner at home (at least five times a week).	1	2	3	4	5
2. I consume vegetables on a daily basis.	1	2	3	4	5
3. I feel my overall dietary habits are very good.	1	2	3	4	5
4. I do not regularly consume meat (chicken, beef, or pork).	1	2	3	4	5
5. I primarily drink water rather than sports drinks, sodas, or juice.	1	2	3	4	5

Total = _____ x 4 = _____ out of 100 = _____%

4. Resting Reset

	1	2	3	4	5
1. I go to bed at the same time each night and wake at the same time each morning.	1	2	3	4	5
2. I do not look at or consult any electronic devices in bed.	1	2	3	4	5
3. I have one day a week when I rest and take a break from my job or schoolwork.	1	2	3	4	5
4. I tend to sleep through the night and do not wake up when I should be sleeping.	1	2	3	4	5
5. I normally sleep six or more hours per night.	1	2	3	4	5

Total = _____ x 4 = _____ out of 100 = _____%

5. Nurturing Relationships

	1	2	3	4	5
1. I spend quality time (either face-to-face or over the phone) each day with at least one family member.	1	2	3	4	5
2. I eat one meal with a family member at least four times a week.	1	2	3	4	5
3. I find it easy to forgive family members and friends, and I rarely hold a grudge.	1	2	3	4	5
4. I have at least two close friends whom I can call for help.	1	2	3	4	5
5. I connect with my close friends at least once a month.	1	2	3	4	5

Total = _____ x 4 = _____ out of 100 = _____%

6. Faith Foundation

	1	2	3	4	5
1. I regularly attend a church, temple, or other house of worship.	1	2	3	4	5
2. I routinely pray, even if I am not under stress.	1	2	3	4	5
3. I believe my life has a higher purpose.	1	2	3	4	5
4. I often turn to God when I need help.	1	2	3	4	5
5. I think it is important in life to have a connection with God.	1	2	3	4	5

Total = _____ x 4 = _____ out of 100 = _____%

7. Positive Mindset

	1	2	3	4	5
1. I feel I have a lot of energy.	1	2	3	4	5
2. Difficulties or challenges rarely get me down or feeling depressed.	1	2	3	4	5

3. I believe that the choices I make in life have the ability to improve my current situation.	1	2	3	4	5
4. I can do just about anything I really set my mind to.	1	2	3	4	5
5. I often feel empowered in dealing with the problems of life.	1	2	3	4	5

Total = _____ x 4 = _____ out of 100 = _____%

8. Helping Hands

1. I volunteer at least once a week to help others.	1	2	3	4	5
2. In the past month I have willingly helped others with a task on two or more occasions.	1	2	3	4	5
3. I daily give a word of encouragement to another person.	1	2	3	4	5
4. I often roll up my sleeves and get to work helping a friend solve a problem.	1	2	3	4	5
5. I enjoy volunteering as well as encouraging and helping others.	1	2	3	4	5

Total = _____ x 4 = _____ out of 100 = _____%

S. Overall Simplified Living

1. For goals I'm setting and working to achieve, I routinely take the best approach for the task rather than a shortcut.	1	2	3	4	5
2. I rarely shop for and purchase items I don't really need.	1	2	3	4	5
3. Outside of work or school, I spend less than one hour each day on my phone or other screen devices.	1	2	3	4	5
4. In the past month, I rarely felt overly stressed by my daily or weekly schedules.	1	2	3	4	5
5. In general, I would consider my overall lifestyle simplistic in nature.	1	2	3	4	5

Total = _____ x 4 = _____ out of 100 = _____%

EVALUATING YOUR SCORE

Now that you've completed the survey, it's time to evaluate your score. Use the scoring rubric below to help you better assess where you stand. If your experience is low in any section, take heart. The program in this book is designed to help you strengthen your overall resiliency.

Excellent SCORE: 90–100%

Congratulations! Based on your score, you are doing an excellent job in this specific resiliency category. Thus far, you and/or your family have found ways to maintain a high level of experience within this resiliency category. You are encouraged to continue to participate in activities that allow you to be engaged with nature, stay active, eat simple foods, rest and reset, spend time with family and friends, have a foundation in faith, have a positive mindset, and/or help others.

Good SCORE: 80–89%

Your score demonstrates that you're doing a good job at maintaining a fairly high level of experience with this specific resiliency category. You are encouraged to find new and creative ways to continue to maintain and even increase your level of resilience and lower stress.

Fair SCORE: 60–79%

While you're doing a fair job, there is definitely room for improvement within this specific resiliency category. If you notice that one area of resilience needs more support compared to others, implement a strategy to improve that area. You're more likely to succeed if you make small, incremental steps toward increasing resilience. Pinpoint one element that needs improvement each day and then make one small change in an effort to boost your practices there. For example, if you realized that you don't expend much energy during the day, you may want to replace an elevator ride with a walk up the stairs. Or you might choose to do a short workout at home. Whether you need to improve in only a few areas or realize that all of them need work, the accumulation of small steps toward increasing resilience will make a powerful impact in your life.

Needs improvement SCORE: LESS THAN 60%

Based on your score, you need to grow in this specific category. Don't be discouraged! Though we all lead busy lives that sometimes make it feel impossible to fulfill all our responsibilities and take care of our health, you can adopt many tips and strategies to increase your resilience. The easiest and fastest way to build resilience is by combining activities that will boost your resilience. For example, attend a local church service and then share a nutritious picnic lunch in the park with friends. Through these two activities, you will participate in nature engagement, faith foundation, resting/reset, family/friends camaraderie, simple foods, and possibly even more. Remember that the ease is in the overlap. By combining activities, you can make the goal of increasing overall whole health much easier and more attainable.

Note: If you scored less than 60% in the Overall Simplified Living category, think of ways to simplify your family's lifestyle (such as reducing your spending, avoiding major purchases, reducing your family's dependence on screen devices and other electronics, and freeing up time in your daily schedules) before working on the other principles.

RESILIENCY PROGRAM WEEKLY EVALUATION

AT THE END OF EACH WEEK, complete the following questions to evaluate your progress over the past seven days:

EVALUATION QUESTIONS FOR THIS WEEK'S RESILIENCY PRINCIPLE

Circle the number that best represents how you feel as you consider each evaluation question. 1 (a complete failure) to 5 (a complete success)

Were you able to accomplish the majority of your new week goal(s)?	1	2	3	4	5
How do you feel about your ability to overcome any potential challenges that might prevent you from reaching your new goal(s)?	1	2	3	4	5
How do you feel about your overall progress with this new principle?	1	2	3	4	5
How do you feel about your ability to maintain your previous goals while adding a new one?	1	2	3	4	5
How ready do you feel to progress to the next week?	1	2	3	4	5

Total = _____ x 4 = _____ out of 100 = _____%

UNDERSTANDING YOUR WEEKLY EVALUATION SCORE

If you scored less than 80 percent in your Weekly Evaluation, consider repeating this week before moving on.

The following self-reflection questions will help you identify the lessons you learned from practicing the principle this week. They will also allow you to consider opportunities for improvement, which will increase the likelihood of your success.

- How did you feel after practicing this week's resiliency principle?
- How easy or difficult was it to stick with your goals?
- Were you able to follow your goals closely or did you deviate from them? If so, in what way?
- Did you face any barriers in reaching your goals? If so, how did you address them?
- How many of your goals encompassed more than one resiliency principle? In what way can you increase the overlap of the resiliency principles in your existing goals?
- Are the rewards working? If not, why not? What other ways can you reward yourself?

RESILIENCY PROGRAM MAINTENANCE SCORECARD

Now that you have completed the program, regularly assessing how well you are sustaining your new habits is important. By taking time at the end of each week to complete the scorecard on page 244, you may be more motivated to continue leading a resilient life.

On a scale of 1 to 5 (1 being a complete failure and 5 being a complete success), rate how you feel you did this week practicing each resiliency principle, as well as how you feel overall about living a more simplified lifestyle. Use the space in the chart to record your thoughts on practicing each principle.

Cornerstone 1 Active Living	Cornerstone 2 Balanced Living	Cornerstone 3 Connected Living	Cornerstone 4 Determined Living	Overall Simplified Living
Principle 1: *Active Movement* ⎯⎯	Principle 3: *Simple Foods* ⎯⎯	Principle 5: *Nurturing Relationships* ⎯⎯	Principle 7: *Positive Mindset* ⎯⎯	*Reduced Spending* ⎯⎯
Principle 2: *Nature Engagement* ⎯⎯	Principle 4: *Resting Reset* ⎯⎯	Principle 6: *Faith Foundation* ⎯⎯	Principle 8: *Helping Hands* ⎯⎯	*Reduced Feelings of Stress* ⎯⎯
Your thoughts:	Your thoughts:	Your thoughts:	Your thoughts:	Your thoughts:
Total ⎯⎯⎯	Total ⎯⎯⎯	Total ⎯⎯⎯	Total ⎯⎯⎯	Total ⎯⎯⎯

Grand Total ⎯⎯⎯ x 2 = ⎯⎯⎯ out of 100 = ⎯⎯⎯ %

EVALUATION OF YOUR SCORECARD

If you achieved 80 percent or greater on your overall total, congratulate yourself on a job well done! If you achieved less than 80 percent overall, then work on improving your practices and enhancing resiliency in any areas with lower scores.

RESILIENCY CAPITAL RECIPES

Given that the Resiliency Capital is a community with a range of races and ethnic backgrounds—African Americans, Asians, Caucasians, and Hispanics to name a few—it should come as no surprise that our recipes are just as diverse. The approach that unites us all is that our diets are typically vegetarian.

In the Resiliency Capital of Loma Linda, a well-known force to reckon with when it comes to nutrition and preparing meals that knock it out of the park is my good friend Krystal Gheen. Krystal is not only a Resiliency Capital mom with two young children, but both she and her husband are major hitters in the food industry. Krystal is a dietitian with a doctoral degree and her husband, Cory Gheen, is the executive chef at Loma Linda University. Together Krystal and I teamed up and compiled some of our favorite recipes to share with you. We hope you and your family enjoy them as much as we do.

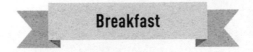

Breakfast

Going Gaga for Green Smoothie

One would think that the children of a vegetarian chef and a dietitian who specializes in taste development would appreciate gourmet food, exotic flavor profiles, and all things "healthy and green." Let's be real, people! They are still kids. Krystal hopes that all her training will one day register a fond food memory, and her kids will choose to expand their palates. Until then, the thrill of them squealing, jumping around, and asking for the "green pineapple" smoothie never gets old.

Ingredients

½ cup almonds or walnuts, whole

1 cup water

2 cups ice

2 cups pineapple, frozen

1 bunch parsley, large stems removed

3 to 5 leaves kale, stems removed

¼ cup apple juice

1. In high-speed blender, blend nuts and water until smooth. (This is important to avoid chewing on chunks of nuts or having them clog your straw!)
2. Add next four ingredients, blend at medium speed, then finish on high speed until smooth. You'll probably need the plunger to get everything mixed up well. To thin, add apple juice, a small amount at a time.

{Serves 4}

Mix It Up Berry Parfait

Yogurt and berry parfaits are a staple in Resiliency Capital households, Krystal's and mine included, for breakfast or dessert. Fresh, nutrient-dense food in minutes—sold! But that simple combo can get old, so kick it up a notch! Adding freshly ground spices not only invigorates your taste buds, but the aromatics stimulate your brain to create more fond food memories. Many spices are also jam-packed with antioxidants and organic compounds with major positive health properties. Try the spice blend listed below, then get creative and make your own. Just remember that a little goes a long way, so don't get carried away with quantity. Plus, you will get the most flavor and health benefits if you eat the ground spices as soon as possible. If you have glass cups/bowls/parfait dishes, use them! This will look fabulous!

Ingredients

2 cups fresh mixed berries

1 cup Greek yogurt, plain or vanilla

2 tablespoons flaxseed, golden

¼ teaspoon cinnamon

¼ teaspoon cloves

¼ teaspoon cardamom

4 sprigs fresh mint

1. Rinse and destem all berries, then divide evenly among four dishes.
2. Top each dish with ¼ cup yogurt.
3. Combine flaxseed and spices in a clean spice grinder (or cleaned coffee grinder); process 20–30 seconds until flaxseed is pulverized.
4. Sprinkle 1 heaping teaspoon ground flaxseed mixture on top of the berries for each portion.
5. Garnish with mint.

{Serves 4}

Fantastic Figs 'n Oats

For opinionated palates, oatmeal is such a fantastic go-to breakfast and just happened to be the staple of most Resiliency Capital centenarians when they were young. The topping combinations and flavor profiles are seriously endless. The trick is to make a good oatmeal base. Straight oatmeal (steel-cut or rolled oats) can be rather *blah-zay* (as Krystal's mama used to say), and can lead to adding too much sweetener to compensate. A few suggestions: Use half water and half your favorite milk product as the liquid (careful—milk can scorch, so keep the temperature at medium-high); then add a pinch of salt and a splash of sweetener (sugar, honey, maple syrup, etc.) to the water-milk base before adding in the oats. Your result will be slightly creamy and super tasty! All the flavors will magically come together in the most delectable dish of oatmeal you've ever had!

Ingredients

4 cups oatmeal, cooked the way you like it

1 cup walnut pieces, lightly toasted

4 fresh figs, quartered (or 8–12 dried figs, quartered)

4 tablespoons balsamic glaze or honey

Salt

Brown sugar

1. Portion oatmeal into bowls.
2. Sprinkle on walnuts and then figs.
3. Drizzle honey or balsamic glaze across the top.
4. Lightly sprinkle a little salt and then a little brown sugar on each serving.

{Serves 4}

Lunch

Lentil Soup

Krystal says that as she was growing up, soup always came condensed in a red and white can. As an adult, she tried for years (literally) to make her own soup but consistently failed. There was always an ingredient that was too hard or too mushy, another possibly burned, a flavorless broth, or any combination of these. Once she began dating a chef and paying keen attention to his techniques, Krystal discovered what she'd been doing wrong! "Remember these few tips," she told me. "Sauté does not mean fry; it means warm slowly until soft; all veggies should be chopped to the same size so they all cook at the same rate; garlic burns and tastes terrible if added to hot oil; salt slows the lentil cooking process; and last but certainly not least, salt is your flavor-boosting friend."

Ingredients

2 tablespoons avocado oil

1 medium white onion, chopped

2 carrots, diced small

2 stalks celery, diced small

3 cloves garlic, minced

28-ounce can diced tomatoes (or 4 cups fresh)

1½ cups lentils, dried

32 ounces vegetable broth

2 to 3 tablespoons fresh thyme, minced (or 2 to 3 teaspoons dried)

Water to desired consistency

Kosher salt

1. In a large soup pot, warm the oil over medium-low heat; sauté the onion and carrot until onions are transparent; add the celery and continue cooking 1–2 minutes. If the onion turns brown, the oil is too hot.

2. When the vegetables are soft, add the minced garlic and tomatoes. Sauté 3–4 minutes.

3. Add dried lentils and vegetable broth; stir. Next add the thyme. Bring to a boil, then let soup simmer on medium-low for 30 minutes.

4. If needed, add water to reach desired consistency.

5. When the lentils are soft and the soup is ready, taste. If needed, add ⅛ teaspoon salt, stir gently, and wait 2–3 minutes. Taste again. Repeat if necessary.

{Serves 4}

No-Plans Veggie Soup

Have you ever forgotten to make lunchtime plans and realized you have fifteen minutes until noon and young stomachs start demanding to be heard? This is my fail-safe meal when I haven't planned ahead but need something quick and nutritious. I typically dash to my fridge, pull out all kinds of veggies, and grab some veggie stock I keep on hand in my pantry. This is a quick and easy soup and can be used with a wide range of vegetables. It also lends itself to freezing; just set aside a portion before adding the pasta—which doesn't freeze well. No one wants to eat shredded, rubbery pasta in soup. Trust me, I tried.

Ingredients

2 cups broccoli, chopped

½ cup peas, frozen

2 carrots, peeled and diced

2 stalks celery, chopped

64 ounces vegetable broth

Salt, to taste

Pepper, to taste

Soy sauce, to taste

2 cups dry pasta (Try elbow, shell, or orecchiette pasta. Even better, mix any two types of pasta together.)

1 cup firm tofu, diced into small cubes

1. Wash all the vegetables, then cut them up.
2. Place the vegetables along with the vegetable broth in a large pot; season with salt, pepper, and soy sauce.
3. Bring the vegetables to a simmer and cook for about 5 minutes.
4. Once the vegetables are softer, add the pasta and tofu to the soup, boil for the time needed to cook on the pasta package. Taste the broth and adjust seasoning with more salt, pepper, or soy sauce if needed. Then serve and enjoy.

{Serves 4}

Cheesy Herb Biscuits

As most families will agree, good soups are even better when accompanied by a tasty bread. This is one of Krystal's favorites because of its flavor and versatility and the fact that it suits her family's opinionated palates. Using the same base dough, Krystal uses a small-portion scoop to make "biscuit rocks" that float in her daughter's soup bowl, and a larger-portion scoop to create soft, dippable biscuits that the rest of her family likes—all baked on the same pan at the same time.

Ingredients

½ teaspoon Kosher salt, finely ground

2 teaspoons baking powder

¾ cup whole wheat flour

¾ cup all-purpose flour

2 tablespoons butter, unsalted, very cold

½ cup strong cheese, shredded (sharp or aged cheddar, Parmesan, Asiago, etc.)

4 teaspoons fresh herbs (or 2 teaspoons dried)[*]

½ cup whole milk[†]

1. Preheat oven to 425°F.
2. Grind salt and baking powder with a mortar and pestle until they are a fine powder.
3. Sift all dry ingredients together into a large mixing bowl.
4. Cut the cold butter into small cubes or shred with a cheese grater, then add to dry mixture. Cut the butter into the dry mixture with a pastry cutter until mixture resembles fine sand. Tiny cold slivers of butter in your final dough will make your biscuits soft and flaky, while big clumps of butter will make them hard and chewy.
5. Sprinkle in cheese and your choice of herb(s). Add milk and stir with a rubber spatula until just combined (a little dry is best).
6. Transfer to a lightly floured work surface and knead a few strokes until mixture just holds together; it will still be lumpy.
7. Option 1: Use a portion scoop to separate dough into 6 mounded biscuits. Option 2: Gently roll out to a thickness of ½ inch. Cut with round cutter or knife into 6 pieces.
8. Transfer to a greased or parchment-lined baking sheet, and bake in hot oven until tops are light brown, approximately 10–12 minutes. Tip: Make sure your oven is at the desired temperature for 5–10 minutes before putting in your biscuits to ensure they rise well and bake evenly.
9. Allow to cool slightly before serving warm.

---

[*] Pick herbs that you like, that you have on hand, and that go with your meal. If herbs are new to you, chives are always a good standard to start with. After that, pick another herb and add it to your biscuit mix. The next time, try a different herb. This will help you learn how the herbs taste and what foods you think each goes well with.

[†] If you use a nut or soy milk, add an extra tablespoon of butter. Be sure the milk is plain and unsweetened.

{Serves 6}

Spinning a Haystack

This new take on the traditional chili or nacho recipe is a staple in the Resiliency Capital community. This is the dish at many gatherings, with attendees asked to bring one of the ingredients listed below. The typical Haystack calls for tortilla chips, but healthier versions swap out the chips for large pieces of lettuce to make lettuce wraps or use whole wheat tortillas. With many options and ways to prepare, this recipe is sure to be a hit at your next gathering.

Ingredients

2 cups Bob's Red Mill 13 Bean Soup Mix

64 ounces vegetable broth

16 ounces tomato sauce

2 tablespoons chili powder

1 teaspoon cayenne pepper

Dash of salt and pepper to taste

1 head of lettuce, shredded or large leaf, depending on your preference

2 cups fresh tomatoes, diced

2 medium white onions, diced

1 can (3.8 ounces) black olives, drained and sliced

2 avocados, diced

2 cups whole-kernel corn

2 cups sour cream

3 cups cheddar cheese, shredded

1 bag of tortilla chips or whole wheat tortillas

1. Soak beans overnight in a pot with water. This will release some of the indigestible sugars from the beans. After soaking, rinse the beans.

2. Next, follow the directions on the back of Bob's 13 Bean Soup Mix to prepare the beans, except leave out the beef and use vegetable broth instead of water and add the tomato sauce. Next add the chili powder, cayenne pepper, and salt and pepper. It takes about 3 hours to cook the beans on the stove, so you can prepare the pot of beans either the day before or the day of your event.

3. Once the chili is prepared, blend a small portion of it in the blender, then combine the blended portion with the original chili—this will give it that great chili soup appearance.

4. About 20 minutes before serving the meal, chop the vegetables, including lettuce (or use the lettuce leaves whole for wraps), tomatoes, onions, olives, and avocados; place all the vegetables, including corn, in individual dishes

for toppings. Include one bowl for the sour cream and one for the shredded cheddar cheese. Voilà—an assembly line of toppings for your chili party! Serve with either tortilla chips, whole wheat tortillas, or lettuce leaves for wraps.

{Serves 6}

Nutty Spinach Pesto

This is a versatile sauce I like to have on hand. You can serve it with toast for a quick and healthy snack, combine it with pasta for a lunchtime meal, or use it as the sauce on a homemade pizza. I usually double the recipe to freeze a batch and give away another container to a friend. Best of all, I like serving this to my children because they get a good dose of spinach, and I like to think they are growing muscles like the old cartoon character Popeye.

Ingredients

5 cups spinach, fresh

1 cup pine nuts (you can substitute walnuts or other types of nuts)

1 cup Parmesan cheese, shredded

3 cloves garlic

½ cup olive oil

Salt to taste

Pepper to taste

1. Wash the spinach and then place 2 cups of it in a food processor. (This sauce is best made with a food processor, but a blender would work too.)
2. Add the pine nuts, Parmesan, garlic, and a little bit of the olive oil just to get going.
3. Turn the food processor on and then slowly add the remaining olive oil.
4. Add the remainder of the spinach and process it all together.
5. Last, add salt and pepper to enhance the flavor.

{Makes 2 cups of sauce}

Potato Bread

Growing up, the Resiliency Capital centenarians often didn't have the luxury of purchasing bread at the local store. They made their own loaves from scratch. The bonus is that their bread didn't contain all the preservatives commonly found in today's grocery store bread.

Ingredients

1 cup milk, scalded

1 cup potato water (water drained from boiled potatoes) or regular water

4 tablespoons butter, melted

1 package dry yeast (1 tablespoon)

¼ cup warm water

½ cup sugar

2 eggs

6 to 6½ cups all-purpose flour

2 teaspoons salt (or can omit)

1. In a bowl, mix together milk, potato water, and melted butter. Allow the mixture to cool slightly. In a separate bowl, dissolve the yeast in ¼ cup warm water and a little sugar. Watch to see if it bubbles to make sure the yeast is still active.

2. To the yeast add the remaining sugar and eggs. Mix potato water mixture and yeast mixture together.

3. Next add half the flour and the salt and let it bubble and rise. Then add the rest of the flour and knead the dough until it is smooth and elastic, no longer sticky. Kneading helps get rid of the air bubbles.

4. Place the dough in a greased bowl, put a damp cloth over it, and let it rise on the counter until it doubles in size, about 1 hour. Then punch down and divide into two equal pieces. Flatten each piece with a rolling pin and roll into a loaf, pinching the end closed. Place each formed loaf into a greased loaf pan. Let the dough rise again until it doubles in size.

5. Bake in the oven at 350 degrees for 45–50 minutes. To check if it is done, tap on top and see if it sounds hollow; if it does, then it's done. Take out of the pans right away after baking and allow to cool.

{Makes 2 loaves}

Good Gorp

Remember that time when all the kids came to you "starving," pleading for you to make them something to eat right then, but they all wanted something completely different? Well, this snack was born in such a moment. Before Krystal headed out for a meeting, her kids asked for a snack. Wanting to give them something quick and nutritious, she flung open her pantry door and pulled out items she had on hand. She asked each of her children what they wanted, tossed it all into a small bowl, and handed it over. When broad smiles spread across their faces, she knew she had a hit. After a little portion refinement, this combo is now a ready-to-go staple that won't melt in the bag, and best of all, it's a nutrient-dense snack the kiddos can grab. What a smart mama!

Ingredients

1 cup almonds, whole or pieces, lightly roasted and salted

1 cup cashew pieces, lightly roasted and salted

1 cup cranberries, dried

1 cup blueberries, dried

½ cup yogurt chips

1. Add all ingredients to bowl or bag; mix gently.
2. Store as desired. (I recommend pre-portioned servings in grab-and-go snack bags.)

{Makes 9 half-cup snacks}

Dinner

Butternut Squash Enchiladas

Krystal has always been a bit of a traditionalist when it comes to food—she likes things simple and fresh. That being said, she was a bit skeptical when her chef husband served up this recipe early in their marriage. One bite and she was sold! Krystal now enjoys taking traditional recipes and adding a vegetarian or vegan twist. This recipe was such a hit at my house, it now holds a place of prominence in my small but growing recipe binder.

Ingredients

1 butternut squash, peeled, seeded, and cut into ¼-inch x 3-inch sticks

1 medium white onion, cut into long slivers, ¼ inch thick

1 red bell pepper, seeded and cut into ¼-inch strips

3 tablespoons vegetable oil

Salt and pepper, to taste

½ cup vegetable oil

12 corn tortillas

12 ounces red enchilada sauce

½ cup queso fresco, crumbled

Cilantro, chopped

1. Preheat oven to 375°F.
2. Toss the squash, onion, and bell pepper in 3 tablespoons oil to coat. Then sprinkle on salt and pepper to taste.
3. Roast vegetables in hot oven for 20 minutes until they are soft and beginning to brown.
4. Heat ½ cup oil in a small skillet on medium or medium low. When the oil is ready, dip each tortilla in the hot oil for 10 seconds per side. Set on paper towels to cool before adding vegetables.
5. Fill each tortilla with squash, onion, and bell pepper, then roll and align in a casserole dish.
6. Pour the red sauce over the enchiladas, being sure to cover/soak all the edges.
7. Bake 20–25 minutes until heated through.
8. Garnish with queso fresco and chopped cilantro.

{Serves 4–6}

Pot Sticker Dumplings

From cornbread in the South to chowder in the Northeast, every region has its heritage dishes. In our neck of the woods, this dumpling recipe is a favorite dish. It makes a great-tasting, veggie-loaded meal that no one passes up!

Ingredients

1½ to 3 tablespoons oil, divided

1 onion, chopped

1 carrot, shredded

3 cloves garlic, minced

½ head of cabbage, cut up

1 (16-ounce) bag frozen spinach, thawed and drained

1 (20-ounce) can of veggie burger

1 (16-ounce) package firm tofu

Soy sauce to taste

Sesame seed oil to taste

Salt to taste

2 packages wonton wrappers

Sweet chili sauce or other sauce as condiment

1. In a skillet with 1 to 2 tablespoons oil, cook the onion and carrot until slightly tender; then add garlic, and last, the cabbage. Just cook the cabbage until slightly wilted. Set aside to cool.

2. In a large bowl, mix the cooked vegetables with the spinach, veggie burger, and tofu. Season this mixture well with soy sauce, sesame seed oil, and salt.

3. On the counter, set up a large cookie sheet to place dumplings on and a soup bowl with water next to the wonton wrappers.

4. Take one wrapper and dip the corners into the water bowl to get them slightly wet. Place a tablespoon of the dumpling mixture in the middle of the wrapper. Then bring all four corners together in the middle, pinch to seal closed, then place sealed side down on the baking sheet.

5. After all wraps are prepared, they are ready to be heated in a covered frying pan in batches. With ½ to 1 tablespoon of vegetable oil heated in a pan, add the wrapped dumplings and heat for a moment. Then add ¼ cup water and cover the pan to steam the dumplings.

6. Once the first batch is complete, repeat frying and steaming the next batch.

7. Serve with sweet chili sauce, soy sauce, or any other sauce you prefer.

{Serves 6–8}

Yellow Curry

From Thai to Indian, Japanese, and beyond, many cultures have their take on a typical curry dish. Here's one of our favorites that's not too spicy!

Ingredients

1 medium white onion, diced small

1 tablespoon avocado oil or vegetable oil

1½ teaspoons yellow curry powder

1 tablespoon fresh ginger, minced (or 1 teaspoon ginger powder)

½ teaspoon salt

1 clove garlic, minced

1½ cups firm tofu, cubed (or 1 can chickpeas, drained)

1 can (13.5 ounces) coconut cream or coconut milk

1 tablespoon honey

1 to 2 teaspoons lime juice

Additions and Garnish Options
- Super-easy addition: a 16-ounce bag of frozen mixed veggies
- More authentic addition: sliced raw bell pepper, lightly steamed broccoli, lemongrass shoots
- Garnish: fresh basil, fresh red bell pepper

1. In a large pot, sauté onion in oil until translucent. If it begins to turn brown, the oil is too hot.
2. Stir in the curry powder, ginger, salt, and garlic; sauté for 1–2 minutes.
3. Add your choice of protein (tofu or chickpeas) and coconut cream, honey, and lime juice; cook 1–2 minutes.
4. Add choice of vegetables from Additions and Garnish Options list, then cover and cook on medium; heat 5–10 minutes.
5. Serve in a bowl over rice or cooked potato, cubed and peeled.

{Serves 4–6}

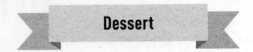

Dessert

When it comes to dessert, remember to keep things simple. Try orange slices (not the candied type, but the kind that comes from a tree) or other seasonal fruit. Cut up the fruit and serve on a colorful plate. Or remember that Berry Parfait? Yes, it too makes a tasty evening treat!

DINNER CONVERSATION KICK-STARTER QUESTIONS

IF YOU WOULD LIKE TO INCREASE conversation around your dinner (or breakfast or lunch) table, try asking a dinner conversation kick-starter question. Two types of questions are listed below—daily support and getting-to-know-you questions.

The daily support questions are to be asked each time you gather for the evening meal—encouraging your family to celebrate any blessings and to work together through any challenges.

Then select one of the getting-to-know-you questions to encourage learning more about the people in your family. Go around the table and take turns answering the question. For grown-ups, answer the question from your childhood experiences (e.g., "When I was young, I wanted to be . . ."). This will help your children learn about you and connect with your childhood.

I recommend printing the questions out on cards and having them on hand at the dinner table. I used a small box with a lid I found at a dollar store. I printed the cards, cut them out, and then laminated them. When you finish the twenty-five questions below, create new cards and add them to your growing box or, better yet, pass on your old cards to a friend.

DAILY SUPPORT QUESTIONS

1. What, if any, great experiences did you have today? What blessings did you experience today?

2. What is something difficult you experienced today? How did you handle it?

GETTING-TO-KNOW-YOU QUESTIONS (PICK A NEW ONE EACH DAY)

1. If you could have any animal in the world as a pet, what would you want to have and why? (Example for grown-ups: If you had a pet, what was it? What was its name?)

2. What is your favorite movie of all time?

3. If you could have any superpower, what would it be and why?

4. Who was your favorite schoolteacher and why?

5. What was your favorite vacation and why?

6. What is your favorite dessert to eat and why?

7. If you could go anywhere in the world, where would it be and why?

8. If you had to play one sport, what would it be and why?

9. If you could be any animal, what would it be and why?

10. Would you prefer to vacation at a lake or the ocean and why?

11. Would you rather visit outer space in a rocket or the bottom of an ocean in a submarine and why?

12. If you had to go back to school for one year to repeat any grade just for the fun of it, what grade would you want to repeat and why?

13. If you were an Olympic athlete, which sport would you compete in and why?

14. If you were granted any wish, what would you want it to be?

15. What is one of the best books you have read? What was it about, and why is it one of your favorites?

16. What is one thing you like best about the person sitting next to you?

17. What is (or was) one of your most favorite things to play with and why?

18. If you could meet anyone famous, who would it be and why?

19. What is one thing you created that you were really happy with how it turned out?

20. If you could set the world record in any event, which record would you want to beat?

21. What is something you'd like to see invented?

22. What is something funny you saw or read that made you laugh?

23. What was a favorite school field trip you went on?

24. Who is your hero (could be real or imaginary) and why?

25. If you could have any job in the world, what would it be and why?

NOTES

INTRODUCTION

1. "History of Blue Zones," Blue Zones website, accessed October 29, 2020, https://www.bluezones.com/about/history/.
2. The quotes from these interviews in the book are as close as possible to the transcripts. In some instances, a word was added or a slight change made to ensure readers better understand what was being reported.

CHAPTER 1: A MOM IN HIDING

1. For more information, see https://adventisthealthstudy.org/studies/AHS-1.
2. Christina D. Bethell et al., "A National and State Profile of Leading Health Problems and Health Care Quality for US Children: Key Insurance Disparities and Across-State Variations," *Academic Pediatrics* 11, no. 3 suppl. (May–June 2011): S22–33, https://doi.org/10.1016/j.acap.2010.08.011.
3. James M. Perrin, L. Elizabeth Anderson, and Jeanne Van Cleave, "The Rise in Chronic Conditions among Infants, Children, and Youth Can Be Met with Continued Health System Innovations," *Health Affairs* 33, no. 12 (December 2014): 2099–105, https://doi.org/10.1377/hlthaff.2014.0832.
4. American Psychological Association, "APA Stress in America Report: High Stress Related to Coronavirus Is New Normal for Many Parents," news release, May 21, 2020, https://www.apa.org/news/press/releases/stress/.
5. Jack P. Shonkoff, W. Thomas Boyce, and Bruce S. McEwen, "Neuroscience, Molecular Biology, and the Childhood Roots of Health Disparities: Building a New Framework for Health Promotion and Disease Prevention," *Journal of the American Medical Association* 301, no. 21 (June 3, 2009): 2252–59, https://doi.org/10.1001/jama.2009.754.
6. Andrew H. Miller and Charles L. Raison, "The Role of Inflammation in Depression: From Evolutionary Imperative to Modern Treatment Target," *Nature Reviews Immunology* 16, no. 1 (January 2016): 22–34, https://doi.org/10.1038/nri.2015.5.
7. Irene Esteban-Cornejo et al., "Inflammatory Biomarkers and Academic Performance in Youth. The UP & DOWN Study," *Brain, Behavior, and Immunity* 54 (May 2016): 122–27, https://doi.org/10.1016/j.bbi.2016.01.010.

8. "National Parent Survey Report," Zero to Three website, June 6, 2016, https://www.zerotothree.org/resources/1425-national-parent-survey-report.

9. "Help Your Parents Get Healthy," Johns Hopkins All Children's Hospital, accessed October 29, 2010, https://www.hopkinsallchildrens.org/Patients-Families/Health-Library/HealthDocNew/Help-Your-Parents-Get-Healthy?id=2066.

CHAPTER 2: A RESILIENCY CAPITAL: UNCOVERING THEIR SECRETS

1. Adverse childhood experiences (ACEs) are potentially traumatic events, such as a parent's abuse, suicide, or substance use disorder, experienced or witnessed by children from infancy through age seventeen.

2. Some of these questions were adapted from a questionnaire provided by the World Health Organization (WHO). See "Adverse Childhood Experiences International Questionnaire (ACE-IQ)," Violence and Injury Prevention, World Health Organization, accessed October 30, 2020, https://www.who.int/violence_injury_prevention/violence/activities/adverse_childhood_experiences/en/.

3. When I began my research, I assumed that people who reached age one hundred had had pretty easy lives. But I was wrong. Most of the centenarians I interviewed carried great burdens in childhood. Although research has shown that people with ACEs are more likely to have chronic diseases and shorter lifespans, the centenarians I talked with proved that people can overcome these early hardships. Soon my line of questioning focused on the hardships in their early lives (ACEs) as well as any factors that might have protected them and made them resilient.

4. V. J. Felitti et al., "Relationship of Childhood Abuse and Household Dysfunction to Many of the Leading Causes of Death in Adults: The Adverse Childhood Experiences (ACE) Study," *American Journal of Preventive Medicine* 14, no. 4 (May 1, 1998): 245–58, https://doi.org/10.1016/s0749-3797(98)00017-8.

5. Rhonda Spencer-Hwang et al., "Adverse Childhood Experiences among a Community of Resilient Centenarians and Seniors: Implications for Chronic Disease Prevention Framework," *Permanente Journal* 22 (May 2018): 17–146, https://doi.org/10.7812/TPP/17-146.

6. Robin Arnette, "The Impacts of Air Pollution on the Immune System," National Institute of Environmental Health Sciences, January 2015, https://factor.niehs.nih.gov/2015/1/science-nadeau/index.htm.

7. Peter A. Wyman et al., "Association of Family Stress with Natural Killer Cell Activity and the Frequency of Illnesses in Children," *Archives of Pediatrics and Adolescent Medicine* 161, no. 3 (March 2007): 228–34, https://doi.org/10.1001/archpedi.161.3.228.

CHAPTER 3: WEEK 1: DIGGING GOATS AND GARDENS

1. Charles Duhigg, *The Power of Habit: Why We Do What We Do in Life and Business* (New York: Random House, 2012).

2. Myrna Oliver, "Hulda Crooks, 101; Oldest Woman to Scale Mt. Whitney," *Los Angeles Times*, November 26, 1997, https://www.latimes.com/archives/la-xpm-1997-nov-26-mn-57923-story.html.

3. Hulda Crooks, *Conquering Life's Mountains* (n.p.: The Quiet Hours, 1996).

4. Sufficient physical activity was defined as at least sixty minutes a day, five days a week. Regina Guthold et al., "Global Trends in Insufficient Physical Activity among Adolescents: A Pooled Analysis of 298 Population-Based Surveys with 1.6 Million Participants," *Lancet Child & Adolescent Health* 4, no. 1 (January 1, 2020): P23–25, https://www.thelancet.com/journals/lanchi/article/PIIS2352-4642(19)30323-2/fulltext.

5. Kids and teens in Tanzania were way out in front, with Estonia and Iceland coming in second and third fastest. Justin J. Lang et al., "International Variability in 20 M Shuttle Run Performance in Children and Youth: Who Are the Fittest from a 50-Country Comparison? A Systematic Literature Review with Pooling of Aggregate Results," *British Journal of Sports Medicine* 52, no. 4 (2018): 276, https://doi.org/10.1136/bjsports-2016 -096224.

6. Laura Chaddock-Heyman et al., "The Importance of Physical Activity and Aerobic Fitness for Cognitive Control and Memory in Children," *Monographs of the Society for Research in Child Development* 79, no. 4 (December 2014): 25–50, https://doi.org/10.1111/mono .12129; Charles H. Hillman, "An Introduction to the Relation of Physical Activity to Cognitive and Brain Health, and Scholastic Achievement," *Monographs of the Society for Research in Child Development* 79, no. 4 (December 2014): 1–6, https://doi.org/10.1111 /mono.12127.

7. See the International Physical Literacy Association website, https://www.physical-literacy .org.uk/.

8. Katie Reilly, "Is Recess Important for Kids or a Waste of Time? Here's What the Research Says," *Time*, October 23, 2017, https://time.com/4982061/recess-benefits-research-debate/.

9. Danielle Cohen, "Why Kids Need to Spend Time in Nature," Child Mind Institute, https:// childmind.org/article/why-kids-need-to-spend-time-in-nature/.

10. Richard Louv, *Last Child in the Woods: Saving Our Children from Nature-Deficit Disorder* (Chapel Hill, NC: Algonquin Books, 2008).

11. See Caleb Smith, *Peacebunny Island* (Carol Stream, IL: Tyndale, 2021).

12. For information on Robbie Bond and Kids Speak for Parks, visit https://www.kidsspeakfor parks.org/. Accessed March 21, 2020.

13. Danielle F. Shanahan et al., "Health Benefits from Nature Experiences Depend on Dose," *Scientific Reports* 6, no. 28551 (June 23, 2016), https://doi.org/10.1038/srep28551; Marilyn Price-Mitchell, "Does Nature Make Us Happy?," *Psychology Today*, March 27, 2014, https://www.psychologytoday.com/us/blog/the-moment-youth/201403/does-nature -make-us-happy.

14. Lara S. Franco, Danielle F. Shanahan, and Richard A. Fuller, "A Review of the Benefits of Nature Experiences: More Than Meets the Eye," *International Journal of Environmental Research and Public Health* 14, no. 8 (August 1, 2017): 864, https://pubmed.ncbi.nlm.nih .gov/28763021/.

15. Tove Fall et al., "Early Exposure to Dogs and Farm Animals and the Risk of Childhood Asthma," *JAMA Pediatrics* 169, no. 11 (November 2, 2015): e153219, https://doi.org /10.1001/jamapediatrics.2015.3219.

16. Casey Gray et al., "What Is the Relationship between Outdoor Time and Physical Activity, Sedentary Behaviour, and Physical Fitness in Children? A Systematic Review," *International Journal of Environmental Research and Public Health* 12, no. 6 (June 8, 2015): 6455–74, https://doi.org/10.3390/ijerph120606455.

17. Kenneth P. Wright Jr. et al., "Entrainment of the Human Circadian Clock to the Natural Light-Dark Cycle," *Current Biology* 23, no. 16 (August 19, 2013): 1554–58, https://doi .org/10.1016/j.cub.2013.06.039.

18. Janke van Dijk-Wesselius et al., "Green Schoolyards as Outdoor Learning Environments: Barriers and Solutions as Experienced by Primary School Teachers," *Frontiers in Psychology* 10 (January 9, 2020): 2919, https://doi.org/10.3389/fpsyg.2019.02919.

19. Ming Kuo, Michael Barnes, and Catherine Jordan, "Do Experiences with Nature Promote Learning? Converging Evidence of a Cause-and-Effect Relationship," *Frontiers in Psychology* 10

(2019): 305, https://doi.org/10.3389/fpsyg.2019.00305; Ruth Ann Atchley, David L. Strayer, and Paul Atchley, "Creativity in the Wild: Improving Creative Reasoning through Immersion in Natural Settings," *PLOS ONE* 7, no. 12 (2012): e51474, https://doi.org/10.1371/journal .pone.0051474; Traci Pedersen, "Nature Play Can Boost Kids' Creativity, Complex Thinking and Social Skills," PsychCentral, February 16, 2020, https://psychcentral.com/news/2020/02 /15/nature-play-can-boosts-kids-creativity-complex-thinking-and-social-skills/154235.html; Dana Miller, Kathy Tichota, and Joyce White, *Young Children's Authentic Play in a Nature Explore Classroom Supports Foundational Learning: A Single Case Study* (Lincoln, NE: Dimensions Educational Research Foundation, 2013), https://dimensionsfoundation.org /wp-content/uploads/2016/07/youngchildrenauthenticplay.pdf.

CHAPTER 4: WEEK 2: CREATING BALANCED KIDS

1. Talia F. Malik and Kiran K. Panuganti, "Lactose Intolerance," National Center for Biotechnology Information, updated June 26, 2020, https://www.ncbi.nlm.nih.gov /books/NBK532285/.

2. "Definition and Facts for Lactose Intolerance," National Institute of Diabetes and Digestive and Kidney Diseases (NIDDK), accessed March 21, 2020, https://www.niddk.nih.gov /health-information/digestive-diseases/lactose-intolerance/definition-facts#common.

3. Susan S. Lang, "Lactose Intolerance Seems Linked to Ancestral Struggles with Harsh Climate and Cattle Diseases, Cornell Study Finds," *Cornell Chronicle*, June 1, 2005, https:// news.cornell.edu/stories/2005/06/lactose-intolerance-linked-ancestral-struggles-climate -diseases#:~:text=According%20to%20the%20National%20Digestive,90%20percent%20 of%20Asian%20Americans; "Prehistoric Man and Lactose Intolerance," Food Intolerance Network, https://www.food-intolerance-network.com/food-intolerances/lactose-intolerance /ethnic-distribution-and-prevalence.html.

4. "US Adult Consumption of Added Sugars Increased by More than 30% over Three Decades," ScienceDaily, November 4, 2014, www.sciencedaily.com/releases/2014/11 /141104141731.htm.

5. "U.S. Adult Consumption of Added Sugars Increased by More than 30 Percent over Three Decades," ScienceDaily, November 4, 2014, https://www.sciencedaily.com/releases/2014 /11/141104141731.htm; Roberto A. Ferdman, "Where People around the World Eat the Most Sugar and Fat," *Washington Post*, February 5, 2015, https://www.washingtonpost.com /news/wonk/wp/2015/02/05/where-people-around-the-world-eat-the-most-sugar-and-fat/.

6. Anna Pia Delli Bovi et al., "Obesity and Obesity Related Diseases, Sugar Consumption and Bad Oral Health: A Fatal Epidemic Mixture: The Pediatric and Odontologist Point of View," *Translation Medicine UniSa* 16, no. 2 (2017): 11–16, https://docksci.com/obesity -and-obesity-related-diseases-sugar-consumption-and-bad-oral-health-a-fat_59eb4ee2d64 ab2aea34de2a4.html.

7. Marcos Paseggi, "It Is Possible to Be a Very Unhealthy Vegetarian," *Adventist Review*, February 28, 2018, https://www.adventistreview.org/church-news/story5903-it-is -possible-to-be-a-very-unhealthy-vegetarian.

8. David Portalatin, "Eating Patterns in America Take a Sharp Turn," October 13, 2020, NPD Group, https://www.npd.com/wps/portal/npd/us/blog/2020/eating-patterns-in -america-take-a-sharp-turn/.

9. Ji Lu, Catherine Huet, and Laurette Dubé, "Emotional Reinforcement as a Protective Factor for Healthy Eating in Home Settings," *American Journal of Clinical Nutrition* 94, no. 1 (July 2011): 254–61, https://doi.org/10.3945/ajcn.110.006361.

10. "Alcohol Use and Your Health," Centers for Disease Control and Prevention, October 1, 2020, https://www.cdc.gov/alcohol/fact-sheets/alcohol-use.htm.

11. Jacqueline Chan et al., "Water, Other Fluids, and Fatal Coronary Heart Disease: The Adventist Health Study," *American Journal of Epidemiology* 155, no. 9 (May 1, 2002): 827–33, https://doi.org/10.1093/aje/155.9.827.

12. "Choose My Plate," US Department of Agriculture (USDA), accessed March 21, 2020, https://www.choosemyplate.gov/.

13. "The Water in You: Water and the Human Body," US Geological Survey (USGS), US Department of the Interior, accessed March 4, 2020, https://www.usgs.gov/special-topic /water-science-school/science/water-you-water-and-human-body?qt-science_center_objects =0#qt-science_center_objects.

14. Erica L. Kenney et al., "Prevalence of Inadequate Hydration among US Children and Disparities by Gender and Race/Ethnicity: National Health and Nutrition Examination Survey, 2009–2012," *American Journal of Public Health* 105, no. 8 (August 2015): e113–18, https://doi.org/10.2105/AJPH.2015.302572.

15. "2015–2020 Dietary Guidelines," Current Dietary Guidelines, Dietary Guidelines for Americans (DGA), accessed March 4, 2020, https://www.dietaryguidelines.gov/current -dietary-guidelines/2015-2020-dietary-guidelines.

16. Redzo Mujcic and Andrew J. Oswald, "Evolution of Well-Being and Happiness After Increases in Consumption of Fruit and Vegetables," *American Journal of Public Health* 106, no. 8 (August 2016): 1504–10, https://doi.org/10.2105/AJPH.2016.303260; Tamlin S. Conner et al., "Let Them Eat Fruit! The Effect of Fruit and Vegetable Consumption on Psychological Well-Being in Young Adults: A Randomized Controlled Trial," *PLOS ONE* 12, no. 2 (February 2017): e0171206, https://doi.org/10.1371/journal.pone.0171206.

17. Na Zhang et al., "Effects of Dehydration and Rehydration on Cognitive Performance and Mood among Male College Students in Cangzhou, China: A Self-Controlled Trial," *International Journal of Environmental Research and Public Health* 16, no. 11 (May 29, 2019): 1891, https://doi.org/10.3390/ijerph16111891.

18. Banafshe Hosseini et al., "Effects of Fruit and Vegetable Consumption on Inflammatory Biomarkers and Immune Cell Populations: A Systematic Literature Review and Meta-Analysis," *American Journal of Clinical Nutrition* 108, no. 1 (July 1, 2018): 136–55, https://doi.org/10.1093/ajcn/nqy082.

19. Andrew Gibson et al., "Effect of Fruit and Vegetable Consumption on Immune Function in Older People: A Randomized Controlled Trial," *American Journal of Clinical Nutrition* 96, no. 6 (December 2012): 1429–36, https://doi.org/10.3945/ajcn.112.039057.

20. Tonje H. Stea and Monica K. Torstveit, "Association of Lifestyle Habits and Academic Achievement in Norwegian Adolescents: A Cross-Sectional Study," *BMC Public Health* 14 (August 11, 2014): 829, https://doi.org/10.1186/1471-2458-14-829.

21. Kate Northstone et al., "Are Dietary Patterns in Childhood Associated with IQ at 8 Years of Age? A Population-Based Cohort Study," *Journal of Epidemiology and Community Health* 66, no. 7 (February 2011): 624–28, http://dx.doi.org/10.1136/jech.2010.111955.

22. Ana Adan, "Cognitive Performance and Dehydration," *Journal of the American College of Nutrition* 31, no. 2 (April 2012): 71–78, https://doi.org/10.1080/07315724.2012.10720011; Bob Murray, "Hydration and Physical Performance," *Journal of the American College of Nutrition* 26, suppl. 5 (October 2007): 542S–548S, https://doi.org/10.1080/07315724.2007.10719656.

23. Jean-Philippe Chaput et al., "Outdoor Time and Dietary Patterns in Children around the World," *Journal of Public Health (Oxford, England)* 40, no. 4 (December 1, 2018): e493–e501, https://doi.org/10.1093/pubmed/fdy071.

CHAPTER 5: WEEK 3: RARING TO GO REBOOT

1. Hulda Crooks, *Conquering Life's Mountains* (n.p.: The Quiet Hours, 1996), 137.

2. Crooks, *Conquering Life's Mountains*, 177–78.

3. University of Chicago Medical Center, "New Study Shows People Sleep even Less than They Think," ScienceDaily, July 3, 2006, www.sciencedaily.com/releases/2006/07 /060703162945.htm.

4. Kenneth P. Wright Jr. et al., "Entrainment of the Human Circadian Clock to the Natural Light-Dark Cycle," *Current Biology* 23, no. 16 (August 19, 2013): 1554–58, https://doi .org/10.1016/j.cub.2013.06.039.

5. Taryn Luna, "California Becomes the First State in the Country to Push Back School Start Times," *Los Angeles Times*, October 13, 2019, https://www.latimes.com/california/story /2019-10-13/california-first-state-country-later-school-start-times-new-law.

6. Jeffrey M. Jones, "In US, 40% Get Less than Recommended Amount of Sleep," Gallup News, December 19, 2013, https://news.gallup.com/poll/166553/less-recommended -amount-sleep.aspx.

7. Neil Howe, "America the Sleep-Deprived," *Forbes*, August 18, 2017, https://www .forbes.com/sites/neilhowe/2017/08/18/america-the-sleep-deprived/#470eb89e1a38.

8. "Paid Time Off Trends in the US," US Travel Association, accessed March 21, 2020, https:// www.ustravel.org/sites/default/files/media_root/document/Paid%20Time%20Off%20 Trends%20Fact%20Sheet.pdf.

9. "Sleep and Sleep Disorders," Centers for Disease Control and Prevention (CDC), accessed March 4, 2020, https://www.cdc.gov/sleep/index.html.

10. Debra Goldschmidt, "The Great American Sleep Recession," CNN, June 23, 2017, https:// www.cnn.com/2015/02/18/health/great-sleep-recession/index.htm.

11. Sumit Bhargava, "Diagnosis and Management of Common Sleep Problems in Children," *Pediatrics in Review* 32, no. 3 (March 2011): 91–99, https://doi.org/10.1542/pir.32-3-91.

12. S. S. Hawkins and D. T. Takeuchi, "Social Determinants of Inadequate Sleep in US Children and Adolescents," *Public Health* 138 (September 2016): 119–26, https://doi .org/10.1016/j.puhe.2016.03.036; Anne G. Wheaton et al., "Short Sleep Duration among Middle School and High School Students—United States, 2015," *Morbidity and Mortality Weekly Report* 67, no. 3 (January 26, 2018): 85–90, https://doi.org/10.15585/mmwr .mm6703a1.

13. "Sleep and Sleep Disorders Data and Statistics," Centers for Disease Control and Prevention (CDC), accessed March 4, 2020, https://www.cdc.gov/sleep/data_statistics.html.

14. "Are Canadian Children Getting Enough Sleep? Infographic," accessed March 4, 2020, https://www.canada.ca/en/public-health/services/publications/healthy-living/canadian -children-getting-enough-sleep-infographic.html; "Six in Ten Children Don't Get Enough Sleep: Warning Poor Parenting and Youngsters Being Glued to TVs or Other Devices Is Leading to a Crisis in Rest Habits," DailyMail.com, May 29, 2016, accessed March 4, 2020, https://www.dailymail.co.uk/news/article-3615602/Six-ten-children-don-t-sleep -Warning-poor-parenting-youngsters-glued-TVs-devices-leading-crisis-rest-habits.html.

15. Dylan Neel, "A Reason to Count Sheep: Is Sleep Deprivation a Global Driver of Metabolic Disease?" *Harvard College Global Health Review*, October 24, 2012, https://www.hcs .harvard.edu/hghr/online/sleep-deprivation/.

16. Andrea Canning and Anna Wild, "Mystery of Sleepless Boy Solved," ABC News, January 22, 2009, https://abcnews.go.com/GMA/OnCall/mystery-sleepless-boy-solved/story?id=6711810.

17. Michikazu Sekine et al., "A Dose-Response Relationship between Short Sleeping Hours and Childhood Obesity: Results of the Toyama Birth Cohort Study," *Child: Care, Health and*

Development 28, no. 2 (March 2002): 163–70, https://doi.org/10.1046/j.1365-2214.2002 .00260.x.

18. Alicja R. Rudnicka et al., "Sleep Duration and Risk of Type 2 Diabetes," *Pediatrics* 140, no. 3 (September 2017): e20170338, https://doi.org/10.1542/peds.2017-0338.

19. Peige Song et al., "Global Prevalence of Hypertension in Children: A Systematic Review and Meta-analysis," *JAMA Pediatrics* 173, no. 12 (October 7, 2019): 1154–63, https://doi .org/10.1001/jamapediatrics.2019.3310.

20. Sonia Sparano et al., "Sleep Duration and Blood Pressure in Children: Analysis of the Pan-European IDEFICS Cohort," *Journal of Clinical Hypertension* 21, no. 5 (May 2019): 572–78, https://doi.org/10.1111/jch.13520.

21. "Hypertension Symptoms and Causes in Children," website of Boston Children's Hospital, accessed November 9, 2020, https://www.childrenshospital.org/conditions-and-treatments /conditions/h/hypertension/symptoms-and-causes.

22. Sheldon Cohen et al., "Sleep Habits and Susceptibility to the Common Cold," *Archives of Internal Medicine* 169, no. 1 (January 12, 2009): 62–67, https://doi.org/10.1001 /archinternmed.2008.505.

23. Kathryn M. Orzech et al., "Sleep Patterns Are Associated with Common Illness in Adolescents," *Journal of Sleep Research* 23, no. 2 (April 2014): 133–42, https://doi.org /10.1111/jsr.12096.

24. Daniel J. Taylor et al., "Is Insomnia a Risk Factor for Decreased Influenza Vaccine Response?" *Behavioral Sleep Medicine* 15, no. 4 (July–August 2017): 270–87, https://doi.org/10.1080 /15402002.2015.1126596.

25. Elsie M. Taveras et al., "Prospective Study of Insufficient Sleep and Neurobehavioral Functioning among School-Age Children," *Academic Pediatrics* 17, no. 6 (August 2017): 625–32, https://doi.org/10.1016/j.acap.2017.02.001.

26. Anna S. Urrila et al., "Sleep Habits, Academic Performance, and the Adolescent Brain Structure," *Scientific Reports* (February 9, 2017): 7, https://doi.org/10.1038/srep41678.

27. Lisa Rapaport, "Strict Bedtime Rules Can Help Kids Get Enough Sleep," Reuters, June 1, 2017, https://www.reuters.com/article/us-health-parenting-child-sleep/strict-bedtime-rules -can-help-kids-get-enough-sleep-idUSKBN18S6F8.

28. Stephen King, *On Writing: A Memoir of the Craft* (New York: Scribner, 2000), 165.

29. Jianghong Liu et al., "Midday Napping in Children: Associations between Nap Frequency and Duration across Cognitive, Positive Psychological Well-Being, Behavioral, and Metabolic Health Outcomes," *Sleep* 42, no. 9 (September 6, 2019): zsz126, https://doi.org/10.1093 /sleep/zsz126.

30. William D. S. Killgore et al., "Sleep Deprivation Impairs Recognition of Specific Emotions," *Neurobiology of Sleep and Circadian Rhythms* 3 (June 2017): 10–16, https://doi.org/10.1016 /j.nbscr.2017.01.001.

31. Cohen et al., "Sleep Habits and Susceptibility"; Orzech et al., "Sleep Patterns Are Associated with Common Illness."

32. Ta-Chien Chan, Tsuey-Hwa Hu, and Jing-Shiang Hwang, "Estimating the Risk of Influenza-Like Illness Transmission through Social Contacts: Web-Based Participatory Cohort Study," *JMIR Public Health and Surveillance* 4, no. 2 (April 9, 2018): e40, https:// doi.org/10.2196/publichealth.8874.

33. Nayyab Asif, Razia Iqbal, and Chaudhry Fahad Nazir, "Human Immune System during Sleep," *American Journal of Clinical and Experimental Immunology* 6, no. 6 (2017): 92–96, https://pubmed.ncbi.nlm.nih.gov/29348984/.

34. Tracey J. Smith et al., "Impact of Sleep Restriction on Local Immune Response and Skin

Barrier Restoration with and without 'Multinutrient' Nutrition Intervention," *Journal of Applied Physiology* 124, no. 1 (January 23, 2018): 190–200, https://doi.org/10.1152 /japplphysiol.00547.2017.

35. Mireia Adelantado-Renau et al., "The Effect of Sleep Quality on Academic Performance Is Mediated by Internet Use Time: DADOS Study," *Jornal de Pediatria* 95, no. 4 (July–August 2019): 410–18, https://doi.org/10.1016/j.jped.2018.03.006.

36. Matthew D. Milewski et al., "Chronic Lack of Sleep Is Associated with Increased Sports Injuries in Adolescent Athletes," *Journal of Pediatric Orthopaedics* 34, no. 2 (March 2014): 129–33, https://doi.org/10.1097/BPO.0000000000000151; Kenneth C. Vitale et al., "Sleep Hygiene for Optimizing Recovery in Athletes: Review and Recommendations," *International Journal of Sports Medicine* 40, no. 8 (August 2019): 535–43, https://doi .org/10.1055/a-0905-3103.

37. Marjo Tourula, Arja Isola, and Juhani Hassi, "Children Sleeping Outdoors in Winter: Parents' Experiences of a Culturally Bound Childcare Practice," *International Journal of Circumpolar Health* 67, nos. 2–3 (June 2008): 269–78, https://doi.org /10.3402/ijch.v67i2-3.18284.

38. Yvonne Harrison, "The Relationship between Daytime Exposure to Light and Night-Time Sleep in 6–12-Week-Old Infants," *Journal of Sleep Research* 13, no. 4 (December 2004): 345–52, https://doi.org/10.1111/j.1365-2869.2004.00435.x.

39. William F. Marshall III, "Can Vitamin D Protect against the Coronavirus Disease 2019 (COVID-19)?" Mayo Clinic, October 2, 2020, https://www.mayoclinic.org/coronavirus -and-vitamin-d/expert-answers/faq-20493088.

40. Justyna Godos et al., "Adherence to the Mediterranean Diet Is Associated with Better Sleep Quality in Italian Adults," *Nutrients* 11, no. 5 (April 28, 2019): 976, https://doi.org /10.3390/nu11050976.

41. Jianghong Liu et al., "The Mediating Role of Sleep in the Fish Consumption–Cognitive Functioning Relationship: A Cohort Study," *Scientific Reports* 7, no. 1 (December 21, 2017): 17961, https://doi.org/10.1038/s41598-017-17520-w.

42. Cibele Aparecida Crispim et al., "Relationship between Food Intake and Sleep Pattern in Healthy Individuals," *Journal of Clinical Sleep Medicine* 7, no. 6 (December 15, 2011): 659–64, https://doi.org/10.5664/jcsm.1476.

43. Asher Y. Rosinger et al., "Short Sleep Duration Is Associated with Inadequate Hydration: Cross-Cultural Evidence from US and Chinese Adults," *Sleep* 42, no. 2 (November 2018): zsy210, https://doi.org/10.1093/sleep/zsy210.

CHAPTER 6: WEEK 4: CULTIVATING LIFE-GIVING RELATIONSHIPS
1. Katharina Buchholz, "This Chart Shows How Much More Common Natural Disasters Are Becoming," World Economic Forum, September 3, 2020, https://www.weforum.org /agenda/2020/09/natural-disasters-global-risks-2019.

2. Katharine Gammon, "Penguins: The Math behind the Huddle," Inside Science, an editorially independent news service of the American Institute of Physics, November 20, 2012, https:// insidescience.org/news/penguins-math-behind-huddle.

3. Robyn Fivush, Marshall Duke, and Jennifer G. Bohanek, "'Do You Know . . . ?': The Power of Family History in Adolescent Identity and Well-Being," *Journal of Family Life* (February 23, 2010), https://ncph.org/wp-content/uploads/2013/12/The-power-of-family-history-in -adolescent-identity.pdf.

4. Steven Ertelt, "Their 'Rescuing Hug' Stunned the World, Now the Twins Are All Grown

Up," LifeNews.com, June 20, 2014, https://www.lifenews.com/2014/06/20/their-rescuing
-hug-stunned-the-world-now-the-twins-are-all-grown-up/.

5. Sheldon Cohen et al., "Does Hugging Provide Stress-Buffering Social Support? A Study of
    Susceptibility to Upper Respiratory Infection and Illness," *Psychological Science* 26, no. 2
    (February 2015): 135–47, https://doi.org/10.1177/0956797614559284.

6. Karen M. Grewen et al., "Effects of Partner Support on Resting Oxytocin, Cortisol,
    Norepinephrine, and Blood Pressure Before and After Warm Partner Contact,"
    Psychosomatic Medicine 67, no. 4 (July–August 2005): 531–38, https://doi.org
    /10.1097/01.psy.0000170341.88395.47.

7. Jenny Tung et al., "Social Networks Predict Gut Microbiome Composition in Wild
    Baboons," *eLife* 4 (March 16, 2015): e05224, https://doi.org/10.7554/eLife.05224.

8. Luke 10:30-37.

9. Kay S. Hymowitz, "Alone: The Decline of the Family Has Unleashed an Epidemic of
    Loneliness," *City Journal*, Spring 2019, https://www.city-journal.org/decline-of-family
    -loneliness-epidemic.

10. Fivush, Duke, and Bohanek, "'Do You Know . . . ?'"

11. Kathleen C. Light, Karen M. Grewen, and Janet A. Amico, "More Frequent Partner
    Hugs and Higher Oxytocin Levels Are Linked to Lower Blood Pressure and Heart Rate
    in Premenopausal Women," *Biological Psychology* 69, no. 1 (May 2005): 5–21, https://doi
    .org/10.1016/j.biopsycho.2004.11.002.

12. Miho Nagasawa et al., "Dog's Gaze at Its Owner Increases Owner's Urinary Oxytocin
    during Social Interaction," *Hormones and Behavior* 55, no. 3 (March 2009): 434–41,
    https://doi.org/10.1016/j.yhbeh.2008.12.002.

13. Cohen et al., "Does Hugging Provide Stress-Buffering Social Support?"

14. Sophie Scott et al., "The Social Life of Laughter," *Trends in Cognitive Sciences* 18, no. 12
    (December 2014): 618–20, https://doi.org/10.1016/j.tics.2014.09.002.

15. Sandra Manninen et al., "Social Laughter Triggers Endogenous Opioid Release in Humans,"
    Journal of Neuroscience 37, no. 25 (June 21, 2017): 6125–31, https://doi.org/10.1523
    /JNEUROSCI.0688-16.2017.

16. JongEun Yim, "Therapeutic Benefits of Laughter in Mental Health: A Theoretical Review,"
    Tohoku Journal of Experimental Medicine 239, no. 3 (July 2016): 243–49; Mary P. Bennett
    et al., "The Effect of Mirthful Laughter on Stress and Natural Killer Cell Activity,"
    Alternative Therapies in Health and Medicine 9, no. 2 (March–April 2003): 38–45, https://
    doi.org/10.1620/tjem.239.243.

17. Lee S. Berk et al., "Neuroendocrine and Stress Hormone Changes during Mirthful
    Laughter," *American Journal of the Medical Sciences* 298, no. 6 (December 1989): 390–96,
    https://doi.org/10.1097/00000441-198912000-00006; Jinping Zhao et al., "A Meta-
    Analysis of Randomized Controlled Trials of Laughter and Humour Interventions on
    Depression, Anxiety and Sleep Quality in Adults," *Journal of Advanced Nursing* 75, no. 11
    (November 2019): 2435–48, https://doi.org/10.1111/jan.14000.

18. Sheldon Cohen et al., "Social Ties and Susceptibility to the Common Cold," *Journal of
    the American Medical Association* 277, no. 24 (June 25, 1997): 1940–44, https://doi.org
    /10.1001/jama.1997.03540480040036; Maija Reblin and Bert N. Uchino, "Social and
    Emotional Support and Its Implication for Health," *Current Opinion in Psychiatry* 21, no. 2
    (March 2008): 201–5, https://doi.org/10.1097/YCO.0b013e3282f3ad89.

19. Janice K. Kiecolt-Glaser, Jean-Philippe Gouin, and Lisa Hantsoo, "Close Relationships,
    Inflammation, and Health," *Neuroscience and Biobehavioral Reviews* 35, no. 1 (September
    2010): 33–38, https://doi.org/10.1016/j.neubiorev.2009.09.003.

20. Julianne Holt-Lunstad, Timothy B. Smith, and J. Bradley Layton, "Social Relationships and Mortality Risk: A Meta-analytic Review," *PLOS Medicine* 7, no. 7 (July 27, 2010): e1000316, https://doi.org/10.1371/journal.pmed.1000316.

21. April Eldemire, "Research Shows a Couple's Friendship Is Key to Reducing Postpartum Depression," The Gottman Institute (TGI), February 8, 2017, https://www.gottman.com /blog/research-shows-couples-friendship-key-reducing-postpartum-depression/.

22. Abdollah Rezaei-Dehaghani, Mahrokh Keshvari, and Somayeh Paki, "The Relationship between Family Functioning and Academic Achievement in Female High School Students of Isfahan, Iran, in 2013–2014," *Iranian Journal of Nursing and Midwifery Research* 23, no. 3 (May–June 2018): 183–87, https://doi.org/10.4103/ijnmr.IJNMR_87_17.

23. Camelia E. Hostinar and Megan R. Gunnar, "Social Support Can Buffer against Stress and Shape Brain Activity," *American Journal of Bioethics Neuroscience* 6, no. 3 (July 1, 2015): 34–42, https://doi.org/10.1080/21507740.2015.1047054.

24. Katarina Habe, Michele Biasutti, and Tanja Kajtna, "Flow and Satisfaction with Life in Elite Musicians and Top Athletes," *Frontiers in Psychology* 10 (2019): 698, https://doi.org /10.3389/fpsyg.2019.00698.

25. Kelly Campbell et al., "Does Love Influence Athletic Performance? The Perspectives of Olympic Athletes," *Review of European Studies* 8, no. 2 (June 2016): 1–7, https://doi .org/10.5539/res.v8n2p1.

CHAPTER 7: WEEK 5: FOLLOWING YOUR SPIRITUAL GPS

1. Ronald F. Inglehart, "Giving Up on God: The Global Decline of Religion," *Foreign Affairs*, September/October 2020, 110–18, https://www.foreignaffairs.com/articles/world/2020 -08-11/religion-giving-god.

2. Gabe Bullard, "The World's Newest Major Religion: No Religion," *National Geographic*, April 22, 2016, https://www.nationalgeographic.com/news/2016/04/160422-atheism -agnostic-secular-nones-rising-religion/.

3. Claire Gecewicz, "Few Americans Say Their House of Worship Is Open, but a Quarter Say Their Faith Has Grown amid Pandemic," Pew Research Center, April 30, 2020, https:// www.pewresearch.org/fact-tank/2020/04/30/few-americans-say-their-house-of-worship-is -open-but-a-quarter-say-their-religious-faith-has-grown-amid-pandemic/.

4. Harold G. Koenig, "Religion, Spirituality, and Health: The Research and Clinical Implications," *International Scholarly Research Notices Psychiatry* (2012): 278730, https:// www.ncbi.nlm.nih.gov/pmc/articles/PMC3671693/; Laura B. Koenig and George E. Vaillant, "A Prospective Study of Church Attendance and Health over the Lifespan," *Health Psychology* 28, no. 1 (January 2009): 117–24, https://doi.org/10.1037/a0012984.

5. Marcie C. Goeke-Morey et al., "Maternal Religiosity, Family Resources and Stressors, and Parent-Child Attachment Security in Northern Ireland," *Social Development* 22, no. 1 (February 2013): 19–37, https://doi.org/10.1111/j.1467-9507.2012.00659.x.

6. Bible Study Fellowship (BSF) International, accessed March 7, 2020, https://www .bsfinternational.org/.

7. Başak Çoruh et al., "Does Religious Activity Improve Health Outcomes? A Critical Review of the Recent Literature," *Explore* 1, no. 3 (May 2005): 186–91, https://doi.org/10.1016 /j.explore.2005.02.001.

8. Camila Csizmar Carvalho et al., "Effectiveness of Prayer in Reducing Anxiety in Cancer Patients," *Revista da Escola de Enfermagem da U S P* 48, no. 4 (August 2014): 683–89, https://pubmed.ncbi.nlm.nih.gov/25338250/; Peter A. Boelens et al., "A Randomized Trial

of the Effect of Prayer on Depression and Anxiety," *International Journal of Psychiatry in Medicine* 39, no. 4 (2009): 377–92, https://doi.org/10.2190/PM.39.4.c.

9. Pat and Tammy McLeod, *Hit Hard* (Carol Stream, IL: Tyndale, 2019).

10. Mohd Ahsan Kabir Rizvi and Mohammad Zakir Hossain, "Relationship between Religious Belief and Happiness: A Systematic Literature Review," *Journal of Religion and Health* 56, no. 5 (October 2017): 1561–82, https://doi.org/10.1007/s10943-016-0332-6.

11. Stuart R. Varon and Anne W. Riley, "Relationship between Maternal Church Attendance and Adolescent Mental Health and Social Functioning," *Psychiatric Services* 50, no. 6 (June 1999): 799–805, https://doi.org/10.1176/ps.50.6.799.

12. James W. Anderson and Paige A. Nunnelley, "Private Prayer Associations with Depression, Anxiety, and Other Health Conditions: An Analytical Review of Clinical Studies," *Postgraduate Medicine* 128, no. 7 (September 2016): 635–41, https://doi.org/10.1080/00325481.2016.1209962.

13. Connie Svob et al., "Association of Parent and Offspring Religiosity with Offspring Suicide Ideation and Attempts," *JAMA Psychiatry* 75, no. 10 (October 1, 2018): 1062–70, https://doi.org/10.1001/jamapsychiatry.2018.2060.

14. Shanshan Li et al., "Association of Religious Service Attendance with Mortality among Women," *JAMA Internal Medicine* 176, no. 6 (June 1, 2016): 777–85, https://doi.org/10.1001/jamainternmed.2016.1615.

15. Tyler J. VanderWeele et al., "Association between Religious Service Attendance and Lower Suicide Rates among US Women," *JAMA Psychiatry* 73, no. 8 (August 1, 2016): 845–51, https://doi.org/10.1001/jamapsychiatry.2016.1243.

16. Christopher P. Salas-Wright et al., "Religiosity Profiles of American Youth in Relation to Substance Use, Violence, and Delinquency," *Journal of Youth and Adolescence* 41, no. 12 (December 2012): 1560–75, https://doi.org/10.1007/s10964-012-9761-z.

17. Simone Croezen et al., "Social Participation and Depression in Old Age: A Fixed-Effects Analysis in 10 European Countries," *American Journal of Epidemiology* 182, no. 2 (July 15, 2015): 168–76, https://doi.org/10.1093/aje/kwv015.

18. Goeke-Morey et al., "Maternal Religiosity, Family Resources and Stressors, and Parent-Child Attachment."

19. H. G. Koenig et al., "Attendance at Religious Services, Interleukin-6, and Other Biological Parameters of Immune Function in Older Adults," *International Journal of Psychiatry in Medicine* 27, no. 3 (1997): 233–50, https://doi.org/10.2190/40NF-Q9Y2-0GG7-4WH6; Celia F. Hybels et al., "Inflammation and Coagulation as Mediators in the Relationships between Religious Attendance and Functional Limitations in Older Adults," *Journal of Aging and Health* 26, no. 4 (April 2014): 679–97, https://doi.org/10.1177/0898264314527479.

20. Patrick F. Fagan, "Religious Practice and Educational Attainment," Marriage and Religion Research Institute, September 2, 2010, https://downloads.frc.org/EF/EF12D59.pdf; Mark D. Regnerus and Glen H. Elder, "Religion and Vulnerability among Low-Risk Adolescents," *Social Science Research* 32, no. 4 (December 2003): 633–58, https://doi.org/10.1016/S0049-089X(03)00027-9.

21. Robert Roy Britt, "Church Attendance Boosts Student GPAs," LiveScience, August 19, 2008, https://www.livescience.com/5051-church-attendance-boosts-student-gpas.html.

22. Mark D. Regnerus, "Shaping Schooling Success: Religious Socialization and Educational Outcomes in Metropolitan Public Schools," *Journal for the Scientific Study of Religion* 39, no. 3 (September 2000): 363–70, http://www.jstor.org/stable/1387820.

23. Terrence D. Hill et al., "Religious Attendance and the Health Behaviors of Texas Adults,"

Preventive Medicine 42, no. 4 (April 2006): 309–12, https://doi.org/10.1016/j.ypmed
.2005.12.005.

24. Tharin Phenwan, Thanarpan Peerawong, and Kandawsri Tulathamkij, "The Meaning of
Spirituality and Spiritual Well-Being among Thai Breast Cancer Patients: A Qualitative
Study," *Indian Journal of Palliative Care* 25, no. 1 (January–March 2019): 119–23,
https://www.ncbi.nlm.nih.gov/pmc/articles/PMC6388600/.

CHAPTER 8: WEEK 6: EMBRACING A MOUNTAIN-MOVING MINDSET

1. Nadja Walter, Lucie Nikoleizig, and Dorothee Alfermann, "Effects of Self-Talk Training
on Competitive Anxiety, Self-Efficacy, Volitional Skills, and Performance: An Intervention
Study with Junior Sub-Elite Athletes," *Sports (Basel, Switzerland)* 7, no. 6 (June 2019): 148,
https://doi.org/10.3390/sports7060148.

2. Magdalena Kruk et al., "Mental Strategies Predict Performance and Satisfaction with
Performance among Soccer Players," *Journal of Human Kinetics* 59 (October 2017): 79–90,
https://doi.org/10.1515/hukin-2017-0149; Antonis Hatzigeorgiadis et al., "Self-Talk and
Sports Performance: A Meta-Analysis," *Perspectives on Psychological Science: A Journal of
the Association for Psychological Science* 6, no. 4 (July 2011): 348–56, https://doi.org
/10.1177/1745691611413136.

3. Nujaree Intasao and Ning Hao, "Beliefs about Creativity Influence Creative Performance:
The Mediation Effects of Flexibility and Positive Affect," *Frontiers in Psychology* 9 (2018):
1810, https://doi.org/10.3389/fpsyg.2018.01810.

4. Hulda Crooks, *Conquering Life's Mountains* (n.p.: The Quiet Hours, 1996), 54.

5. See Nick Vujicic's website Life without Limbs, accessed April 5, 2020, https://www.life
withoutlimbs.org/.

6. Boris Vujicic, "My Son Was Born with No Arms or Legs and It's Nothing like You're
Thinking," *Fatherly*, July 29, 2016, https://www.fatherly.com/health-science/nick-vujicics
-father-on-raising-a-boy-with-no-arms-or-legs/.

7. Rosie Perper, "Photos and Charts Show How the Natural World Is Thriving Now That
Humans Are Staying Indoors," Insider, April 22, 2020, https://www.insider.com/photos
-videos-earth-planet-thriving-coronavirus-2020-4.

8. Robert A. Emmons and Michael E. McCullough, "Counting Blessings versus Burdens:
An Experimental Investigation of Gratitude and Subjective Well-Being in Daily Life,"
Journal of Personality and Social Psychology 84, no. 2 (February 2003): 377–89, https://
doi.org/10.1037/0022-3514.84.2.377.

9. Izabela Krejtz et al., "Counting One's Blessings Can Reduce the Impact of Daily
Stress," *Journal of Happiness Studies* 17 (2016): 25–39, https://doi.org/10.1007
/s10902-014-9578-4.

10. Charles S. Carver, Michael F. Scheier, and Suzanne C. Segerstrom, "Optimism," *Clinical
Psychology Review* 30, no. 7 (November 2010): 879–89, https://doi.org/10.1016/j.cpr.2010
.01.006.

11. Sheldon Cohen et al., "Emotional Style and Susceptibility to the Common Cold,"
Psychosomatic Medicine 65, no. 4 (July–August 2003): 652–57, https://doi.org/10.1097
/01.psy.0000077508.57784.da.

12. Franklin G. Miller, Luana Colloca, and Ted J. Kaptchuk, "The Placebo Effect: Illness and Interpersonal Healing," *Perspectives in Biology and Medicine* 52, no. 4 (Autumn 2009): 518–39, https://doi.org/10.1353/pbm.0.0115.

13. Marjolein M. Hanssen et al., "Can Positive Affect Attenuate (Persistent) Pain? State of the Art and Clinical Implications," *Current Rheumatology Reports* 19, no. 12 (2017): 80, https://doi.org/10.1007/s11926-017-0703-3.

14. Barbara L. Fredrickson, "The Broaden-and-Build Theory of Positive Emotions," *Philosophical Transactions of the Royal Society of London: Series B, Biological Sciences* 359, no. 1449 (September 29, 2004): 1367–78, https://doi.org/10.1098/rstb.2004.1512.

15. Barbara L. Fredrickson and Christine Branigan, "Positive Emotions Broaden the Scope of Attention and Thought-Action Repertoires," *Cognition and Emotion* 19, no. 3 (May 1, 2005): 313–32.

16. Ivan Vargas, Christopher L. Drake, and Nestor L. Lopez-Duran, "Insomnia Symptom Severity Modulates the Impact of Sleep Deprivation on Attentional Biases to Emotional Information," *Cognitive Therapy and Research* 41, no. 3 (May 2017): 842–52, https://doi.org/10.1007/s10608-017-9859-4.

17. Astrid Nehlig, "The Neuroprotective Effects of Cocoa Flavanol and Its Influence on Cognitive Performance," *British Journal of Clinical Pharmacology* 75, no. 3 (March 2013): 716–27, https://doi.org/10.1111/j.1365-2125.2012.04378.x; "New Studies Show Dark Chocolate Consumption Reduces Stress and Inflammation, While Improving Memory, Immunity and Mood," Loma Linda University Health, April 24, 2018, https://news.llu.edu/for-journalists/press-releases/new-studies-show-dark-chocolate-consumption-reduces-stress-and-inflammation-while-improving-memory-immunity-and-mood.

18. Siri Carpenter, "That Gut Feeling," *Monitor on Psychology* 43, no. 8 (September 2012): 50, https://www.apa.org/monitor/2012/09/gut-feeling.

CHAPTER 9: WEEK 7: BECOMING THE SOLUTION

1. "60 Minutes Presents: Amazing Kids," *60 Minutes*, CBS News, February 2, 2014, https://www.cbsnews.com/news/60-minutes-presents-amazing-kids/.

2. Leanne Arsenault, "Research on Household Chores," *Raising Strong Girls* podcast, Society for the Psychology of Women, July 2017, https://www.apadivisions.org/division-35/news-events/news/household-chores.

3. "Should You Make Your Child Do Chores? Majority of Kids 'Get Away with NO Cleaning,'" *Express*, October 25, 2017, https://www.express.co.uk/life-style/life/870542/children-chores-majority-kids-no-cleaning-parents; Marc Montgomery, "Children and Household Chores: Developing Life Skills," Radio Canada International, March 30, 2016, https://www.rcinet.ca/en/2016/03/30/children-and-household-chores-developing-life-skills/; Shi Li, "'It's All about Me, Me, Me!' Why Children Are Spending Less Time Doing Household Chores," The Conversation, October 6, 2016, https://theconversation.com/its-all-about-me-me-me-why-children-are-spending-less-time-doing-household-chores-66134.

4. Richard Rende and Jen Prosek, *Raising Can-Do Kids: Giving Children the Tools to Thrive in a Fast-Changing World* (New York: TarcherPerigee, 2015).

5. Barbara Rogoff, "Learning by Observing and Pitching In to Family and Community Endeavors: An Orientation," *Human Development* 57, no. 2 (2014) 69–81, https://www.jstor.org/stable/26764709.

6. Richard M. Sherman and Robert B. Sherman, "A Spoonful of Sugar," from *Mary Poppins Original Soundtrack*, Walt Disney Records, 1964.

7. "Responsibility and Chores: Part 1—Benefits of Chores," Center for Parenting Education,

accessed April 10, 2020, https://centerforparentingeducation.org/library-of-articles
/responsibility-and-chores/part-i-benefits-of-chores/.

8. For more about Roman McConn and Project Freedom Ride, see their website at http://
projectfreedomride.org/; "Meet the 7-Year-Old Boy Who Has Rescued More than 1,000
Dogs from Kill Shelters," Inside Edition, July 13, 2018, https://www.insideedition.com
/meet-7-year-old-boy-who-has-rescued-more-1000-dogs-kill-shelters-44973.

9. Ryan Hreljac, "Ryan's Story," Ryan's Well Foundation, https://www.ryanswell.ca/about-ryans
-well/ryans-story; for an overview of the foundation's work, see https://www.ryanswell.ca/.

10. Kathryn Spink, *Mother Teresa: A Complete Authorized Biography* (New York: HarperCollins,
1997), 6–12.

11. See Michael Collopy, *Works of Love Are Works of Peace* (San Francisco: Ignatius Press, 1996).

12. Marjorie Joseph tells her story in her autobiography, *God Has Brought Me This Far* (Fort
Oglethorpe, GA: TEACH Services, 2007).

13. One such group I'm familiar with is Maranatha Volunteers International. Learn more at
https://maranatha.org.

14. Jerf W. K. Yeung, Zhuoni Zhang, and Tae Yeun Kim, "Volunteering and Health Benefits in
General Adults: Cumulative Effects and Forms," *BMC Public Health* 18 (2018): 8, https://
doi.org/10.1186/s12889-017-4561-8.

15. Lara B. Aknin, J. Kiley Hamlin, and Elizabeth W. Dunn, "Giving Leads to Happiness in
Young Children," *PLOS ONE* 7, no. 6 (June 14, 2012): e39211, https://doi.org/10.1371
/journal.pone.0039211.

16. Hannah M. C. Schreier, Kimberly A. Schonert-Reichl, and Edith Chen, "Effect of
Volunteering on Risk Factors for Cardiovascular Disease in Adolescents: A Randomized
Controlled Trial," *JAMA Pediatrics* 167, no. 4 (April 2013): 327–32, https://doi.org
/10.1001/jamapediatrics.2013.1100.

17. Eric S. Kim and Sara H. Konrath, "Volunteering Is Prospectively Associated with Health
Care Use among Older Adults," *Social Science and Medicine* 149 (January 2016): 122–29,
https://doi.org/10.1016/j.socscimed.2015.11.043.

18. Yannick Griep et al., "Can Volunteering in Later Life Reduce the Risk of Dementia? A
5-Year Longitudinal Study among Volunteering and Non-Volunteering Retired Seniors,"
PLOS ONE 12, no. 3 (March 16, 2017): e0173885, https://doi.org/10.1371/journal
.pone.0173885; Jeffrey A. Burr, Sae Hwang Han, and Jane L. Tavares, "Volunteering and
Cardiovascular Disease Risk: Does Helping Others Get 'Under the Skin'?" *Gerontologist* 56,
no. 5 (October 2016): 937–47.

19. Cassie Mogilner, Zoë Chance, and Michael I. Norton, "Giving Time Gives You Time,"
Psychological Science 23, no. 10 (September 12, 2012): 1233–38, https://doi.org/10.1177
/0956797612442551; Cassie Mogilner, "You'll Feel Less Rushed If You Give Time Away,"
Harvard Business Review, September 1, 2012, https://hbr.org/2012/09/youll-feel-less
-rushed-if-you-give-time-away.

20. Seoyoun Kim and Hyunwoo Yoon, "Volunteering, Subjective Sleep Quality, and Longitudinal
Risk of Inflammation: Potential Pathways?," *Innovation in Aging* 2, suppl. 1 (November 2018):
270, https://doi.org/10.1093/geroni/igy023.999.

CHAPTER 10: WEEK 8: BUILDING A LEGACY OF HEALTH (AND HAPPINESS!)

1. Annie Murphy Paul, "The Protégé Effect: Why Teaching Someone Else Is the Best Way to
Learn," *Psychology Today*, June 13, 2012, https://www.psychologytoday.com/us/blog/how-be
-brilliant/201206/the-prot-g-effect.

RECIPE INDEX

ABOUT THE AUTHOR

RHONDA SPENCER-HWANG, who holds a doctorate in public health, is an epidemiologist, an associate professor in the School of Public Health at Loma Linda University, and a member of the world's first identified Resiliency Capital, a Christian community known for its healthy lifestyles. Dr. Spencer-Hwang's groundbreaking research on centenarians offers a unique perspective on developing whole health and resilience, which are especially important for families today. Despite adverse childhood experiences (ACEs) and stressors faced throughout their lifetimes, from pandemics to pollution and economic recession, these centenarians offer valuable insights on healthy living.

With over twenty-five years of experience in public health, Dr. Spencer-Hwang has appeared in multiple international documentaries discussing her findings and lifestyle practices, has written for numerous peer-reviewed publications, has given presentations around the world, and has stewarded funding from various government agencies as she promotes resiliency and a culture of health, especially for children. She is an expert at using art and play to promote health in both children and adults. Furthermore, Dr. Spencer-Hwang has worked the front lines as an epidemiologist combating the spread of infectious disease. Now through her research-based Resiliency Program, she helps children and adults develop healthy and resilient lifestyles to withstand whatever life throws their way.

Dr. Spencer-Hwang and her husband enjoy raising their children, Jayden, Joelle, and Julia, in Loma Linda, California.